Uncommon Tongues

Uncommon Tongues

Eloquence and Eccentricity in the English Renaissance

Catherine Nicholson

PENN

UNIVERSITY OF PENNSYLVANIA PRESS

PHILADELPHIA

Published by
University of Pennsylvania Press
Philadelphia, Pennsylvania 19104-4112

www.upenn.edu/pennpress

Printed in the United States of America on acid-free paper

10 9 8 7 6 5 4 3 2 1

Library of Congress Cataloging-in-Publication Data
ISBN 978-0-8122-4558-5

Contents

Introduction

Antisocial Orpheus

In the late sixteenth century, just as England began to assert its integrity as a nation and English its value as a literate tongue, vernacular writing took a turn for the eccentric. John Lyly's *Euphues: The Anatomy of Wit* (1578), Edmund Spenser's *Shepheardes Calender* (1579), and Christopher Marlowe's *Tamburlaine the Great* (1587) loudly announced their authors' ambitions for the English language, but in their extravagant ornamentation, obscure archaism, and violent bombast they stood at a seemingly deliberate remove from the tongue whose reputation they helped to secure. Indeed to some early critics, the inaugural achievements of what Richard Foster Jones has termed "the triumph of the English language" seemed in their extremity hardly English at all.[1] Edward Blount credited *Euphues* with inventing a "new English," but Philip Sidney likened its showy effects to the glittering of a bejeweled "Indian."[2] Joseph Hall dismissed *Tamburlaine*'s blank verse as a "Turkish" concoction of "big-sounding sentences" and "termes Italianate."[3] Ben Jonson carped that Marlowe had taken the poet's privilege to "differ from the vulgar somewhat" as license to "fly from all humanity," and he praised the matter of Spenser's poems but lamented that in them he "writ no language."[4] Indian, Turkish, Italianate, inhuman—in laying claim to eloquence, it appears, English became increasingly strange to itself.

That estrangement is the subject of this book, which situates eccentricity at the paradoxical heart of sixteenth-century pedagogical, rhetorical, and literary culture. In doing so it departs from, or at least qualifies, a fantasy that has shaped both the English Renaissance and our perception of it. According to the founding myth of the classical rhetorical tradition, eloquence is the essence of sociability: mankind's natural vagrancy yields to the attractive power of language.[5] "Because there has been implanted in us the power to persuade each other and to make clear to each other what we desire . . . we have come together and founded cities and made laws and invented arts," Isocrates declares in his defense of rhetoric.[6] Before the invention of rhetoric, as Cicero writes in the opening chapter of *De Inventione*, humankind "wandered at large . . . scattered in the fields and hidden in sylvan retreats"; only when men had learned the art of persuasion could this wayward flock be "assembled and gathered . . . in a single place," reconciled to domesticity and society.[7] In the *Ars Poetica* Horace identifies the eloquence of the aboriginal poets Orpheus and Amphion with the power to "distinguish the public from private weal, things sacred from things profane," to "plan out cities," and to "engrave laws on tables of wood."[8] "I cannot imagine," declares Quintilian in his *Institutio Oratoria*, "how the founders of cities would have made a homeless multitude come together to form a people, had they not moved them by their skillful speech."[9]

Sixteenth-century English rhetoricians found in this fantasy a potent justification for their efforts on behalf of the vernacular: if eloquence was the original antidote to errancy, more eloquent English would make for a stronger and more cohesive England. According to Thomas Wilson's 1560 *Arte of Rhetorique*, the cultivation of the vernacular is thus England's chief safeguard from the perils of what he punningly terms "roming"—which is to say, both "roaming" speech and "Rome-ing" souls, wayward tongues and Papist hearts.[10] In a similar vein, George Puttenham's 1589 *Arte of English Poesie* names Orpheus and Amphion as "the first Legislators and polititians in the world," cites their verses as "th'originall cause and occasion" of civil society, and interprets poetic precepts as guides to social and political acculturation. When Puttenham hails Queen Elizabeth I as England's "most excellent Poet," the compliment redounds to poetry, which is reimagined as a rarefied form of statecraft.[11] "Nothing can bee more excellently giuen of Nature then Eloquence," declares Richard Rainolde in his 1563 *Foundacion of Rhetorike*, "by the which the florishyng state of commonweales doe consiste [and] kyngdomes vniuersally are gouerned."[12] Even Henry Peacham, whose 1577 *Garden of Eloquence* is a barely elaborated listing of tropes and figures, claims a patriotic motive for his text: "My wel meaning," he declares, "is . . . to profyte this my country."[13]

And profit it did. Indeed we are now likely to credit the flourishing of the vernacular not simply with enriching England but with inventing it. As a large body of recent scholarship attests, the ascendancy of English as a learned and eloquent tongue in Shakespeare's day fostered a new and durable form of collective identification: an "imagined community," in Benedict Anderson's influential formulation, founded on the "deep, horizontal comradeship" of reading and writing in a common tongue. Anderson's account of the origins of modern nationalism updates the mythology of eloquence for the purposes of modern literary and political history: now poets, playwrights, and pamphleteers play the part of Orpheus, as the once atomized inhabitants of premodern England are, beginning in the sixteenth century, "connected through print, form[ing], in their secular, visible invisibility, the embryo of the nationally imagined community."[14]

Although critics continue to debate the contours of this emergent nationalism—is it English or British, Elizabethan or more broadly Tudor?[15]—there is widespread agreement about its origins in literary practice. In the sixteenth century, Richard Helgerson argues, vernacular authors in virtually every genre worked "to articulate a national community whose existence and eminence would then justify their desire to become its literary spokesmen," participating in "what retrospectively looks like a concerted generational project": the "writing of England."[16] Defining and consolidating "Englishness," by means of what Claire McEachern calls "the poetics of nationhood," is now understood as a central ambition and defining achievement of Renaissance literature; in the age of Shakespeare and Spenser, McEachern argues, imaginative writing worked "to syncretize and synchronize competing interests in utopian visions of union."[17] As Andrew Escobedo argues, literary authors used "narrative representations of nationhood" to compensate for an otherwise hopelessly fractured sense of history, knitting together "the English past, present, and future in a complete and continuous story."[18] In the context of "writing England," the work of promoting and improving the mother tongue mattered more than ever, for as Ian Smith claims, "on both the local and, more strikingly, the national scale, speaking English amount[ed] to a performative act of being English, a performance of the nation."[19]

But such arguments rely on what sixteenth-century writers and rhetoricians would have recognized as a partial version of the classical account of eloquence, which, as Derek Attridge points out in his seminal book on literature as "peculiar language," "seems to be based on two mutually inconsistent demands—that the language of literature be recognizably different from the language we encounter in other contexts, and that it be recognizably the same."[20] Indeed, from its inception within the rhetorical theory of ancient Greece, eloquence has had as much to do with estrangement as with intimacy and familiarity. At the outset of his *Art of Rhetoric*, Aristotle defines eloquence as the realization of common bonds in and through language: an orator succeeds in both his particular task and his larger social function by establishing "what seems true to people of a certain sort," wooing men to consensus by accommodating his argument to "instances near their experience."[21] But when it comes to style, he acknowledges, the reverse holds true: the skilled speaker should make his "language unfamiliar, for people are admirers of what is far off, and what is marvelous is sweet."[22] In this regard, eloquence belongs not only to the poet-legislator who founds the rhetorical "commonplace" but also—even especially—to the outsider whose marginal glamour disturbs and dazzles that community.

Following Aristotle, rhetoricians parsed style ever more finely in an effort to adjudicate between the rival virtues of accessibility and wonder: Dionysius of Helicarnassus contrasted Attic simplicity to Asiatic flamboyance; Cicero's triad of high, middle, and low styles assigned plainness to certain subjects and occasions and extravagance to others; Hermogenes's seven-part taxonomy of stylistic "ideas" ranged from the fundamental virtues of clarity and distinctness to the more striking effects of dignity, solemnity, and brilliance. Such rubrics did not resolve the tension between likeness and difference within Aristotle's account, however; on the contrary, they codified and elaborated it, enshrining strangeness as both the antithesis and the epitome of style.[23]

In other words, sixteenth-century English writers inherited a rhetorical culture that was doubly far-fetched: literally far-fetched in that it entailed a deepening investment in remote antiquity; but also far-fetched as a matter of principle in that it had long regarded eloquence as *no one's* native speech. As Puttenham acknowledges in book 3 of his *Arte*, "there is yet requisite to the perfection of this arte, another maner of exornation, which resteth in the fashioning of our makers language and stile, to such purpose as it may delight and allure as well the mynde as the eare of the hearers with a certaine noueltie and strange maner of conueyance, disguising it no litle from the ordinary and accustomed."[24] Rhetoric and poetry might thus beautify and enrich English, conferring upon it the allurements of novelty and strangeness, but in doing so they threatened to deprive the vernacular of its most essential and widely acknowledged virtue, its status as the common—"the ordinary and accustomed"—tongue. Puttenham hastens to allay this anxiety: the cultivation of an eloquent style should, he insists, make the poet's or orator's words "nothing the more vnseemely or misbecomming, but rather decenter and more agreable to any ciuill eare and vnderstanding."[25] But classical precedent suggested that the effects of eloquence might in fact seem uncivil and misbecoming. Quintilian observes that Cicero's own superlative eloquence led the decorous denizens of the Roman courtroom to applaud wildly, forgetful of their sober surroundings. "Nor," Quintilian explains, "would his words have been greeted with such extraordinary approbation if his speech had been like the ordinary speeches of every day":

> In my opinion, the audience did not know what they were doing, their applause sprang neither from their judgment nor their will; they were seized with a kind of frenzy and unconscious of the place in which they stood, burst forth spontaneously into a perfect ecstasy of delight.

> (Atque ego illos credo qui aderant nec sensisse quid facerent nec sponte iudicioque plausisse, sed velut mente captos et quo essent in loco ignaros erupisse in hunc voluptatis adfectum.)[26]

What Quintilian describes as being "unconscious of . . . place" and Puttenham allegorizes as "strange conveyance" is identified by both rhetoricians as the consummation of rhetorical skill—even though it is also an exact inversion of the sensitivity to local circumstance that is the essence of rhetorical wisdom: what the Greeks call *to prepon* and the Romans *decorum*.[27] The eloquence that anchors men in place thus also transports them, turning the common language into something profoundly and singularly strange. In order to be recognized as such, eloquence must exceed to the point of superseding the very sense of communal identification it is tasked with creating.

As the myth of Orpheus itself suggested, the pressure of such irreconcilable impulses could prove violently disintegrative. The aboriginal orator presented himself to sixteenth-century readers in two guises: not simply as the voice that summons vagrant and bestial mankind into civilized communion but also as the half-mad, self-exiled singer who reviles marriage, dotes on boys, and plays his lyre to an inhuman audience of trees, stones, and wild animals. In book 11 of Ovid's *Metamorphoses*, the latter Orpheus faces a doom that is the antithesis of his earlier achievement: his scorn incites the Ciconian women to turn the instruments of agriculture and religion into blunt objects; they brandish "mattocks, rakes, and shouels," as Arthur Golding writes in his 1567 translation, and batter the poet with "their thyrses greene . . . which for another use than that invented been." In a gruesome inversion of Cicero's fantasy of the gathering of scattered mankind, Orpheus's bruised limbs are flung "in sundrie steds," and his still-singing head, washed downstream from Thrace to Lesbos, is "cast aland" on a "forreine coast."[28]

It is this antisocial, outcast Orpheus who presides over the most significant stylistic innovations of the late sixteenth century, so much so that outlandishness becomes not simply the point of departure for English authors but the point of arrival as well. Lyly, Spenser, and Marlowe achieve renown by subjecting English to extreme elaborations, even deformations, in the name of eloquence. Rather than affirming vernacular literature as the medium of cultural and political synthesis, they foreground its departures from both ordinary speech and the decorums of classical rhetoric and poetry.

Far from mythologizing eloquence as a force that binds vagrant individuals into social communion, they allegorize its effects in narratives of willful unsociability, featuring protagonists whose astonishing powers of persuasion dislodge them from anything resembling stable community: Euphues's witty tongue leads away from a home to which he can never truly return; Colin Clout retreats from pastoral fellowship into sullen isolation; Tamburlaine struts across the civilized world leaving rubble and ashes in his wake. These are paradigmatic figures of English style from the late sixteenth century, but they are hardly representatives of a "common tongue" around whom a new national community might form.

Nor are they meant to be. Throughout the sixteenth century, in theoretical treatises and literary works alike, tropes of intimacy and sociability, the traditional virtues of artful speech, were made to coexist with unexpectedly compelling fantasies of alienation, errancy, and disunity. The appeal of those fantasies stems from a peculiar confluence of historical and cultural pressures, as English scholars, rhetoricians, and literary authors discovered both practical and theoretical advantages to what had once seemed like linguistic infirmities. Primed by their sensitivity to "England's classical nowhereness,"[29] they prove keenly alert to the contradictory stances on familiarity and foreignness that structure classical accounts of eloquence, and the very moments at which they seem most urgently concerned with the particularities of their own Englishness are often the moments at which they come closest to the preoccupations of their Greek and Roman predecessors. The mutually inconsistent demands of classical rhetorical theory mirrored the mutually inconsistent demands exerted upon English writers by the classical tradition as a whole, that enticing yet alienating corpus of speeches, poems, and plays that both invited their efforts at emulation and impugned their status as barbarous outsiders. Relative to classical Greek and Latin, after all, English was *already* a peculiar language: haphazardly composed, indiscriminately mixed, awkwardly pronounced, and indelibly strange. Capitulation to the alien order of eloquence could thus seem curiously like doubling down on a native eccentricity.

As Jones documents in his magisterial study of the vernacular in English Renaissance culture, in a brief span of years beginning around 1575 the status of English was revised dramatically upward. Novel achievements in prose, verse, and drama earned for the vernacular the reputation of an "eloquent tongue," and decades of skepticism give way to the assertive experiments of an age that, in Jones's words, "believed wholeheartedly in the literary value of its language."[30] But this belief was not identical to—or even, perhaps, compatible with—faith in the vernacular's power to organize and sustain the body politic, for making English eloquent was also a way of dislocating it from the imagined community of native speakers. As Jones observes, the first fruits of this new faith were often willfully off-putting: "No longer was the vernacular only a practical instrument, the efficacy of which depended upon simple clarity and humble plainness; it was, instead, a free medium of expression, in which brave new words and elaborate figures could puzzle or displease whom they would."[31] Jones does not dwell on this curiously negative formulation of poetic license, nor have subsequent scholars taken it up, but sixteenth-century critics were sensitive to its implications for the mother tongue. Although the authors of rhetorical and poetic handbooks promoted artful English as the expression of a well-fashioned England, others identified eloquence as a more disorienting and disruptive force.

Thus William Harrison writes in his *Description and Historie of England*, printed in 1577 as part of the first volume of Holinshed's *Chronicles*, that the unprecedented investment of literary writers in their mother tongue seems to have made it both more excellent and less English than ever before. "Our tongue," Harrison allows, "never came unto the type of perfection until the time of Queen Elizabeth, wherein . . . sundry learned and excellent writers have fully accomplished the ornature of the same," but he cautions that "not a few other doo greatlie seeke to staine the same, by fond affectation of forren and strange words, presuming that to be the best English, which is most corrupted with externall termes of eloquence."[32] Harrison was not alone in identifying the pursuit of eloquence with the affectation of strangeness or externality. Samuel Daniel's 1603 *Defence of Ryme* deplores the "affectation" of poets who show themselves "to be both unkinde and vnnaturall to our owne natiue langue, in disguising or forging strange or vnusuall words, as if it were to make our verse seeme another kind of speech out of the course of our vsuall practice," while the preface to Robert Cawdrey's 1604 dictionary, *A Table*

Alphabeticall, adapts a passage from Wilson's *Arte of Rhetorique* to its own homogenizing purposes, urging readers that unless they are prepared to "make a difference of English, and say, some is learned English, and othersome is rude English, or the one is Court talke, the other is Country-speech," they "must of necessitie banish all affected Rhetorique, and vse altogether one manner of language."[33] Such admonishments remind us that, notwithstanding the myth of eloquence's attractive power, the promotion of the vernacular as a literary tongue was not easily aligned with the promotion of a unified national identity. If laying claim to "the best English" meant disavowing the obligations of familiarity and mutual intelligibility, then the triumph of English begins to look like a more equivocal—even self-defeating—achievement.

The mingled pride and concern Harrison expresses is in some respects typical of his moment, a moment at which England appeared to its inhabitants as simultaneously provincial and cosmopolitan, isolated and expansive. Both perspectives can be grounded in historical fact. As David Wallace points out, only in 1558, with the loss of Calais, did England lose its foothold on the Continent and "become . . . an island."[34] At the same time, however, travel and trade brought the rest of Europe, and even Asia, closer: foreigners—and foreign books—swarmed London; the wool trade boomed; Englishmen crossed the channel in pursuit of wealth, learning, and pleasure; and the authors of texts such as Richard Hakluyt's *Principle Navigations of the English Nation* (1589) took pride in representing England's reach as unprecedentedly large. "Whoever heard of Englishmen at Goa before now?" Hakluyt asks. "What English ships did heretofore . . . range along the coast of Chile, Peru, and all the backside of Nova Hispania?"[35]

It is not surprising that the excitement and anxiety elicited by such changes inflect English authors' perceptions of what Thomas Nashe half-jokingly calls "our homely Island tongue."[36] Nashe tells readers who object to his "huge words," "I had as lieve have . . . no clothes rather than wear linsey wolsey";[37] the language that Thomas Wilson likens favorably to "our Countrie cloth"[38] strikes him as too homespun altogether.[39] So too George Chapman, who in the preface to his translation of Homer refuses to apologize for his "farre fetcht and, as it were, beyond sea manner of writing": English would be better off, he insists, if its native authors did not restrict themselves to "nothing but what mixeth it selfe with ordinarie table talke."[40] For Richard Mulcaster, Spenser's grammar-school master and a fierce advocate for the mother tongue, the mobility of England's merchant class was a sign of the vernacular's own potential for expansion and enrichment: "Will all kindes of trade, and all sorts of traffik, make a tung of account?" he asks. "If the spreading sea, and the spacious land could vse anie speche," he declares, "theie would both shew you, where, and in how manie strange places, theie haue sene our peple, and also giue you to wit, that theie deall in as much, and as great varietie of matters, as anie other peple do, whether at home or abrode."[41]

But the success of England's efforts to extend its influence across the globe could intensify as well as assuage concerns about the value of English. Those far-flung merchants and travelers could hardly expect to use English in their dealings with foreigners.[42] Puttenham worries in his *Arte* that the vernacular would suffer from such encounters, as the English of "Secretaries and Marchaunts and trauailours" was inevitably corrupted by the "straunge termes of other languages."[43]

Debates about the vernacular's literary potential thus intersected with, reflected, and informed more widespread debates about England's place in the world—historically marginal, newly insular, increasingly mobile, and uncertainly bounded. Throughout the sixteenth century terms such as insularity and estrangement, homeliness and exoticism, proximity and distance served as analogies for a whole range of (often contradictory) attitudes toward English eloquence, and the immediate experiences of geographic expansion and isolation supplied vernacular writers with a rich fund of metaphors for their linguistic predicament. Like England in the sixteenth century, English seemed poised to embark on a potentially enriching, potentially ruinous venture beyond its native plot. Indeed the ambivalence with which many authors allude to England's geographic circumstances—its long-standing marginality, its burgeoning global reach—turns out to be a useful guide for articulating their ambivalence about eloquence. If geographic insularity was both an asset and an impediment to England's cultural, moral, and intellectual development, so too was confining oneself to the strict limits of common usage both an aid and an obstacle to rhetorical success. If travel, trade, and other foreign engagements were either the key to the nation's growth and enrichment or the fastest route to degradation and decline, so too was the allure of strange terms either the vernacular's greatest hope or its most persistent source of error.

Compounding this ambivalence was the fact that, as Paula Blank has shown, it proved impossible to position oneself as a defender of linguistic commonality without exacerbating the problem of linguistic diversity.[44] Language reformers who appealed to the notion of a common tongue invariably also highlighted divisions within the language: the alternative to banishing rhetoric is, as Cawdrey writes, "mak[ing] a difference of English," dismembering the vernacular in order to distinguish good uses from bad, proper from improper, usual from eccentric. Harrison's account works at just such cross-purposes of consolidation and differentiation, and his repeated invocations of the phrase "our tongue" jar with a tendency to characterize the vernacular's virtues in terms of narrowness and exclusivity. English is, he acknowledges, just one of "the languages spoken in this Iland"; its "excellency" is found only "in one, and the south part of this Iland," and strangers to that part find its sounds and syntax near impossible to master.[45] Instead of producing English as the locus of "deep, horizontal community," then, the promotion of the vernacular depended on discriminatory judgments that threatened to undo the pretense of a common tongue. The terms of that adjudication exerted further stress on the ideal of commonality: even Harrison's mistrust of eloquence's "externall termes" does not preclude him from reaching for a neo-Latinate loan-word—"ornature"—to characterize the achievements of the vernacular's truly English stylists, the "learned and excellent" writers whose style he distinguishes from that of their fondly affected rivals.[46]

We might point out in Harrison's defense that the identification of eloquence with the classical tongues makes "externall termes" nearly impossible to avoid. As Wayne Rebhorn has observed, like the Roman rhetoricians before them, who depended on a theoretical lexicon borrowed from Greece, English rhetoricians and language reformers had "almost no choice but to use literally outlandish words from foreign languages."[47] However firmly he might wish to draw the boundaries of vernacularity, then, Harrison, like any Renaissance critic, had to look elsewhere for a language to describe its literary virtues. That necessity yields a minor dissonance in Harrison's prose, but it resonated in a far more consequential way through the literature and literary theories of his time. That is to say, the tension between insularity and externality in sixteenth-century debates about eloquence is not exclusively, or even primarily, a function of the vernacular's "real-world" contexts; it is also the residue of its immersion in the classical tradition. The efforts of pedagogues and rhetoricians to fix rules and examples by which the best English might be recognized and perpetuated had the disorienting effect of embedding norms of vernacularity in the emulation of frankly alien tongues, the "peculiar languages" of ancient Athens and Rome. To speak English eloquently was, by definition, to speak it strangely.

Indeed, although modern historians and literary critics have characterized sixteenth-century rhetorical culture as "unequivocally and resolutely social in outlook," its rituals of argument aimed at producing "a community of individuals sharing a common language,"[48] the translation of this culture into England and into English pushed Renaissance writers up against the limits of the assumed virtues of community and commonality. To begin with, as Sean Keilen has emphasized, English scholars and writers working to augment their notoriously deficient tongue were repeatedly confronted with reminders of their insularity and marginality; looking for models in the classical past, they discovered a legacy of barbarous exclusion, remedied only through submission to conquest.[49] As Jenny Mann's work on figures of speech reveals, even small-scale transactions between antiquity and the present could trigger a jarring sense of dislocation and devaluation: vernacular rhetoricians may have fantasized the nation as "an ideally united community of native English speakers," but in ferrying schemes and tropes out of classical prose and poetry and into English, they upset that native unity, "threaten[ing] to overwhelm their vernacular with foreign devices."[50] All too often, then, as Carla Mazzio demonstrates, vernacular texts that modeled themselves on classical literature became sites of "language trouble," marred by stammering, mumbling, lexical confusion, and other forms of inarticulacy.[51]

Like these critics, I am interested in the distorting, even disabling pressure that classical antiquity exerts on the theory and practice of vernacular eloquence—in particular in the impossibility of validating modern native practice without resorting to the definitively ancient and nonnative. But this paradoxical conflation of eloquence and alienation, although it speaks in seemingly direct ways to the belated and marginal predicament of English writers, is by no means particular to the sixteenth century; it is a legacy of the classical tradition's unresolved attitude toward linguistic difference. In this sense the very incommensurability of the classical past and the vernacular present could prove enabling for English writers, for even as their study of ancient rhetoric and poetry taught them to recognize their estrangement from antiquity, it also taught them to perceive in that estrangement—or any estrangement of language—the essence of literary value. Thus within any number of sixteenth-century English texts, the expressed desire to domesticate eloquence, reconciling antique precepts to the rhetorical imperatives of the here and now, clashes with an equally pervasive tendency to privilege distance and difference as the ideal attributes of eloquent speech. This willful embrace of strangeness is not, as William Harrison assumes, the purview of the unlearned, those self-alienated "other[s]" whose perversity threatens the ideal course of linguistic progress. On the contrary, it is a *learned* technique, cultivated in deference to the very texts and theories that made English seem so strange.

*   *   *

That learning is the first subject of this study. However radically innovative they appeared, the stylistic experiments of the late 1570s and early 1580s are rooted in theoretical ground prepared by an earlier humanism, as two seemingly antagonistic strains of linguistic reform worked to alter the nature and status of the English language. The earlier decades of the sixteenth century bear witness, on the one hand, to the concerted effort to imbue a generation of English schoolboys with perfect Latinity and, on the other hand, to the equally concerted effort to define rhetorical and poetic standards for the vernacular, achieving parity with antiquity by giving English an eloquence of its own. Although they aim at distinct, even rivalrous, visions of linguistic achievement, in practice the two movements shared significant overlap: those who sought to inculcate Latinity necessarily wrote in English and, in consequence, valued the vernacular more highly and altered its course more definitively than is often allowed; meanwhile the authors of vernacular arts of rhetoric and poetics served as conduits for conspicuously foreign terms, concepts, and writerly practices—for an ideal of Englishness that remains in constant, jostling contact with tongues elsewhere. In a more basic sense, both Latin pedagogues and vernacular rhetoricians presented readers with an essentially paradoxical vision of what it might mean for England, as a whole, to lay claim to eloquence. Although each movement addresses itself to a broad audience, invoking a self-justifying rhetoric of intimacy and domesticity— proper instruction will make Latin "familiar" and "easy" to any learner; the vernacular merits development because it is the "common" and "mother" tongue—each ends by accepting, and even valorizing, estrangement and exile as the necessary conditions of a properly English eloquence.

Conventional narratives of vernacularization and nation-building tend to obscure both the sympathies between these two movements and the tensions within them. To begin with, although the rise of vernacular literature is often yoked to the "fall" or "dethronement" of the classical tongues,[52] this equation is misleading. For much of the sixteenth century, as I argue in my opening chapter, a stubborn attachment to frankly impracticable fantasies of Latinization was a primary motive for the cultivation of the vernacular by literate authors. The elegant and inventive use of English in Sir Thomas Elyot's *Boke named the Governour* (1531) and Roger Ascham's *Scholemaster* (1570) anticipates the outpouring of vernacular literature that marks the end of the sixteenth century, but the two texts manifest as well a seemingly self-abnegating devotion to the cultivation of the classical tongues. Critics have responded by treating their stylistic influence as distinct from, even opposed to, their expressed pedagogical commitments. In fact, however, both Elyot's unself-conscious neologizing and Ascham's artfully balanced syntax arise out of their philosophies of foreign language study: what they bequeath to English is an indelible sense of its own difference from Latin and Greek.

As architects of ambitious new programs for the study of classical literature, men tasked with managing the transfer of eloquence from one time and place to another, radically unlike it, Elyot and Ascham scrutinize the relationship of learning to intimacy and estrangement. Both their pedagogical theories and their prose work to remedy the seemingly catastrophic fact of England's alienation from classical civilization—what Elyot calls the "infelicitie of our tyme and country." They arrive, however, at very different conceptions of how that infelicitous gap ought to inform the pursuit of eloquence. For Elyot, both pedagogy and language are sustained by acts of hospitality, inviting strangeness into the home so as to be transformed and enriched by it: classical authors (and foreign loan-words) are akin to the Greek wet nurses who raised Roman infants, foreigners welcomed as intimate familiars. For Ascham, such receptivity to outside influence is morally perilous, pedagogically ineffective, and rhetorically unwise: remoteness and insularity may be obstacles to linguistic sophistication, but they are sure safeguards of virtue. Thus while Elyot's pedagogy and prose work to reduce the distance between English and Latin, Ascham—more pragmatically and more radically—embraces distance as the engine of linguistic refinement. His pedagogical method and his prose style foreground the necessity and virtue of *mediation*: for him, classical authors are not wet nurses but sea captains, guides on a necessarily prolonged and difficult journey between tongues. This forced detour, enshrined in the artificially arduous practice of double translation, returned a generation of English writers to their mother tongue as, in effect, a second language—what was once the enforced predicament of the exile and the barbarian becomes the deliberately cultivated pose of the would-be eloquent author.

Estrangement—temporal, geographic, cultural, and linguistic—is urgently and obviously a concern for those who would transplant Latin eloquence to England, those who measure their own language and culture by its distance from antiquity. It is less clearly an issue for the authors of the first vernacular arts of rhetoric and poetics: in these texts, it would seem, the goal is to establish eloquence as an essentially homely value. But as I have suggested above, their acquaintance with classical rhetoric brings English rhetoricians and poetic theorists into conversation with a tradition *already* divided between allegiance to home and attraction to the remote and alien. Chapter 2 explores the outworkings of that internal division within a corpus of texts that stake their own highly contested value on a myth of linguistic sociability that proves inadequate, or even opposed, to their visions of linguistic transport. As Thomas Wilson emphasizes in the first full-fledged English art of rhetoric, the claims that rhetoric makes to truth are essentially local in character; proximity is the guarantor of plausibility, and ordinary or common speech therefore exerts a particularly strong claim on the attention and commitment of an audience. But persuasion, as Wilson also allows, is not simply a matter of plausibility: style, ornament, and figuration have always been acknowledged to play some part in the achievement of eloquence, and in this regard, rhetorical success depends not on the familiarity of one's speech but precisely on its novelty and difference. The sense that eloquence resides elsewhere is endemic to rhetoric, however emphatically "Englished." The archive of rhetorical handbooks and poetic treatises that is often invoked as evidence of literature's nationalizing force is thus equally available as testimony to literature's appeal as *uncommon* speech: especially in the guise of what William Harrison calls "ornature," eloquence retains persistent associations with foreignness.

Like their predecessors in Athens and Rome, English rhetoricians identify the orator's and the poet's power both with the fashioning of community and with the uncircumscribed pleasures of travel, with familiarity and estrangement. Wilson abjures those who affect "outlandish English" in the name of eloquence, but he praises the beauty of "farre fetcht" figures of speech.[53] Richard Sherry apologizes that the title of his 1550 *Treatise of Schemes and Tropes* will sound "all straunge unto our English eares," but he also imagines that the strangeness of terms such as "scheme" and "trope" may appeal to readers who are "moued with the noueltye thereof."[54] Puttenham defines "the best English" as that used in "London and the shires lying about London within sixty miles, and not much above," but he urges vernacular poets to ornament their language with "rich Orient colours," to embrace the "forraine and coloured talke" of figuration, and to risk "trespasses in speech" in order to achieve the "novelty of language evidently (and yet not absurdly) estranged from the ordinary."[55] Without the cultivation of a certain degree of alienation—without translation and metaphor—eloquence collapses into mere talk; taken too far, the exoticism of eloquence becomes affectation and absurdity. Of course, the distance between evident estrangement and absurdity proves much more difficult to gauge than the sixty miles between London and its outermost suburbs:

far from securing the vernacular as the locus of communal identification, sixteenth-century efforts to define eloquence in (and on) native terms make the province of "the best English" increasingly difficult to map.

Decoupling the trajectories of vernacularity and nationhood in this fashion allows us to regain an appreciation of the productive role that affectation—that most maligned of literary strategies—plays in the effort to claim eloquence for the mother tongue. The vernacular rhetorician joins with the Latin schoolmaster in calculating both the hazards and the rewards of lin-guistic eccentricity; together they fashion the conceptual frame within which Lyly, Spenser, and Marlowe enact their self-consciously bold experiments in vernacular style. In other words, the extravagantly strung-on clauses of *Eu-phues*, the exaggeratedly "uncouth" terms of *The Shepheardes Calender*, and *Tamburlaine*'s savage bombast are not incidental to the bids these texts make on behalf on the vernacular; they are, rather, the means by which English asserts itself in an age that places a premium on the alienating force of artful speech. I have called strangeness a learned achievement, and as I will empha-size in my readings, eccentricity is in many ways a calculated effect of Lyly's prose, Spenser's verse, and Marlowe's drama: these writers and the styles they promote are not quite as strange as they strive to appear. Lyly's hyperabundant prose arises from utterly conventional compositional practices; the oddity of Spenser's pseudo-archaic diction is exaggerated by E. K.'s gloss; Marlowe's blank-verse line has closer antecedents in English than we usually recall, or than Marlowe admits. Their efforts earned them outrage as well as admira-tion, but in either case they succeeded in fixing their individual achievements within a much larger conversation about the nature and purpose of vernacular eloquence. Commonality might be the premise from which that conversa-tion began, but estrangement was where it invariably tended: thus the writers credited with accomplishing the most in and for the mother tongue were those who underscored its freaks, fissures, and indecorums, transferring it "by a strange maner of conveyance," as Puttenham might say, into the mouths of errant cosmopolitans, exiled shepherds, and barbarian warlords.

Reading Lyly, Spenser, and Marlowe in this light means acknowledging that eccentricity is the ideal that shapes their visions of eloquence. Euphues, Colin Clout, and Tamburlaine articulate new forms of English, and of English-ness, but they also enact the dramas of displacement, alienation, and trespass that make those innovations possible—and, what is perhaps more important, legible as such. The substance of their stylistic eccentricity—Lyly's assiduously balanced clauses, Spenser's quasi-medieval diction, Marlowe's chest-thumping orotundity—is well known, but the motives and mechanisms for announcing that eccentricity to readers are not. For this reason I am less concerned to delineate what is new or distinctive in each style—less, perhaps, than critics have tended to assume—than I am to show how novelty and distinction are promoted, theorized, and critiqued with the texts themselves: how and why familiar words, forms, and literary techniques are burdened or burnished with strangeness.

In Lyly's case, the romance of estrangement was built into the commonplace tradition. My third chapter highlights the interplay within Erasmus's rhetorical handbooks—the most influential and prestigious source for Lyly's style—of the satisfactions of stylistic amplitude and the pleasures of geographic errancy. The *De Copia* taught a generation of English schoolboys to define eloquence as the ability to speak as expansively as possible on any subject—and to identify that ability with a more literal freedom of movement, a protocosmopolitan approach to being at home in the world. Erasmus demonstrates *copia* by generating over a hundred versions of a single sentence—"your letter greatly pleased me"—and the link between letter writing and stylistic abundance persists throughout his pedagogical program. In *De Conscribendis Epistolis* (another staple of the sixteenth-century English schoolroom), Erasmus makes clear that he favors letter writing as an educational exercise because the epistle, like the ideal of *copia*, defies the usual boundaries governing speech, passing from one rhetorical context to another with the same ease that a well-trained schoolboy might pass from one commonplace to the next. It is no coincidence, then, that vernacular *copia* finds its limit in a text filled to bursting with both letters and commonplaces. Incorporating similitudes, sententiae, and exempla from an array of classical and contemporary sources, including many from Erasmus, the ornate rhetorical set-pieces of Lyly's *Euphues* are as wide ranging—and as hard to pin down, logically speaking—as his eponymous hero. Frequently, however, neither Euphues nor Lyly arrives at his projected end, succumbing to an errant superfluity that overrides the more local demands of narrative and rhetorical coherence. Generations of readers have taxed *Euphues* with this as an oversight, charging Lyly with allowing his enthusiasm for *copia* to carry him past the boundaries of stylistic decorum. But Lyly is hardly blind to the eccentricities of his style: on the contrary, his failure to inaugurate a sustainable model of vernacular eloquence is prefigured in the pages of his 1580 sequel, *Euphues and His England*, which exiles Euphues to the margins of his own plot, branding him as a perpetual outsider. Lyly does not succumb to Erasmian excess so much as he deliberately subjects English to its hidden costs.

A similarly self-marginalizing drive fuels Edmund Spenser's efforts to invent a poetic diction that redeems the vernacular's onerous debt to the classical tradition. Chapter 4 argues that *The Shepheardes Calender* adopts a poetics of deliberate self-estrangement, foregrounding England's remoteness from antiquity and poetry's remoteness from ordinary speech. Despite its conventional associations with poetic and even political ambition, pastoral is a singularly inhospitable genre for an English poet: in Virgil's first eclogue Britain appears as the antithesis of pastoral contentment, a place of exile and colonial abjection. By treating English as a quasi-foreign tongue and adopting the errant and alienated persona of Colin Clout, Spenser repeats this marginalizing gesture, finding in exile a means to reinvigorate vernacular poetry. The pedantic E. K. plays a crucially paradoxical role in this endeavor: positioned as guide to the odd corners and rough edges of Spenser's verse, he often serves as a means of detaining and dislocating our attention, supplying the poem as a whole with an aura of estrangement in excess of its own peculiarities. Ultimately his insistence on the virtues of this kind of deliberate self-alienation allows Spenser to find a place for pastoral—and for Colin Clout—in England's own abject colonial sphere, beyond the Irish pale.

Chapter 5 takes up the persistent problem of how to set limits for poetic expression, especially given the lack of a universally accepted system of measuring English verse. Hailed as the source of English verse's "mighty line"—the iambic pentameter that gives classical shape to unruly rhyme—Marlowe's *Tamburlaine the Great* nevertheless offers an ominous vision of linguistic trespass, in the person of a barbarous yet eloquent Scythian whose disdain for territorial limits is matched by his tendency to rhetorical excess. The violence that attends persuasion in Marlowe's poetry suggests that abuse is the inevitable counterpart of eloquence—and that cages, bits, and harnesses are the necessary implements of linguistic refinement. However, if we situate Marlowe's play within the context of debates over rhyme and metrical form, we discover a multiplicity of Tamburlaines: in addition to Marlowe's famous overreacher, there are the unexpectedly terse—even measured—Timur Cutzclewe of book 2 of Puttenham's *Arte of English Poesie* and the Tamburlaine of Daniel's *Defence*, who emerges as the unwitting progenitor of a cultural movement—Renaissance humanism—that Daniel indicts precisely for its neglect of so-called barbarian culture. Marlowe's Tamburlaine, Puttenham's Timur Cutzclewe, and Daniel's Tamburlaine chart very different courses for English verse, but they stand together as figures for a more expansive definition of linguistic excellence, what Daniel calls eloquence "in what Scythian sorte soeuer."[56]

As a group, these Scythian warrior-poets remind us that at the end of Elizabeth I's reign and the height of what we now call the Renaissance, English writers were far from agreed on the ideal trajectory of the English literary tradition—a tradition whose contours they refused to equate with those of England (or even Britain). Why, then, do we continue to associate their age with the consolidation of English identity under the banner of language? Clearly the answer has something to do with Shakespeare, the Orpheus around whom the idea of an English literary tradition still coheres. But as I remark in a brief coda, Shakespeare is not an obvious candidate for that role. To seventeenth- and eighteenth-century critics, the extremity of linguistic experimentation in the late sixteenth century cried out for reform, and no one needed disciplining more than Shakespeare. As those early critics recognized, the poet who is largely hailed today for the universal accessibility of his art thrived in his own time by imitating and even exaggerating the excesses of his most outrageous peers and predecessors. It is no coincidence that, in the sequence of plays that for many modern critics exemplify the "poetics of nationhood," Falstaff speaks with the voice of Euphues and Pistol in the tones of Tamburlaine. These disreputable companions, figures for the outlandishness that has always haunted eloquence, both aid and impede the articulation of Hal's (eventually) kingly English; vagabonds and strays can also serve as scouts, marking by their trespasses the boundaries of authorized expression. In the end, of course, they must be banished—but they very nearly take Shakespeare with them. Indeed the poet we continually invoke as a figure for language's unifying power may have more to teach us about the self-alienating gestures on which our vernacular literary tradition is founded.

Chapter 1

Good Space and Time:
Humanist Pedagogy and the
Uses of Estrangement

A rich body of criticism attests to the imprint left on Renaissance writers by their grammar-school education in classical literature,[1] but a basic feature of this pedagogical program has received little attention: in order to promote their vision of Latinity, sixteenth-century humanist pedagogical theorists first had to reinvent English. As Ardis Butterfield points out, the training bestowed on educated Englishmen from the medieval period through the sixteenth century gave them "much greater eloquence and indeed fluency in [Latin] than they possessed in the vernacular"; far from representing a reversion to a more natural voice, writing in English "was thus a source of strain, a sense that there was a gulf to cross between one form of language and the other."[2] And yet such men were, of necessity, some of the first to publish in the vernacular, eager to disseminate their methods of study to an audience that had not yet achieved perfect Latinity. In pedagogical treatises such as Thomas Elyot's *The Boke named the Governour* (1531) and Roger Ascham's *The Scholemaster* (1570), the fashioning of English as a literate tongue thus models, in reverse, the fashioning of English schoolboys as literate classicists: the vernacular is advanced, with self-conscious effort, as a means to its own supersession.

For many critics, this ambivalent stance toward the vernacular constitutes an essential difference between humanist writers of the early and mid-sixteenth century and their late Elizabethan successors. If, as Richard Foster Jones argues, the final decades of the sixteenth century were marked by whole-hearted faith in the vernacular's expressive powers, this is a faith that Elyot and Ascham evidently did not share. The fact that such writers "employed the vernacular is no proof that [they] admired it," Jones observes: Elyot, though he "did not disdain to use the vernacular in *The Governour*," treats eloquence as "a quality beyond the abilities of the vernacular," while Ascham "gives [in *The Scholemaster*] unmistakable evidence that the language he is using has no claim to eloquence."[3] In a broader sense, Latin-promoting humanists such as Elyot and Ascham are understood to have chosen the wrong side in an unfolding rivalry between the vernacular and the classical tongues: English "triumphs" at the necessary expense of Latin and Greek.[4] Or, in Richard Helgerson's more neutral phrasing, "the sufficiency or insufficiency of the English language . . . came to matter with a special intensity" only when "other sources of identity and cultural authority mattered less."[5]

But such formulations cannot account for the pains both Elyot and Ascham took to shape their prose and the cause that justified those pains: these are texts whose innovative and artful English is crafted in the service of Latinity. Indeed, *The Governour* and *The Scholemaster* suggest that for early English humanists—who might otherwise, and with greater ease, have written in Latin—the vernacular came to matter precisely because other sources of cultural authority mattered so much more. For the most part, however, the formal achievements of Elyot's and Ascham's prose have been read against the grain of their pedagogical commitments: for literary critics, *The Governour* and *The Scholemaster* are exemplary of a movement at odds with itself, obtusely blind to the real value of its own investment in the vernacular. Thus C. S. Lewis credits Elyot as a "convinced and conscious neologizer," the composer of "lucid" and "literary" sentences, and one of the first English writers to be "aware of prose as art," but he insists that, as a work of pedagogical theory, *The Governour* has "nothing in it which suggests a mind of the first order." Ascham he hails as an "irresistible" writer, but only if one pays minimal attention to his educational precepts: "the literary historian can have no opinion on the mischief of 'making Latines' or the virtues of the 'two paper bokes,'" he writes, but "once get [Ascham] out of the schoolroom and he pleases us all."[6] In more recent criticism, Lewis's instinctive distaste for humanism's classicizing ambitions has ramified into a consensus about the adversarial relationship between pedagogy (and, above all, foreign language learning) and literature in the sixteenth century. According to this consensus, humanist pedagogy, with its emphasis on rote learning and unthinking submission to authority, threatened to develop in English schoolboys the very qualities least conducive to linguistic experimentation and literary achievement, and the vernacular Renaissance testifies to the happy failure of its methods.[7] Classical education is still acknowledged as a shaping influence on Elizabethan writers, but attention has fixed on "the slippage between the august ideals of humanist education and its practical shortcomings, between its ambitions and its unintended consequences."[8]

In a similar way, by dint of their prowess as writers and their influence as theorists, Elyot and Ascham continue to find their way into studies of sixteenth-century literature, but the lines of formal influence are traced across a more basic plot of departure: prodigality, opposition, rebellion, and critique.[9] Thomas Greene's admiration for Elyot and (especially) Ascham as prose stylists prompts him to offer the most generous possible version of this plot. The crucial feature of early English humanism, he writes, is that "it lacked still a sure sense of where it was headed": what seems like a rigid adherence to antique precepts is simply a not-yet-realized sense of literary and linguistic ambition.[10] But if Jones's description of Elyot and Ascham exaggerates their disdain for English, Greene's account understates their confidence in the classical tongues. To say that early English humanism lacked a clear sense of where it was headed dismisses the one thing Elyot and Ascham thought they knew for sure: "[A]ll men couet to haue their children speake Latin: and so do I verie earnestlie too," Ascham reassures readers of *The Scholemaster*. "We bothe, haue one purpose: we agree in desire, we wish one end: but we differ somewhat in order and waie, that leadeth rightlie to that end."[11] From Ascham's perspective, the end of the journey was its only fixed point: well-intentioned humanists might disagree about how to arrive at fluency in the Latin tongue (and, as we shall see, he and Elyot emphatically do), but it never occurs to him that anyone might question the goal itself.

It is precisely the firmness, even the stubbornness, with which *The Governour* and *The Scholemaster* cling to this end that draws them closest to the vernacular poets and playwrights of a later generation, with whom they share—to whom they communicate—the notion that eloquence both depends and thrives on estrangement. Indeed it is in the writing of men strenuously committed to a linguistic ideal anchored in classical antiquity, and prone to see England in terms of its remoteness from that ideal, that we find a rationale for the willfully eccentric literary vernaculars of the late sixteenth century: in the context of the humanist schoolroom, English is a language constituted and regenerated by its difference and distance from the classical tongues. We find, moreover, a precedent for the impulse to *narrate* the experience of linguistic estrangement, projecting one's own rhetorical maneuvers onto characters whose actions allegorize fraught transactions within and between languages.

The self-reflexive stories of errancy, alienation, and trespass in *Euphues, The Shepheardes Calender*, and *Tamburlaine* riff on fantasies of estrangement and transport original to scenes of foreign language learning in *The Governour* and *The Scholemaster*. In their eloquence and their indelible strangeness Euphues, Colin Clout, and Tamburlaine are kin to a cluster of imaginary figures who preside over the transmission of eloquence in Elyot's and Ascham's treatises: classical writers reimagined in the guise of foreign-born nursemaids and native archers, expert sea captains and wayward exiles, figures whose skill resides precisely in their negotiation of estrangement. From our own perspective, the linguistic transactions such figures are asked to mediate can appear, as Richard Halpern writes of humanist education as a whole, like "miracle[s] of impracticality."[12] That impracticality is, in fact, a central preoccupation for Elyot and Ascham, manifested most clearly in their self-conscious reflections on their own use of the vernacular—a practical necessity that begets a sense of possibility. For both writers, the strain of moving between tongues is initially legible only as an obstacle to their ambitions for England, a country whose historic marginality and insularity seem to condemn it to rusticity, if not outright barbarity. Each ultimately arrives, however, at a more positive sense of what distance and difficulty might mean for English culture and language: the labor of translating their classical ideals into the vernacular subtly refashions their conceptions of eloquence.

Virgil the Nursemaid

When Ascham says that he and his fellow pedagogues "differ somewhat in [the] order and waie" of language study, he points to a debate that swirls around a single, fundamental question: how were sixteenth-century English schoolmasters, self-appointed heirs to classical antiquity, to accommodate the fact of living in sixteenth-century England? As he observes in *The Scholemaster*, "if ye would speake as the best and wisest do, ye must be conuersant, where the best and wisest are, but if yow be borne or brought vp in a rude contrie, ye shall not chose but speake rudelie: the rudest man of all knoweth this to be trewe."[13] For Elyot, this truth is a source of frequent embarrassment, a recurring impediment to his desire to "devulgate or sette fourth" the substance of classical learning.[14] The difficulties arise literally from the start. As he acknowledges in the opening pages of *The Governour*, classical theories of education have little to say about language instruction for infants: most "olde authors holde oppinion that, before the age of seuen yeres [the moment at which the care of the mother or nursemaid yields to the supervision of the *pedagogue*] a chylde shulde nat be instructed in letters." But Elyot insists that it is only by distinguishing itself from the classical example in this one particular that the English can hope to equal Greece and Rome in any other: "[For] those writers were either grekes or latines, amonge whom all doctrine and sciences were in their maternall tonges; by reason wherof they saued all that longe tyme whiche at this dayes is spente in understandyng perfectly the greke or latyne. Wherfore it requireth nowe a longer tyme to the understandynge of bothe. Therfore that infelicitie of our tyme and countray compelleth us to encroche some what upon the yeres of children, and specially of noble men, that they may sooner attayne to wisedome and grauitie" (18$_r$). This apology reveals the double bind at the heart of Elyot's approach to foreign language study: for sixteenth-century English schoolboys, the infelicitous circumstances of time and place have made it difficult to access learned speech, and that difficulty compounds the burden of temporal and geographic alienation. The "longer time" that must be devoted to the acquisition of classical tongues—the years spent in grammar school grasping painfully by rote what was once held by birthright—both exposes and exacerbates England's distance from civilized antiquity.

But Elyot's perception of the doubling of lost time and wasted space that occurs whenever a seven-year-old English boy opens his Greek or Latin grammar for the first time points him toward a possible solution: a pedagogy that makes the acquisition of foreign learning an experience of immediacy, intimacy, and domesticity—a pedagogy that conceals its own "encroachment" on the infant by masking itself as something like maternal care. "Hit is expedient," he therefore urges, "that a noble mannes sonne, in his infancie, haue with hym continually onely suche as may accustome hym by litle and litle to speake pure and elegant latin," and even "the nourises and other women aboute hym, if it be possible, [are] to do the same" (19$_v$). In this manner, he insists, "nothing can be more conuenient than by litle and litle to trayne and exercise [a child] in spekyng of latyne: infourmyng them to knowe first the names in latine of all thynges that cometh in syghte, and to name all the partes of theyr bodies: and gyuynge them some what that they couete or desyre, in most gentyl maner to teache them to aske it agayne in latine" (18$_r$). Such convenient and gentle exchanges supply the infant with a foreign speech adapted to his own possessions, his own body, his own desires: what the child acquires almost as a matter of course in Elyot's imaginary nursery is a fully domesticated Latinity, an ease and comfort with the alien tongue that mimics the always already intimate knowledge of native speech. If Englishmen cannot possess Latin as a "maternall tongue," they may at least adopt it as a nursemaid tongue: any well-born child might come to "use the latin tonge as a familiar langage," Elyot promises, provided that his familiars, those "seru[ing] him or kepyng hym company," are all "suche as can speake latine elegantly" (30_{r-v}).

There is an obvious flaw in this plan: where, in sixteenth-century England, are such companions to be found? If, as Lynn Enterline urges, it is time to look more skeptically at the promises made by humanist pedagogical theorists, this far-fetched scheme to entrust the basics of classical instruction to nursemaids and playmates (a plan that arouses Lewis's particular scorn[15]) would seem an excellent place to begin.[16] Here Elyot's logic is conspicuously self-defeating: the effort to imagine a way out of the constraints of time and country merely returns the reader to them. After all, as Elyot laments, English parents who shared his enthusiasm for classical learning were hard-pressed to find qualified tutors or schoolmasters, since even men boasting university training often possessed but a "spone full of latine" (61_r). The idea of a wet nurse who speaks "pure and elegant latin" to the child at her breast may provide an appealing imaginary contrast to the scant intellectual nourishment afforded in actual English schoolrooms, but it is hardly an "expedient" basis for pedagogical practice.[17]

The fantasy of the Latin-speaking wet nurse nonetheless proves generative for Elyot, for it supplies him with a conceptual model both for his pedagogical program and for his prose. Both *The Governour*'s pedagogy and its prose gently enlarge the meaning of supposedly familiar terms, forging increasingly capacious—even far-fetched—boundaries for concepts such as "home," the "mother tongue," and "eloquence." The very absurdity of the idea of a classically fluent wet nurse triggers one such subtle expansion: conscious that no such nurses exist in sixteenth-century England, Elyot quickly amends his suggestion to allow for nurses who, "at the leste way, . . . speke none englisshe but that which is cleane, polite, perfectly and articulately pronounced" (19_v). The Latin-speaking wet nurse figures one strategy by which eloquence might be domesticated—through the adoption of Latin as a familiar tongue—but her English replacement figures another: by differentiating the vernacular from itself, creating an incremental critical distance between English speakers and their native speech.[18] The Latin-speaking nurse shows how learning might be permitted to encroach on an ideal of domesticity; the English-speaking nurse shows how the vernacular might be permitted to encroach on an ideal of eloquence. If "pure" and "elegant" are not exact synonyms for "clean," "polite," and "perfectly and articulately pronounced," the passage from one set of adjectives to another nonetheless begins to effect a transfer of linguistic standards from a purely classical tradition to its no longer homely counterpart.

The two strategies are not identical—Elyot's "at the leste way" marks a significant capitulation—but that too is the point. The fact that the Latin-speaking wet nurse is so quickly supplanted by a more attainable ideal does not undo the logic of the original proposal so much as intensify it: surrogacy is the name of the game. As Robert Matz observes, the efficacy of Elyot's *Boke* depends on the reader's willingness to assent to a sequence of necessary but potentially unconvincing analogies: virtue is like dancing, reading like eating, study like leisure, and scholarly achievement like aristocratic honor.[19] The same holds true of Elyot's philosophy of linguistic refinement, which even as it is characterized by its investment in immediacy, intimacy, and ease is distinguished as well by a pragmatic willingness to effect the illusion of those qualities through substitution or approximation. "If not this, then *at least* that" is the modest mechanism by which one begins to narrow the gap, "by little and little," as Elyot might say, between eloquence and an infant (which is to say, inarticulate) tongue. Each substitution or similitude repeats the service provided by the imaginary Latin-speaking nursemaid, taking the place of an elusive ideal—approximating but also distancing us from that original fantasy of truly maternal Latinity.

Thus the initial attempt to immerse the infant in Latin from birth yields to an effort to populate his world with companions who speak only pure and elegant Latin, or perhaps clean and polite English, and then to descriptions of exercises and games that provide in a more piecemeal and painstaking way the illusion of familiarity with the classical tongue. Finally the companions fall away, and the conversation becomes purely textual: nursemaids are replaced by books. But here too the pedagogical ideal is an experience of intimacy, familiarity, and proximity—by way of analogy, at least. Virgil's poetry, Elyot writes, ought to be the first Latin any English child reads because it "so nighe approcheth to the commune daliaunce and maners of children" that nothing "can be more familiar" (32ᵥ). According to Elyot, the bucolic landscape of Virgil's pastorals evokes the child's own favored haunts, the husbandry of the georgics appeals to his practical instincts, and Aeneas's escapades satisfy his longing for adventure. Indeed, Elyot insists, "there is nat that affect or desire, wherto any childes fantasie is disposed, but in some of Virgils warkes may be founden matter therto apte and propise." Virgil thus presents himself as compensation for the impossible fantasy of the Latin-speaking wet nurse, for he "like to a good norise, giueth to a childe, if he wyll take it, euery thinge apte for his witte and capacitie" (34ᵣ). This nurselike Virgil is not just a surrogate for the unobtainable actual Latin nursemaid; he is also the stand-in for a more arduous and potentially alienating course of study. Elyot's ideal classical education begins with Homer, "from whom as a fountaine, proceded all eloquence and learning"—"there is no lesson . . . to be compared with Homer," he declares (31ᵥ–32ᵣ). But finding a comparable lesson proves necessary: Greek is more difficult than Latin, and Homer's long epics "require therefore a great time to be all lerned and kanned," so Virgil presents himself as the next best thing, being "most lyke to Homere, and all moste the same Homere in latine" (32ᵥ).

Elyot's term for this miraculous *aptness* of Virgil's poetry, its dual kinship both to Homer and to the interests and experiences of the English child, is "eloquence." And although he insists on the necessity of learning Latin in order to access eloquence where it is most readily found, he insists that eloquence transcends disciplinary and linguistic boundaries, enfolding all other intellectual and cultural achievements. "They be moche abused, that suppose eloquence to be only in wordes or coulours of Rhetorike," he declares, "for . . . in an oratour is required to be a heape of all maner of lernyng: whiche of some is called the worlde of science, of other the circle of doctrine, whiche is in one worde of greke *Encyclopedia*" (48ᵥ). Such a vast, indeed global, competence necessarily extends far beyond "the elegant speking of latin": "latine," Elyot observes, "is but a naturall speche, and the frute of speche is wyse sentence, whiche is gathered and made of sondry lernynges" (47ᵥ). Precisely because it transcends the boundaries of any particular language, eloquence is—paradoxically—accessible to all, inherent "in euery tonge . . . whereof sentences be so aptly compact that they by a vertue inexplicable do drawe unto them the mindes and consent of the herers" (47ᵥ–48ᵣ). It is this generous perception of linguistic potential and rhetorical efficacy, of the *sameness* of eloquence whenever and wherever it is heard—as much as any hopefulness about the hitherto untapped linguistic talents of nursemaids—that sustains Elyot's vision of an otherwise impossible intimacy with classical antiquity. To read Virgil is to escape the infelicitous constraints of time and country: to traverse a world of learning but to experience it as inexplicably familiar, aptly compact.

However, that is not exactly the lesson one takes away from Virgil's great poem of civilization building and travel, which takes a rather darker view of the satisfactions afforded by nurses. The *Aeneid* is all about generative displacements—Troy is rubble and must be rebuilt in Rome—but Aeneas's encounter with Dido makes clear that the logic of substitution is not infallible: some forms of intimacy only increase the hunger they are meant to satisfy. Indeed, as J. S. C. Eidinow has suggested, book 4 of Virgil's poem—and in particular Dido's fantasy of fostering Ascanius as a *parvulus Aeneas*—can be read as a historically topical meditation on the limits of cross-cultural and extrafamilial intimacy.[20] Dido may romanticize herself as the wet nurse of Aeneas's ambitions, but Virgil ironizes the image, recasting the nurse or foster mother as an emblem of mutually unsatisfactory exchanges and unfulfilled yearning, of losses that cannot be made good.[21] *The Boke named the Governour* remains defensive about the implications of this lesson for its own nursemaidlike endeavors: that is, both the substitution of Virgilian nutriments for easier and more natural bodies of knowledge—the exchanges on which Elyot's pedagogy depends—and the translation of classical learning and culture into English— the exchanges on which Elyot's prose depends. What must be displaced? What will get left behind? For much of book 1, Elyot's anxiety is clearly on behalf of the classics. "I am (as god iuge me)," he writes in the opening lines of the dedicatory epistle to King Henry VIII, "violently stered to devulgate or sette fourth some part of my studie, trustynge therby tacquite me of my dueties to god, your hyghnesse, and this my contray" (aii_r). This declaration, David Baker writes, "marks one of the first significant attempts by English humanists to make their learning accessible to a vernacular reading public," but, as Baker observes, even the violent steering to which Elyot has been subjected persuades him only to publish "some part" of his own wide reading.[22] Baker attributes this incompleteness to reticence: wary of the heretical and revolutionary potential of classical learning, Elyot provides only a partial account of his study, insisting on maintaining the boundaries between the learned and the unlearned. But while diplomacy and piety may help to define *The Governour*'s boundaries, Elyot tends to attribute its defects to the constraints of vernacularity.

Repeatedly throughout book 1 he interrupts the flow of his argument to redirect our attention to his labored, at times frustrated, efforts to put it into English. The very "name" of the *Governour*, he confesses early in book 1, is not quite apt as a descriptor for the sort of educated nobleman his text is designed to produce, as governance properly speaking belongs to the sovereign alone: "herafter," he explains, "I intende to call them Magistratis, lackynge a more conuenient worde in englisshe" (14_r). But then, reminding himself that his subject in book 1 is not governance but the education and virtue necessary to produce good government, which learning and virtue noblemen "haue in commune with princes," Elyot reconsiders, concluding that he might "without anoyance of any man, name them gouernours at this tyme," trusting readers to maintain the necessary distinction between this general term and the "higher preeminence" reserved to kings and princes. Other lexical impasses prove absolute: Elyot recommends Aristotle's *Ethicae* and Cicero's *De Officiis* as indispensable sources of moral instruction, revealing the "propre significations of euery vertue," but insists that the former is "to be lerned in greke; for the translations that we yet haue be but a rude and grosse shadowe of the eloquence and wisedome of Aristotell." As for the latter, he confesses, even the title must remain obscure to English readers, since there "yet is no propre englisshe worde to be gyuen" for the Latin "officium" (41$_{r-v}$).

He writes enthusiastically of the learning to be attained by the reading of classical poetry too, boasting that he "coulde recite a great nombre of semblable good sentences" out of Ovid and other "wantone poets" but then declining to do so, for they "in the latine do expresse them incomparably with more grace and delectation to the reder than our englisshe tonge may yet comprehende" (51$_v$). Even when he turns from the study of literature to more practical ethical and political matters, Elyot often finds himself thrown back on the classical tongues in order to describe virtues that have no precise vernacular analogue: "constrained to usurpe a latine worde" such as "maturitie" for "the necessary augmentation of our langage" (85$_{r-v}$), or to clarify the meaning of a term such as "modestie," "nat . . . knowen in the englisshe tonge, ne of al them which under stode latin, except they had radde good authors" (94$_r$), or to invent words altogether, hoping that they, "being . . . before this time unknowen in our tonge, may be by the sufferaunce of wise men nowe receiued by custome . . . [and] made familiare" (94$_v$).

Elyot's success in expanding the boundaries of the language is rather remarkable, it must be said,[23] and his strategies can be quite subtle. Philologists have long cited Elyot as a devotee of the "neologistic couplet," a syntactical unit that pairs a new or strange term with a more familiar vernacular counterpart.[24] Thus, in the opening lines of the *Governour*, the phrase "to devulgate or sette fourth" facilitates the introduction of the Latinate coinage "devulgate" by yoking it to the homely Anglo-Saxon "sette fourth." Elyot was proud of his couplets: in 1533, in the preface to *Of the Knowledge which Maketh a Wise Man*, he writes that, although in the *Governour* he "intended to augment our Englyshe tongue," nonetheless "through out the boke there was no terme newe made by me of a latine or frenche worde, but it is there declared so playnly by one mene or other to a diligent reder that therby no sentence is made derke or harde to be understande."[25] From Elyot's perspective, then, the phrase "to devulgate or sette fourth" gracefully performs what it promises.[26] But as Stephen Merriam Foley points out, the neologistic couplet also highlights the author's anxiety that he will not be understood: Elyot's compulsive pairings are, Foley argues, "the traces of a mind insecurely poised between competing discourses of intellectual authority."[27]

In this regard the neologistic couplet is yet another rhetorical counterpart for the Latin-speaking nursemaid; it simultaneously exposes and disguises a cultural defect by drawing together two unlike and perhaps incompatible terms. Like any wet nurse, the neologistic couplet risks the charge of redundancy: if the familiar term is adequate to express the meaning of the borrowed or invented term, why borrow or invent? If it is not, how useful is it as a guide to the unfamiliar word? What is forestalled (but also registered) by such a compound is the vexed question of linguistic and cultural parity. That question—as much or more than any political or religious fears—accounts for the violence and the coercion attendant upon Elyot's admittedly partial devulgation of learning: if the approximations attendant upon the work of translation necessarily entail a loss of meaning or value, how, nonetheless, is meaning or value to be transferred without such fudged equations, such compromised and compromising resemblances? Because he understands eloquence as a quality that speaks across linguistic, cultural, geographic, and temporal divides—as the most mobile of linguistic effects—Elyot can conceive of the study of remote, long-dead tongues as an experience of profound, near-perfect intimacy, and he can write prose that effaces lexical difference even as it testifies to persistent gaps in expressive capability. In addition he can dream of a time when such education and such prose produce an English home, and perhaps even a mother tongue, whose walls enclose the "encyclopedia" of eloquence.

But would such a home, and such a tongue, remain English? In his 1533 preface to *Knowledge*, Elyot scoffs at the question, berating for their ingratitude those readers who are "offended (as they say) with my strange terms."[28] But in *The Governour* he seems—briefly and obliquely—to wonder. In the final chapter of book 1, having just urged the *Governour*'s readers to set themselves vigorously to the work of translating classical wisdom into England, he departs conspicuously from that wisdom. Citing, but then disavowing, Cicero's injunction against sports and games, he proceeds to make a rather plaintive case for the merits of the dying art of English longbow shooting, a skill that "is, and always hath ben" England's security "from outwarde hostilitie" and the source of its fame throughout the world, "as ferre as Hierusalem" (99_v–100_r). Elyot attributes the decline of longbow shooting to an encroaching cosmopolitanism, as foreign and new-fangled modes of defense—crossbows and handguns—have eroded a skill that "continuell use" made "so perfecte and exacte amonge englisshe men" (102_r). "O what cause of reproche shall the decaye of archers be to us nowe liuyng?" he demands. "Ye what irrecuperable damage either to us or them in whose time nede of semblable defence shall happen?" (100_r).

This plangent appeal for the preservation of an already (or once) "perfect" native art—an art that has shored up England's defenses against outsiders and extended its renown to the far corners of the world—makes for an odd conclusion to the litany of *not yets* that propels the rest of book 1 and justifies its radical conflations of domesticity and estrangement. Indeed, Elyot rather casually observes at one point, midway through his attack on English legal discourse, that eloquence is no different than embroidery, drawing, or sculpture: if Englishmen are not able or willing to cultivate a particular skill at home—if, that is, they are to face the fact that they inhabit a realm where "the langage is barberouse" and "the steering of affections of the mind," rhetoric itself, "was never used" (56_r)—they must "be constrained . . . to abandone [their] owne countraymen and resorte unto straungers" (55_r). That matter-of-fact resorting unto strangers exacts an unexpected toll in the final pages of book 1, as Elyot imagines a future England enervated and demoralized by its blind embrace of things novel and strange, its neglect of what it once knew and practiced best.

Cicero the Sea Captain

It is a bit of an interpretive leap to link this elegiac defense of the longbow to a latent concern for the vernacular, but I am nudged to make that leap by the fact that Elyot's most important sixteenth-century reader—the heir to his zeal both for the English longbow and for foreign-language study—seems to have made it too. In 1545, a year before Elyot's death, Roger Ascham, the young Cambridge lecturer in Greek, made his debut as an author, publishing a pseudo-Socratic dialogue on the merits of longbow shooting, citing Elyot's enthusiasm for the sport as inspiration for his own labors on its behalf.[29] "[T]o haue written this boke either in latin or Greke . . . had bene more easier and fit for mi trade in study," he confesses in the dedicatory epistle to *Toxophilus: The Schole of Shotyng*, "yet neuerthelesse," he deems it best to "haue written

this Englishe matter in the Englishe tongue, for Englishe men" (x). The epistle
to readers amplifies this claim by way of a fable borrowed from Herodotus:

> Bias the wyse man came to Cresus the ryche kyng, on a tyme,
> when he was makynge newe shyppes, purposyng to haue subdued
> by water the out yles lying betwixt Grece and Asia minor: What
> newes now in Grece, saith the king to Bias? None other newes, but
> these, sayeth Bias: that the yles of Grece haue prepared a wonderful
> companye of horsemen, to ouerrun Lydia withall. There is nothyng
> vnder heauen, sayth the kynge, that I woulde so soone wisshe, as
> that they durst be so bolde, to mete vs on the lande with horse. And
> thinke you sayeth Bias, that there is anye thyng which they wolde
> sooner wysshe, then that you shulde be so fonde, to mete them on
> the water with shyppes? And so Cresus hearyng not the true newes,
> but perceyuyng the wise mannes mynde and counsell, both gaue
> then ouer makyng of his shyppes, and left also behynde him a won-
> derful example for all commune wealthes to folowe: that is euer-
> more to regarde and set most by that thing whervnto nature hath
> made them moost apt, and vse hath made them moost fitte. (xii)

"By this matter," Ascham explains, "I mean the shotynge in the long bowe, for
English men," but the fable—like *Toxophilus*—serves equally well as defense
of the practice of writing in the vernacular: English, after all, is the language
that nature and use have conspired to make most apt and fit for his own
undertaking; to write in Latin or Greek would be to set sail in unseaworthy
vessels. Indeed, as Ryan Stark and Thomas Greene have suggested, Ascham's
interest in archery is always also an interest in eloquence: the strengths
developed by the former (clarity of vision, precision of aim) are, to his mind,
exactly correspondent to the skills requisite for the latter.[30] In his epistle to
Toxophilus Ascham elucidates the analogy: "Yf any man wyll applye these
thynges [that is, writing and shooting] togyther, [he] shal nat se the one farre
differ from the other," he alleges, for "[i]n our tyme nowe, . . . very many
do write, but after suche a fashion, as very many do shoote . . . , tak[ing] in
hande stronger bowes, than they be able to mayntayne" (xiii). For Ascham, his
defense of the longbow and his advocacy for the vernacular are interchangeable
commitments, and he scoffs at "any man [who] woulde blame me, eyther for
takynge such a matter in hande, or els for writing it in the Englyshe tongue"
(xiii).

Ascham's attitude toward his mother tongue is hardly uncritical, but neither does it partake of Elyot's faith in the enriching effect of intimacy with
foreign tongues. Indeed what Ascham seems to have taken from his reading of
Elyot—and especially from his reading of the mournful conclusion to book
1—is a keen awareness of the dangers of false intimacy or overeager identification. Like Elyot, he frames his decision to write in English in terms of a desire
to improve the tongue and profit his vernacular readership, but he betrays
no optimism that such improvement or profit will come easily or without
cost. Where Elyot emphasizes likeness, contiguity, and kinship, Ascham insists
on a radical and perhaps insuperable estrangement: "as for ye Latin or greke
tonge, euery thing is so excellently done in them, that none can do better," he
bluntly declares, but "in the Englysh tonge contrary, euery thinge in a maner
so meanly, bothe for the matter and handelynge, that no man can do worse"
(xiv). Rather than search for terms or syntactical arrangements that might,
like Elyot's neologistic couplets, ease the passage between the learned and the
vulgar, Ascham advocates for prose that eschews foreign affectations and neologistic borrowings, arguing that "[h]e that wyll wryte well in any tongue,
muste . . . speake as the common people do" and lamenting the fact that
"[m]any English writers haue not done so, but vsinge straunge wordes as latin,
french and Italian, do make all thinges darke and harde" (xiv).

As for the possibility that the vernacular requires such augmentation, he
dismisses it summarily: "Ones I communed with a man whiche reasoned the
englyshe tongue to be enryched and encreased therby, sayinge: Who wyll not
prayse that feaste, where a man shall drinke at a diner, bothe wyne, ale and
beere? Truely quod I, they be all good, euery one taken by hym selfe alone, but
if you putte Maluesye and sacke, read wyne and white, ale and beere, and al in
one pot, you shall make a drynke, neyther easie to be knowen, nor yet holsom
for the bodye" (xiv). Where Elyot sees nurturing and intimacy—the infant
at his nurse's breast—Ascham sees the threat of contamination, an unwhole-
some and unpalatable brew. This is not to suggest that Ascham believed the
vernacular had nothing to learn from the classical tongues, nor English youth
from the study of classical literature. His career as a writer and a teacher was
founded on the promotion of Greek and Latin literacy, and indeed in the very
next lines he hints that not all attempts at linguistic enrichment are doomed
to failure, noting that "Cicero in folowyng Isocrates, Plato and Demosthenes,
increased the latine tounge after an other sorte" (xiv). Of this "other sorte" or
"waye" he will say only that it has fallen into neglect and disrepute—"bycause
dyuers men that write, do not know, they can neyther folowe it, bycause of

theyr ignorauncie, nor yet will prayse it, for verye arrogauncie"—but it is clear that it must bear little resemblance to Elyot's own methods.

For Ascham, the infelicities of time and country that have consigned England and English to the cultural and intellectual margins are to be remedied not by a pedagogy that simulates proximity, familiarity, and immediacy but rather by a pedagogy that makes distance, strangeness, and the very passage of time into instruments of instruction. Estrangement may be the root cause of barbarism, but it is also the guarantor of purity: this conviction undergirds *The Scholemaster*'s fierce objection to the practice of sending English youths to study in Catholic Italy, and it governs the treatise's pedagogical philosophy no less. *The Scholemaster* advertises itself as a method of teaching a young boy Latin "with ease and pleasure, and in short time" (1ᵥ). But in truth Ascham has little regard for—or confidence in—ease, pleasure, or quickness. He famously prefers "hard" to "quick" wits on the grounds that the former, however resistant to instruction, are liable to retain what they learn, while the latter "commonlie, be apte to take" but "vnapte to keepe," "more quicke to enter spedelie, than hable to pearse farre," and "delit[ing] them selues in easie and pleasant studies, . . . neuer passe farre forward in hie and hard sciences" (4ᵥ). That eloquence itself is such a high and hard science follows from Ascham's insistence that, contrary to Elyot's notion of it as a universal inheritance, proper to any "natural" tongue, true eloquence is to be found only in the remote and rarefied provinces of antiquity: "[I]n the rudest contrie, and most barbarous mother language, many be found [that] can speake verie wiselie," he observes, "but in the Greeke and Latin tong, the two onelie learned tonges, we finde always wisdome and eloquence, good matter and good vtterance, neuer or seldom asunder" (46ᵣ).

For Ascham, as for Elyot, the rudeness of the English vernacular—its grammatical inconsistency, its inability to replicate the rhythms of classical prose and verse, its impoverished vocabulary and patchwork etymologies—is a natural consequence of England's own inescapable rusticity, its alienation from Athens and Rome, the wellsprings of learning and eloquence. But in Ascham's ideal schoolroom the distance between antiquity and modernity, Rome and England, becomes a productive and necessary guard against moral corruption and linguistic vulgarity. To begin with, in direct opposition to Elyot's promotion of the use of Latin as a familiar tongue—indeed, if possible, as a *family* tongue—Ascham insists that Latin must not be spoken at all, neither at home nor at school, until students have mastered fully the arts of translation and composition. "In very deede," he allows, "if children were brought vp, in soch a house, or soch a Schole, where the latin tonge were properlie and perfitlie spoken, as Tib[erius] and Ca[ius] Gracci were brought vp, in their mother Cornelias house, surelie, than the dailie vse of speaking, were the best and readiest waie, to learne the latin tong" (2ᵥ). But such homes and such mothers did not exist in sixteenth-century England, as Ascham's notorious anecdote of Lady Jane Grey, born to parents whose crudity is matched only by their cruelty, makes plain. Indeed when he reflects on the kind of language learning that might plausibly occur in an English home, it is only to offer a cautionary tale: "This last somer," he recalls, "I was in a Ientlemans house: where a yong childe, somewhat past fower years olde, cold in no wise frame his tonge, to saie, a little shorte grace: and yet he could roundly rap out so manie vgle othes, and those of the newest facion, and some good man of fourscore yeare olde hath neuer hard named before. . . . This Childe vsing moche the companie of servinge men, and geuing good eare to their taulke, did easily learne, whiche he shall hardlie forget, all daies of his life hereafter" (16ᵥ). This recollection exactly inverts Elyot's fantasy of the child nurtured with ease and companionship into pure Latinity, or even clean and polite vernacularity: here easy learning and a good ear are the agents of moral and linguistic corruption. The best parents can hope for, Ascham suggests, is to preserve their children from the "confounding of companies" (16ᵥ): domestic intimacies are imagined strictly in negative terms.

The schoolroom presents a similar challenge, for even in "the best Scholes" the habitual use of poor Latin by masters and schoolboys alike means that "barbariousnesse is bred vp so in yong wittes, as afterward they be, not onelie marde for speaking, but also corrupted in iudgement: as with moch adoe, or neuer at all, they be brought to right frame againe" (2ᵥ). Ascham's own pedagogical precepts work to provide this "right frame": a space where children's instinct for imitation—so often, for him, a source of danger—can be put to safe and profitable use. The basic method is simple: Ascham requires the student to translate a passage from Latin or Greek to English and then back again, using the original classical text to correct his own. Through its carefully regulated employment of classical models, such "double translation" remedies the estrangement of rude English from classical eloquence, facilitating exchanges between the learned and unlearned tongues, but it also guards against the dangers of straying too far from the classical precedent, by imposing a calculated retreat from and return to its bounds.

Much as Elyot's neologistic couplets modeled for readers the enriching effects of intimacy with foreign tongues, Ascham's distinctive prose mirrors the controlled comparisons on which his pedagogy depends: ideas are worked out by way of "fit similitude" (19ᵣ), in cautiously elaborated analogies whose resemblances are expressed in neatly balanced parallel clauses. Thus he writes of the distinction between educated and uneducated noblemen:

> The greatest shippe in deede commonlie carieth the greatest burden, but yet alwayes with the greatest ieoperdie, not onelie for the persons and goodes committed vnto it, but euen for the shyppe it selfe, except it be gouerned, with the greater wisedome. But Nobilitie, gouerned by learning and wisedome, is in deede, most like a faire shippe, hauyng tide and winde at will, vnder the reule of a skilfull master: whan contrarie wise, a shippe, caried, yea with the hiest tide & greatest winde, lacking a skilfull master, most commonlie, doth either, sinck it selfe vpon sandes, or breake it selfe vpon rockes. And euen so, how manie haue bene, either drowned in vaine pleasure, or ouerwhelmed by stout wilfulnesse, the histories of England be able to affourde ouer many examples vnto vs. (13ᵥ–14ᵣ)

"But yet," "not onelie," "but euen," "except," "but . . . in deede," "whan contrarie wise," "and euen so": where Elyot might have compressed the comparison into a single suggestive metaphor, Ascham attenuates it over several sentences, parsing the original commonplace formulation—men are like ships—into an ever more precise diagnosis of the difference between virtue and vice, wisdom and folly. Indeed the similitude, a figure of likeness, becomes in Ascham's hands an instrument for the expression of otherwise elusive distinctions, and the ideal figure for a pedagogical philosophy founded on mistrust of what is close at hand. For as he explains via another similitude:

> [T]here be manie faire examples in this Court, for yong Ientlemen to follow. . . . But they be, like faire markes in the feild, out of a mans reach, to far of, to shote at well. The best and worthiest men, in deede, be somtimes seen, but seldom taulked withall: A yong Ientleman, may somtime knele to their person, smallie vse their companie, for their better instruction. But yong Ientlemen ar faine commonlie to do in the Court, as yong Archers do in the feild: that is take soch markes, as be nie them, although they be neuer so foule to shote at. I meene, they be driuen to kepe companie with the worste: and what force ill companie hath, to corrupt good wittes, the wisest men know best. (14ᵣ)

Here again the initial comparison between imitation and archery is revised and revised again, yielding a taxonomy of likeness and difference: fair marks versus foul, far off versus nigh, worthy men versus the worst, seeing versus talking, kneeling versus keeping company, instruction versus corruption. In every case virtue is aligned with remoteness: if archery and seamanship are Ascham's favored analogies for the work of moral and rhetorical education, that is surely because each case skill increases with distance.

So it is with double translation, for the crucial step of the process, what transforms it from a display of rote repetition or memory to an exercise of elo-quence in the making, is the *gap* that Ascham imposes at its center. Once the child has completed his initial translation, from Latin into English, the master is to "take from him his latin booke, and *pausing an houre, at the least,* than let the childe translate his owne Englishe into latin againe, in an other paper booke" (1$_v$, emphasis mine). The hour or more that intervenes between the two Latin versions—Cicero's original and the child's imitation—during which the child is left alone with his own English, recapitulates in miniature the infelicitous gap of time, country, and language that divides sixteenth-century England from ancient Rome. What survives that lapse is an inevitably partial reconstruction, akin to "the shadow or figure of the ancient Rhetorique" that Elyot just barely discerns in English legal discourse (56$_v$). Of course the loss of an original perfection is not the only problem: in the schoolroom as in the course of history, errors and barbarisms accumulate in the interval. The child, as Ascham confesses, is likely to "misse, either in forgetting a worde, or in chaunging a good with a worse, or misordering the sentence" (1$_v$). As Jeff Dolven suggests, this "meantime" between tongues is "a window of necessary risk" since learning "depend[s] . . . on the hazards of the middle."[31]

But such language is perhaps unduly monitory, for Ascham is surpris-ingly sanguine about the likelihood of forgetfulness and confusion, urging the teacher not to "froune, or chide with him, if the childe haue done his diligence, and vsed no trewandship therein" (1$_v$–2$_r$). Indeed such errors are what the pause of an hour or more is designed to produce; they are essential to the cultivation of eloquence. "For I know by good experience," Ascham assures his readers, "that a childe shall take more profit of two fautes, ientlie warned of, then of foure thinges, rightly hitt. . . . For than, the master shall haue good occasion to saie vnto him. *Tullie* would haue vsed such a worde, not this: *Tullie* would haue placed this word here, not there: would haue vsed this case, this number, this person, this degree, this gender" (2$_r$). Lynn Enterline describes this friendly colloquy as "connect[ing] master and student via the student's likeness to Tullie,"[32] but in fact the emphasis falls on difference: it is only when he lays his own Latin next to that of Cicero that the child learns to measure and value the distance between them, only then that he perceives the countless tiny calculations of diction, syntax, arrangement, and style that distinguish eloquence from mere speech. It is this final act of correction that prevents the student from wandering off course, even as he cultivates his own expressive style, but the errors that will so often precede it are no less necessary or productive. Allow the child "*good* space and time" to complete the exercise, Ascham urges schoolmasters (31ᵥ, emphasis added). Because double translation assumes error as the precondition of learning, it redeems both distance and time, and the waywardness they enable, from their roles as the agents of barbaric decline.

It is not surprising that the "Tullie" who presides over these interlingual exchanges bears no resemblance to Elyot's nurselike Virgil, who entices the child with sweetly familiar morsels. Instead, Ascham imagines Cicero as an "expert Sea man" who "set[s] vp his saile of eloquence, in some broad deep Argument, [and] caried with full tyde and winde, of his witte and learnyng," outdistances all rivals, who "may rather stand and looke after him, than hope to ouertake him, what course so euer he hold, either in faire or foule" (63ᵣ). Ascham's method allows the inexpert schoolboy to accompany Cicero on those perilous rhetorical journeys, with the full expectation that he will run off course in the attempt: translation, which Ascham initially champions as an alternative to travel abroad because "learning teacheth safelie" while the traveler is "made cunning by manie shippewrakes" (18ᵣ₋ᵥ), in fact mimics the perils of foreign travel, recuperating the shipwreck as the point of the voyage. We might recall here the fable that introduces *Toxophilus,* in which a barbarian landlubber is persuaded to give up shipbuilding in order to confront his Greek antagonists on (literally) familiar ground. *The Scholemaster* offers a less stark take on the folly of meeting an ancient civilization (or its most eloquent exponent) at sea: imitation by way of double translation allows rude and hardwitted schoolboys to set themselves up in direct competition with Cicero and recuperates their inevitable losses as gain.

Ultimately, Ascham allows himself to dream of an England so enriched by such exchanges that even Cicero might prefer it to the nurseries of his own eloquence. Recalling that "Master *Tully*" once declared of England that "[t]here is not one scruple of siluer in that whole Isle, or any one that knoweth either learning or letter," he imagines making a triumphant rejoinder: "But now master *Cicero*, . . . sixteen hundred yeare after you were dead and gone, it may trewly be sayd, that . . . your excellent eloquence is as well liked and loued, and as trewlie followed in England at this day, as it is now, or euer was, sence your owne tyme, in any place of *Italie*, either at *Arpinum*, where ye were borne, or els at *Rome* where ye were brought vp" (62$_{r-v}$). Such a fantasy would seem to answer Elyot's yearning for perfect intimacy with the past, for an erasure of distance and difference; but, in fact, it is precisely Ascham's consciousness of his remove from that past, and of England's inglorious place within it, that gives his fantasy its savor. The sixteen hundred years (and thousands of miles) that separate Ascham's England from Cicero's Arpinum or his Rome are here not the source of cultural and linguistic shame but rather evidence of a triumph—the triumph of a pedagogy that turns the "infelicitie of . . . tyme and countray" into time and space for learning.

Sallust the Exile

In Ascham's fantasy of an England made eloquent, the natives speak and write in Cicero's Latin, but he insists that a similar transformation may eventually be effected in the mother tongue. Indeed his first allusion to double translation, *Toxophilus*'s reference to the "other" method followed by Cicero, comes in a discussion of how best to enrich "the englyshe tongue" (xiv). In addition his gleeful rebuke to Cicero in *The Scholemaster* is prompted not by the improved Latinity of his countrymen but by their growing skill as *vernacular* writers. This is as he hopes and expects: the rigorous method of double translation, he writes, is intended "not onelie to serue in the *Latin* or *Greke* tong, but also in our own English language. But yet, bicause the prouidence of God hath left vnto vs in no other tong, saue onelie in the *Greke* and *Latin* tong, the trew preceptes, and perfite examples of eloquence, therefore must we seeke in the Authors onelie of those two tonges, the trewe Paterne of Eloquence, if in any other mother tongue we looke to attaine, either to perfit vtterance of it our selues, or skilfull iudgement of it in others" (56$_v$). But when Ascham describes the results of that patterning in England, he has less to say about what vernacular writers do well than about what they now (rightly) perceive themselves to do badly: like the boys in his imaginary schoolroom, English authors are learning to "know the difference" between themselves and antiquity (60$_r$). He applauds, therefore, the sentiments behind recent efforts to replace "barbarous and rude Ryming" (60$_r$) with verses modeled on classical quantitative measures, but he is cheered less by results of those experiments than by the knowledge that English writers have, at last and at least, become conscious of their own barbarity: "I rejoice that euen poore England preuented Italie, first in spying out, than in seekying to amend this fault" (62$_r$). That those amendments so far have yielded verses that "rather trotte and hobble, than runne smoothly in our English tong" (60$_v$) is, to his way of thinking, further proof of the virtue of the undertaking itself: those who dissent are lazy homebodies who, for "idleness" or for "ignorance," "neuer went farder than the schole . . . of Chaucer at home" (61$_v$)—home, as ever, being the very worst place to take one's schooling.

Helgerson cites Ascham's misguided faith in English quantitative measures as an instantiation of a larger truth: "at the historic root of national self-articulation," he writes, "we find . . . self-alienation."[33] It is this self-alienating investment in the authority of classical example, he argues, that later Elizabethan writers must learn to overcome in order to fashion English as a truly national tongue.[34] But alienation and eloquence are more complexly entwined, both in the sixteenth century and in Cicero's Rome, as Ascham is fully aware. On the one hand, as he insists, the greatest classical writers became great because of their willingness to depart from common practice: he cites approvingly Cicero's dictum that by studying at Rhodes, he exchanged the speech he received at home for a better one (though Ascham adds, characteristically, that he doubts that study abroad helped Cicero as much as "binding himself to translate" the great Attic orators [44$_v$]). On the other hand, he acknowledges that those who leave home may struggle to find their way back: thus *The Scholemaster* concludes with an uneasy meditation on the difference between Cicero and Sallust, each living "whan the Latin tong was full ripe" (63$_r$), each blessed with wisdom and learning, and only one capable of eloquence.

As Ascham recalls, his beloved former tutor John Cheke, whom he credits with the invention of double translation, once cautioned him that it "was not verie fitte for yong men, to learne out of [Sallust], the puritie of the Latin tong," for "he was not the purest in proprietie of wordes, nor choisest in aptnes of phrases, nor the best in framing of sentences," and his writing was all too often "neyther plaine for the matter, nor sensible for mens vnderstanding" (64$_v$). When Ascham asks how a well-educated Roman of Cicero's time should have succumbed to such awkwardness and bad taste, Cheke confesses that he does not know but adds that he has developed a private "fansie." Sallust's youth was, he observes, marked by "ryot and lechery," and it was only "by long experience of the hurt and shame that commeth of mischief" that he was brought to "the loue of studie and learning." His reward for this conversion of mind and habits was a post as "Pretor in *Numidia*," a North African outpost of the empire, "where he [was] absent from his contrie, and not in-ured with the common talke of Rome, but shut vp in his studie, and bent wholy to reading" (65$_r$). This geographic and scholarly isolation was produc-tive insofar as it yielded Sallust's great *Historiae*, Cheke observes, but the voice of the work betrays the stress of its author's alienation: depending on older authors, especially Cato and Thucydides, for his matter, arrangement, and style, Sallust lapses into archaisms and—when he can find no suitable word for his purposes in Cato or Thucydides—invents new terms wholesale. The worst defect of his style, Cheke continues, is "neyther oldnes nor newnesse of wordes" but the "strange phrases" that result when "good Latin wordes" are recast in imitation of Greek, "placed and framed outlandish like" (65$_v$). It is this outlandish quality that distinguishes Sallust from Cicero: like his model Thucydides, who "wrote his storie, not at home in Grece, but abrode in Italie, and therefore smelleth of a certaine outlandish kinde of talke" (66$_r$), Sallust loses the ease and familiarity of the native speaker, holding his mother tongue at an awkward and unmistakable remove.

Cheke offers Sallust as proof of the urgency of choosing one's models wisely: Plato and Isocrates, "the purest and playnest writers, that euer wrote in any tong," are the "best examples for any man to follow whether he write, Latin, Italian, French, or English" (66$_r$). But his fanciful vision of Sallust la-boring in a North African study with only Cato and Thucydides for company bears a striking resemblance to Ascham's vision of the ideal English school-room, in which scripted interchanges with dead Latin authors take the place of conversation, and the familiar contours of the mother tongue are gradually refashioned to fit the impress of a language now found only in books. *The Scholemaster* ends shortly after these reflections, with Ascham noting simply that "these . . . reules, which worthie Master *Cheke* dyd impart vnto me con-cernyng *Salust,*" are to be taken as guides for the "right iudgement of the *Latin* tong" (67$_r$). His readers are left with the surmise that, as far as the English tongue is concerned, the pedagogy of Cheke and Ascham seems liable to pro-duce not a nation of Ciceros but an island of Sallusts.

As far as we can tell, few English schoolboys were subjected regularly to the rigors of double translation,[35] and even fewer, if any, must have learned Latin at the breast, but the ideals of English humanist pedagogical theory nonetheless threatened to alter the course of vernacular usage.[36] So argues Richard Mulcaster, master of London's Merchant Taylors' School (where his pupils included a young Edmund Spenser) and outspoken critic of human-ist efforts to impose classical standards on the mother tongue. Mulcaster was a humanist by training, steeped in the example of classical authors, but he took from his study of antiquity a very different lesson than Elyot or Ascham did: rhetoric and pedagogy are, he concludes, essentially local arts. As he writes in *Positions*, his 1581 treatise on the education of children, in seeking to fashion England along the lines of Athens or Rome, a schoolmaster may overlook the fact that "the circunstance of the countrie, will not admit that, which he would perswade." This inattention to local particularities makes the schoolmaster like the biblical parable's foolish builder who erects his house on sand: "mistaking his ground, [he] misplaceth his building, and hazardeth his credit."[37] The same care, he points out, is required of the orator: it is only by "mastering of the circunstance"—that is, both the rhetorical circumstances of his case and the actual circumstances of the place in which he speaks—that he may effectively instruct and persuade his fellow citizens. Both travel and an undue regard for alien traditions jeopardize such mastery, since they distance the orator from the ground on which his argument must be built. In the very causes he chooses to espouse, Mulcaster writes, an orator reveals the depth of his loyalty to his native land: "by it each countrie discouereth the travellour, when he seeketh to enforce his forreigne conclusions, and clingeth to that countryman, which hath bettered her still, by biding still at home" (9). Excessive devotion to Greek or Latin, he emphasizes, constitutes just such an enforcement of "forreigne conclusions." Even the most revered ancient authorities must bow to the imperative of local circumstance, for in rhetorical matters, "where circunstance is prescription, it is no proufe, bycause *Plato* praiseth it, bycause *Aristotle* alloweth it, bycause *Cicero* commendes it, bycause *Quintilian* is acquainted with it . . . that therfore it is for vs to vse." "What if our countrey honour it in them," Mulcaster asks, "and yet for all that may not vse it her selfe, bycause circunstance is her check" (11)?

On this basis Mulcaster makes his radical case for a pedagogy of the mother tongue: an orthography, grammar, rhetoric, and poetics fashioned specifically for English, according to English models and English habits. He challenges fidelity to Latin exemplars as a servile remainder of England's colonial past: as he reminds readers of his 1582 treatise on English spelling, *The First Part of the Elementarie*, "[t]he Romane autoritie first planted the Latin among vs here, by force of their conquest," and "the vse thereof for matters of learning, doth cause it continew, tho the conquest be expired."[38] He reproaches "the opinion of som such of our peple, as desire rather to please themselues with a foren tung, wherewith theie ar acquainted, then to profit their cuntrie, in hir naturall language, where their acquaintance should be" (255); such misplaced allegiance, he argues, grants the classical tongues and the contemporary continental languages an unjust advantage over the English vernacular. "No one tung is more fine then other naturallie," Mulcaster argues, "but by industrie of the speaker, . . . [who] endeuoreth himself to garnish it with eloquence, & to enrich it with learning" (254). To claim that rude countries inevitably breed rude tongues is, he continues, to misunderstand the character of eloquence, which thrives in every place such industry is employed; sounding rather like Elyot, he writes that true eloquence is "neither limited to language, nor restrained to soil, whose measur the hole world is" (258). But where Elyot deplores England's provinciality, blaming its rusticity for the roughness of its speech, Mulcaster proclaims his pride in all aspects of English identity: "I loue Rome, but London better, I fauor Italie, but England more, I honor the Latin, but I worship the English" (255). Instead of being "pilgrims to learning by lingring about tungs," he argues, English authors may find "all that gaietie [to] be had at home, which makes vs gase so much at the fine stranger" (256).

To the charge that English is "vncouth," Mulcaster responds that it is merely "vnused" and must attain praise "thorough purchace, and planting in our tung, which theie [that is, Greeks and Romans] were so desirous to place in theirs" (256–57). His own treatise, devoted to the establishment of rules for pronunciation and spelling in the vernacular, is meant as a mere pretext to such purchase and planting; ultimately, he writes, the English language must cultivate the whole of the art of rhetoric, becoming "enriched so in euerie kinde of argument, and honored so with euerie ornament of eloquence, as she maie vy with the foren." In pursuit of that enrichment, he cheerfully advocates the adoption of foreign words and phrases, cautioning only that spelling be anglicized: "For if the word it self be english in dede, then is it best in the natural hew, if it be a stranger, & incorporate among vs, let it wear our colors, sith it wil be one of vs" (227). In Mulcaster's view, England's relationship to foreign languages ought not to be construed as a choice between alienation and dependence. Instead, he urges, English may partake freely of all other linguistic models while retaining a strong sense of its own local virtues.

Mulcaster admits that England's geographic insularity and remoteness have contributed to its lack of rhetorical polish; he acknowledges that the vernacular has been treated as if it were "of no compas for ground & autoritie" because "it is of small reatch" and "stretcheth no further then this Iland of ours, naie not there ouer all." But concerns about England's isolation and peripherality miss the mark, he argues. The very geography responsible for the vernacular's modest reach is also the guarantee of its rhetorical sufficiency:

"[t]ho it go not beyond sea, it will serue on this side." In the same way he admits that England's place in the world is limited—"our state is no Empire to hope to enlarge it by commanding ouer cuntries," and "no stranger, nor foren nation, bycause of the bounder & shortnesse of our language, wold deal so with vs, as to transport from vs as we do from other"—but this too he regards as a point in its favor: "tho it be neither large in possession, nor in present hope of great encrease, yet where it rules, it can make good lawes, and as fit for our state, as the biggest can for theirs, and oftimes better to, bycause of confusion in greatest gouernments, as most vnwildinesse in grossest bodies" (257).

He concludes by revising England's history of foreign conquest and colonial subordination, imagining a newly pacific invasion of its borders by strangers who come not to conquer or pillage but to satiate their desire for learning and eloquence. If Latin is the language of England's colonial past, English is the tongue of its mercantile future: "Why maie not the English wits . . . in their own tung be in time as well sought to, by foren students for increase of their knowledge," he wonders, "as our soil is sought to at this same time, by foren merchants, for encrease of their welth?" As yet, he concedes, wisdom and eloquence are not counted among the island's domestic riches, but that may change: as England's "soil is fertile, bycause it is applyed," he remarks, "so the wits be not barren if theie list to brede" (257). If those fertile wits are cultivated—in the Merchant Taylors' School and in schoolrooms throughout the nation where Mulcaster's grammatical precepts are applied—then England need no longer choose between exile from the mother tongue or isolation in a rude vernacular: the homely island tongue may play host to a world of learning.

This vision of an England (and an English) whose relationship to the outside world is one of mutual increase offers those invested in the vernacular—and Mulcaster encourages the mercantile metaphor—an alternative to slavish dependency and close-minded insularity. Destiny, he writes, elects some particular age in the history of each tongue and culture to bless it with perfection: "Such a period in the Greke tung was that time, when Demosthenes liued, and that learned race of the father philosophers: such a period in the Latin tung, was that time, when Tullie liued, and those of that age: Such a period in the English tung I take this to be in our daies, for both the pen and the speche."[39] "[T]he question," he concludes, "is wherein finenesse standeth." When it comes to Latin, he is no different than any other well-read sixteenth-century Englishman, making Cicero his standard and Sallust his cautionary tale: "So was Salust deceiued among the Romans, liuing with eloquent Tullie, and writing like ancient Cato" (160). The consequences of that deceived attachment to a past provide the motive for Mulcaster's own career and his passionate advocacy for the embrace of English on its own terms and merits. If eloquence is to be found, he argues, it will be found here and now, and if patterns of that eloquence are required, they too must be local ones: "it must nedes be, that our English tung hath matter enough in hir own writing, which maie direct her own right, if it be reduced to certain precept, and rule of Art, tho it haue not as yet bene thoroughlie perceaued" (77).

However, in seeking to avoid the fate of Sallust for a generation of English schoolboys, Mulcaster may well help to bring it about. For a native speaker, after all, nothing is more alienating than the effort of relearning one's mother tongue in the form of precepts and rules of art; what was easy and instinctive threatens to become, in Mulcaster's schoolroom, laborious and artificial. As Ascham might point out, this is not necessarily a bad thing. The internalized sense of strangeness for which Mulcaster blames his humanist colleagues is, in some sense, the essential precondition for a full-fledged art of English eloquence. Answering what Mulcaster calls the question of "finenesse"—"thoroughly perceiving" what one has learned at the breast—demands a certain strategic distance. The late sixteenth century bears witness to a revolution on what can seem, at first, like Mulcaster's terms: in rhetorical handbooks and literary texts alike, the English tongue begins to "direct her own right." But direction comes, as ever, from afar: within the new vernacular rhetorics and poetics, the distance between English and antiquity becomes, if anything, an even more pressing concern. At the same time strangeness emerges as an essential aspect of eloquence in *any* tongue, the element that distinguishes artful from ordinary speech and gives rhetoric and poetry their power. Shaped by their long detour in the classical tongues, English writers reconstitute their mother tongue as a second language, self-consciously belated and usefully eccentric. Errancy and exoticism, the instruments of Sallust's corruption as a writer, are promoted as the master tropes of rhetorical and poetic fineness.

The Commonplace and the Far-Fetched: Mapping Eloquence in the English Art of Rhetoric

As Thomas Elyot reminds readers of *The Boke named the Governour*, rhetoric was the foundation of the earliest commonwealths: "[I]n the firste infancie of the worlde, men, wandring like beastes in woddes and on mountaines, regardinge neither the religion due unto god, nor the office pertaining unto man, ordred all thing by bodily strength: untill Mercurius (as Plato supposeth) or some other man holpen by sapience and eloquence, by some apt or propre oration, assembled them to geder and perswaded to them what commodite was in mutual conuersation and honest maners."[1] When Elyot surveys sixteenth-century England, he is therefore dismayed to find in it only "a maner, a shadowe, or figure of the auncient rhetorike": the stunted ritual of "motes," or moot courts, observed by students at the law schools. Such mock trials insured that educated men were acquainted with the rudiments of invention and arrangement, but they failed to produce anything like the eloquence of Mercury, Orpheus, or Amphion. On the contrary, Elyot laments, far from fostering "mutual conversation," the speech of most English lawyers verges on unintelligibility: "voyde of all eloquence," it "serveth no commoditie or necessary purpose, no man understanding it but they whiche haue studied the lawes" (53ᵥ). He attributes this defect to ignorance of eloquence's higher purpose: "the tonge wherin it is spoken is barberouse, and the sterynge of affections of the mynde in this realme was neuer used," he observes, "and so there lacketh Eloquution and Pronunciation, the two principall partes of rhetorike" (56ᵣ₋ᵥ). Only if educated Englishmen address themselves to the cultivation of *style*, marrying "the sharpe wittes of logicians" and "the graue sentences of philosophers" to "the elegancie of the poetes," will England possess "perfect orators" and "a publike weale equiualent to the grekes or Romanes" (57ᵥ, 59ᵥ).

In 1531, when *The Governour* first appeared in print, "elegancie" was literally absent from the English art of rhetoric. The only existing rhetorical handbook in the vernacular, Leonard Cox's *Art or Crafte of Rhetoryke* (c. 1524–30), sets elocution and pronunciation pointedly to the side. "[M]any thynges be left out of this treatyse that ought to be spoken of," Cox allows in his preface, but not, he insists, in a handbook to be read only by "suche as haue by negligence or els fals persuacions" failed to "attayne any meane knowlege of the Latin tongue." For an audience defined by linguistic incompetence, he reasons, the rudiments of invention and arrangement "shall be sufficyent"—what Roger Ascham calls "good utterance" is no plausible object.[2] Some twenty years later, however, a pioneering English rhetorician cited Elyot as proof of the elegancy of the mother tongue. The title page of Richard Sherry's 1550 *Treatise of Schemes and Tropes* advertises it as an aid to "the better vnderstanding of good authors," and those who picked it up probably assumed that the authors in question were classical writers: here, presumably, was a handbook to help schoolboys recognize and reproduce a Ciceronian *paraphrasis* or a Virgilian *metalepsis*. The *Treatise*'s preface initially reinforces this assumption, as Sherry apologizes for the conspicuous classicism of his title, which must sound "all straunge vnto our Englyshe eares" and may cause "some men at the fyrst syghte to marvayle what the matter of it should meane." He urges readers to consider that "use maketh straunge thinges familier": with time, alien terms such as "scheme" and "trope" may become as common "as if they had bene of oure owne natiue broode."[3]

But as Sherry soon reveals, the strange things his treatise seeks to domesticate are not strictly the property of the classical tongues: on the contrary, what is foreign to English readers is the virtue of their own native speech. "It is not vnknowen that oure language for the barbarousnes and lacke of eloquence hathe bene complayned of," he writes,

> and yet not trewely, for anye defaut in the toungue it selfe, but rather for slackenes of our countrimen, whiche haue always set lyght by searchyng out the elegance and proper speaches that be ful many in it: as plainly doth appere not only by the most excellent monumentes of our auncient forewriters, Gower, Chawcer and Lydgate, but also by the famous workes of many other later: inespeciall of yᵉ ryght worshipful knyght syr Thomas Eliot, . . . [who]

as it were generallye searchinge oute the copye of oure language
in all kynde of wordes and phrases, [and] after that setting abrode
goodlye monumentes of hys wytte, lernynge and industrye, aswell
in historycall knowledge, as of eyther the Philosophies, hathe herebi
declared the plentyfulnes of our mother tounge. (A2ᵥ–[A3]ᵣ)

The "good authors" of the title page thus include not simply Cicero and Virgil
but also Thomas Elyot and the "manye other . . . yet lyuyng" (sig. [A3]ᵥ) whose
very familiarity—whose Englishness—has obscured the "copye" or riches of
their speech.

   In truth, it is hard to imagine any reader consulting the litany of arcane
tropes and figures that ensues and finding Elyot's prose easier to read as a consequence, but that perhaps is the point. English schoolboys were accustomed
to the notion that understanding a classical text meant retreating from the
immediate perception of meaning to a more remote appreciation of artifice:
"surely," writes Ascham, "the minde by dailie marking, first, the cause and
matter: than, the words and phrases: next, the order and composition: after
the reason and arguments: than the forms and figures . . . [and] lastelie, the
measure and compass of euerie sentence, must nedes, by litle and little, draw
vnto it the like shape of eloquence, as the author doth vse, which is red."[4]
When Sherry promises his readers "better understanding" of a writer such as
Elyot, he therefore offers them a mode of access to their mother tongue that
is also a process of alienation from it—the strange things made familiar are
also familiar things made enticingly strange. We—and presumably sixteenth-
century readers—do not need Sherry's definition of the figure he calls "Meta-
phora" or "translacion"—"a worde translated from the thynge that it properlye
signifieth, vnto another whych may agre with it by a similitude" (C4ᵥ)—to
understand what Elyot means when he describes moot-court exercises as the
"shadow or figure" of an ancient rhetoric, but the label and the definition call
our attention to the artfulness of the phrase, its capacity to suggest the way
time has attenuated and flattened a once substantive art. In this sense the
domestication of classical rhetorical precepts and practices brings with it a deliberate and profitable remove from the mother tongue, whose own shadows
and figures come into fresh relief.

   In its foregrounding of the vernacular's capacity for figuration, Sherry's
Treatise marks the beginning of a decisive shift in the discipline of English
rhetoric. Throughout the second half of the sixteenth century, a rapidly proliferating corpus of vernacular arts redefines eloquence almost exclusively in

terms of elocution, and elocution itself in terms of an ever-burgeoning catalog of figures of speech.[5] Historians of rhetoric have tended to look askance at this metastasis of style, naming "attention to ornament alone" as the "chief Renaissance abuse of the classical system" and dismissing the ubiquitous catalogs of rhetorical figures, with their elaborate taxonomies of scheme and trope, as "derivative . . . patchworks" of more comprehensive classical and continental treatises.[6] More recently, however, critics have recovered a sense of what elocution (or its absence) signified to Thomas Elyot and his successors in sixteenth-century England, recuperating the style-obsessed English art of rhetoric as a crucial instrument in the fashioning of a self-consciously literate mother tongue. Far from signaling the decline of a robust art of public discourse into a scholarly fetish, Wolfgang G. Müller argues, its investment in elocution constitutes "the most original part" of the English rhetorical treatise: a singular space of linguistic and national self-assertion.[7] By making the "elegancie" of English speech and writing their concern, the authors of sixteenth-century vernacular arts of rhetoric and poesy display a novel kind of interest and confidence in the vernacular, expecting it to serve not simply their commodity but their pleasure. As the editors of a recent collection of essays on Renaissance figures of speech point out, "it was in the area of *elocution*—and specifically the theory and description of the figures—that Renaissance rhetoric managed actually to take classical theory forwards," adding to the stock of ancient devices and doing "something new with them."[8] No longer merely ornamental, schemes and tropes become "flowers" and "colours" whose multiplication in the pages of vernacular treatises proves, as Jenny Mann argues, England's fitness "as a garden or field where rhetoric can grow and thrive."[9]

But in doing something new with figuration, ensconcing it at the center of rhetorical theory and practice and asking it to shore up their claim to eloquence as a common good, English rhetoricians run up against a very old dilemma. In an almost literal sense, as rhetorical theorists from Aristotle onward discover, style *reorients* rhetoric, transforming its defining investments in commodity and commonality into a fascination with exoticism and excess. In this sense elocution and pronunciation are not so much ancient rhetoric's "principal partes" as its most problematic: even in ancient Athens and Rome, style remains stubbornly unassimilated to accounts of eloquence as civic discourse, retaining dangerous and enticing associations with the uncivilized beyond. Elyot allows that the attractions of eloquence are not necessarily identical to the imperatives of the common good: "divers men . . . will say," he admits, "that the swetnesse that is contayned in eloquence . . . shulde utterly withdrawe the myndes of yonge men from the more necessary studie of the lawes of this realme" (55ᵥ). He dismisses this suspicion rather glibly, first by urging that legal doctrine be made eloquent, recast "either in englisshe, latine, or good French, written in a more clene and elegant stile," and second by insisting that greed and ambition guarantee that the law will always have its devotees (55ᵥ–56ᵣ), but it unsettles the sturdily civic-minded foundation of his pedagogical program, hinting at a potentially prodigal future for English eloquence.[10] And indeed, as they proceed through invention, arrangement, and memory into the alien precincts of style, sixteenth-century rhetoricians find themselves promoting the vernacular in radically altered guise: not as the necessary and commodious instrument of social communion but as a medium of transfiguration and transport—most potently attractive when it is most conspicuously far-fetched.

"Neither Cesar, nor Brutus, Builded the Same": England as *Topos*

Leonard Cox and Richard Sherry may have written the first English arts of rhetoric, but Thomas Wilson wrote the first art of *English* rhetoric: a work that takes for granted its interest and value as an account of the mother tongue and that establishes England as the necessary measure of eloquence in the vernacular. Cox justifies his vulgarization of classical rhetoric on the principle that "euery goode thynge, . . . the more commune that it is the better it is," but to his mind commonness is all English has to recommend it: he assumes that an educated readership will greet his vernacular rhetoric as "a thyng that is very rude and skant worthe the lokynge on."[11] For Wilson, by contrast, commonness is at the heart of "the orator's profession," which is fulfilled when he "speake[s] only of all such matters, as may largely be expounded . . . for all men to heare them": what is intelligible to all Englishmen is thus neither rude nor scant but the very fullness of rhetorical decorum.[12] He therefore conjures for his 1553 *Arte of Rhetorique* a readership not of poor Latinists but "*of all suche as are studious of Eloquence*": "Boldly . . . may I aduenture, and without feare step forth to offer that . . . which for the dignitie is so excellent, and for the use so necessarie," he announces in his prologue to the revised and expanded edition of 1560 (Aivᵣ). He dedicates both the 1553 and 1560 editions to his patron John Dudley, Earl of Warwick, whose "earnest . . . wish" that he "might one day see the precepts of Rhetorique set forth . . . in English" Wilson attributes not to his defects as a Latinist but to the "speciall desire and

Affection" he "beare[s] to Eloquence" (Aii$_v$). He anticipates a time when the "perfect experience, of manifolde and weightie matters of the Commonweale, shall haue encreased the Eloquence, which alreadie doth naturally flowe" in Dudley to such an extent that his own *Arte* will be "set . . . to Schoole" in Dudley's home, "that it may learn Rhetorique of . . . daylie talke"—for men learn best, he concludes, by following "their neyghbours deuice" (Aiii$_v$).

The fancy that eloquence might be schooled by an Englishman's "daylie talke" or patterned on one's "neyghbours deuice" upends Elyot's fantasy of the English home as a nursery for Latinity and issues a bracing challenge to Ascham's conviction that the "trewe Paterne of Eloquence" must be sought not "in common taulke, but in priuate bookes."[13] Indeed, although for Ascham the imitation of foreign eloquence recommends itself as a more profitable, less perilous alternative to actual travel abroad, in Wilson's view the two pursuits are dangerously kin. Having forsaken their mother country and mother tongue, he observes, "some farre iorneid ientlemen at their returne home, like as thei loue to goe in forraine apparel, so thei will pouder their talke with oversea language," but no less foolish are those would-be eloquent speakers who "seeke so far for outlandish English, that they forget altogether their mothers language." Orphaned and alienated by their own affectations, they "will say, they speake in their mother tongue," but "if some of their mothers were aliue, they were not able to tell what they say." The hybrid tongues that result from such excursions, whether literal or rhetorical, are invariably ludicrous and ineffective, "as if an Oratour that professeth to vtter his mind in plaine Latin, would needes speake Poetrie, and farre fetched colours of straunge antiquitie" (86$_r$). Actual foreign loan-words, Wilson implies, are merely the most obvious sign of linguistic corruption: the enticements of "straunge antiquitie"—excessive ornamentation, pseudo-archaisms, and pretentious classicisms—lure even educated speakers beyond the bounds of rhetorical community. "But thou saiest, the olde antiquitee doeth like thee best, because it is good, sobre, & modest," he jibes. "Ah, liue man as thei did before thee, and speake thy mynde now, as menne do at this daie." Instead of fretting over England's infelicitous isolation or the distinctions between its speech and the language of classical authors, he urges readers to learn from the classics precisely the integrity of their own native speech: "[R]emember that, whiche Cesar saith, beware as long as thou liuest, of straunge woordes, as thou wouldest take hede and eschewe great rockes in the Sea" (2$_r$).

When Wilson urges would-be vernacular orators to "seke . . . such words as are commonly receiued" (87$_v$), he represents the cultivation of rhetorical skill as an inquiry into a shared English life, depicted vividly in his anecdotes of Lincolnshire clergymen, Tindale ruffians, and London lawyers. He returns often to the image of bad oratory as a transgression of that secure and bounded existence, an ill-advised journey most often aimed in the direction of a Rome that is no longer Caesar's but the pope's. The folly of those who identify eloquence with circumlocution, "swaruing from their purpose" and introducing matters "farthest" from it, reminds him, for instance, of the cautionary example of an Anglican preacher who, intending to speak "of the generall resurrection," instead "hath made a large matter of our blessed Ladie, praysing her to bee so gentle, so curteous, and so kinde, that it were better a thousand fold, to make sute to her alone, then to Christ her sonne." He imagines the audience for such a speech responding with indignation—"Now, whether the deuill wilt thou, come in man againe for very shame"—for such errant discourse is "both vngodly, and nothyng at al to the purpose." Ultimately, Protestant England is abandoned, as rhetorical laxity makes way for heresy: "[A]ssuredly," he concludes, "many an vnlearned and witlesse man, hath straied in his talke much farther a great deale, yea truly as farre as hence to Roome gates" (48ᵣ).

Such jests have led critics to discern "a decidedly nationalistic spirit" in Wilson's *Arte of Rhetorique*.[14] The "goal that he established for himself," Albert Schmidt argues, "was less to teach Englishmen . . . rhetoric than to teach citizenship."[15] There is indeed little doubt that Wilson's rhetorical precepts reflect his political commitments: the language he uses against foreign loan-words, for instance, is very like the language he uses in a 1571 parliamentary speech against vagabonds, in which he urges Englishmen that it is "no charity to give to such a one as we know not, being a stranger unto us."[16]

But any vernacular rhetorician who quotes Caesar to persuade English orators not to be seduced by the luster of "olde antiquitee" has a rather complicated sense of what belongs to England and what is foreign to it. In reading Wilson's stylistic injunctions as proof of his nationalizing ambitions, critics have disregarded the complexity of "England" and "Englishness" within his *Rhetorique*, a text whose nativism is bound to—and shadowed by—its classicism. Insofar as he *theorizes* his resistance to foreign loan-words, pointless digressions, and ostentatious Latinity, justifying his preference for familiar speech in terms of rhetoric's own bias toward shared understanding, Wilson plants his English *Arte of Rhetorique* in what he identifies as foreign ground: the classical theory of topical invention. Wilson comes to the topics by way of rhetoric's sister art, dialectic, which he introduces to English readers in a

1551 treatise titled *The Rule of Reason, Conteinyng the Arte of Logique* (1551). Despite its name, Wilson's *Logique* draws most directly on theories of invention outlined in Aristotle's *Art of Rhetoric* and Quintilian's *Institutio Oratoria*. And yet his *Logique* appears to readers—and has been treated by critics—as a very different undertaking than his *Rhetorique*, largely because it displays such a different attitude toward its source material: if Wilson claims eloquence as England's native property, he regards the apparatus of logical reasoning as a distinctly foreign import.

Compared to the preface he wrote for his *Rhetorique*, the preface to his *Logique* is modest, even tentative, in tone. He insists that the endeavor was undertaken "not as though none could dooe it better; but because no Englishman until now, hath gone through with this enterprise." He cautions that the result may alienate some readers: "this fruit being of a straunge kind (soche as no Englishe ground hath before this tyme, and in this sort by any tillage brought forthe) maie perhaps in the firste tastyng, proue somewhat rough and harsh in the mouthe, because of the straungenesse." And yet the very strangeness of the art is indicative of its value: Wilson compares his "strange labour" and "earnest trauaile" as translator to the work of "some poore meane man, or simple personne, whose charge were to be a lodesman to conuey some noble princesse into a straunge land where she was neuer before." Nevertheless he continues, believing that "the capacitie of my country men the English nacion is . . . not inferiour to any other," hopeful that logic will prove "apte for the English wittes," and convinced that its precepts "myght with as good grace be sette forth in Thenglishe [tongue], I . . . enterprised to ioyne an acquaintaunce betwiene Logique, and my countrymen from the whiche they haue bene hetherto barred" and "make Logique familiar to Thenglishe man."[17]

Ironically, given his insistence on its strangeness to England, it is the art of logic—or rather the art of topical invention he draws from classical rhetoric and names logic—that secures Wilson's faith in England's fitness as a home for the arts of "reason[ing] probably" (*Logique*, A4$_v$–A5$_r$).[18] As he explains to readers, probability is intimately linked to place in the classical tradition. By consulting a familiar repertoire of mental "commonplaces"—abstract categories such as cause and effect, possibility or impossibility, virtue or vice—a speaker discovers the content of his argument: each "place" is "the restyng corner of an argumente, or els a marke whiche geveth warning to our memorie" (*Logique*, J5$_v$–[J6$_r$]). This process of invention is localized in a more literal fashion: tailored to fit the contours of a particular subject, audience, time, and place. Wilson illustrates this premise by way of an analogy he adapts from the *Institutio*

Oratoria, in which Quintilian likens the skilled orator's knowledge of the *loci communes* to an Italian fisherman's knowledge of the Mediterranean coast: "For just as all kinds of produce are not provided by every country, and as you will not succeed in finding a particular bird or beast, if you are ignorant of the localities where it has its usual haunts or birthplace, as even the various kinds of fish flourish in different surroundings, some preferring a smooth and others a rocky bottom, and are found on different shores and in diverse regions (you will, for instance, never catch a sturgeon or wrasse in our [Italian] seas), so not every kind of argument can be derived from every circumstance, and consequently our search requires discrimination."[19] Wilson, however, rewrites the analogy so that the classical *loci communes* become features of a recognizably English landscape:

> Those that bee good harefinders will soone finde the hare by her fourme. For when thei see the ground beaten flatte round about, and faire to the sighte: thei have a narrowe gesse by al likelihode that the hare was there a litle before. Likewise the Huntesman in hunting the foxe, wil soone espie when he seeth a hole, whether it be a foxe borough or not. So he that will take profeicte in this part of Logique [that is, invention], must bee like a hunter, and learn by labour to know the boroughs. For these places bee nothing else but coverts or boroughs, wherein if any one searche diligently, he maie finde game at pleasure. Therfore if any one will do good in this kynde, he must go from place to place, and by serching euery borough, he shall haue his purpose vndoubtedlie in moste part of them, if not in all. (*Logique*, J5$_v$–[J6$_r$])

This transformation of Quintilian's Italian fisherman into the English hare finder or huntsman reflects Wilson's determination that English readers be made to feel at home in places from which they were formerly barred—in this case in the places of invention. It shows as well his understanding of the topics, which demand such local accommodations.

Indeed, homely as it may seem, Wilson's metaphor of the hunt is rigorously classical in its account of the genesis of plausibility or "likelihode": it is only when the hare finders thoroughly acquaint themselves with the environs near the hare's burrow and "see the ground beaten flatte round about" that they are able to call upon the resources of probability, knowing "by al likelihode that the hare was there a litle before." This notion, that familiarity with one's surroundings ("know[ing] the boroughs") yields proximity to the truth ("a narrowe gesse"), is the central premise of Aristotle's *Art of Rhetoric*, which elevates the "narrowe gesse" to a valid form of knowledge—valid, that is, within the strictly delineated space of local deliberation. By transforming the topics or "commonplaces" of sophistic oratory from mere rhetorical shortcuts to a method of reasoning, Aristotle's *Rhetoric* attempts to rescue rhetoric from both the stringent criticisms of Plato's Socratic dialogues and the excessive relativism of the sophists, anchoring the art's disciplinary and epistemological legitimacy in a new conception of the relationship between persuasion and place.[20] Aristotle's *topoi* establish rhetoric as a "situated competence," as Walter Jost and Michael J. Hyde explain: they are "the places—issues, values, commitments, beliefs, likelihoods—that we hold in common with others, that we dwell in and argue over."[21] They are also the "place" rhetoric holds in common with its neighbor, dialectic. Finally, they are in an important sense linked to literal experiences of place, to those communal sites of "public" or "social" discourse that make up the arena of "practical knowledge in use."[22]

In Plato's *Gorgias,* Socrates insists that truth must be universally recognizable as such, declaring that even though "almost everyone in Athens" would find his opponent's defense of rhetoric plausible, as long as "there's still a dissenting voice, albeit a single one—mine," Gorgias cannot claim to have established his argument as true.[23] In his *Rhetoric*, Aristotle pointedly sidesteps both the issue of individual conviction and the question of universal or abstract truth by insisting that the orator does not "theorize about each opinion—what may seem so to Socrates or Hippias—but about what seems true to people of a certain sort."[24] From the law courts, the political forum, and the public gathering places of Athens, the orator therefore draws the materials he needs to fashion his arguments.[25] The local specificity of this knowledge is crucial because audiences make judgments "on the basis of what [particulars] they know and instances near their experience."[26] Such advice may sound ominously similar to the kind of appeasement that, according to Socrates, casts rhetoric into "the same province" as sophistry, [27] but by focusing on the importance of locating an argument within a particular context, Aristotle defines a valid role for argument by approximation. His definition of rhetorical truth, that is, pertains to arguments "not . . . only from what is necessarily valid"—so-called "inartificial" proofs, such as eyewitness testimony—"but also what is true for the most part," what, by virtue of its affinity with received wisdom and commonly held opinions, comes *close* to the truth.[28] The arguments produced by topical invention are thus intimately shaped by the orator's knowledge of actual locales, for plausibility is contingent upon time, place, and persons. But the *theory* of the topics is eminently and necessarily portable; otherwise rhetoric would be no teachable art.

In this sense Wilson's *Logique* and his *Rhetorique* collaborate in a sleight-of-hand: as the abstract basis of probable reasoning, the topics constitute the classical tradition's movable goods; as the engines of purely local conviction, the topics remain anchored in—indeed help to produce—a specifically English discursive community. Wilson seems to have taken pleasure in this irony, using his accounts of the individual topics in both treatises as occasions to meditate, playfully, on the idea of England as *topos*, both the product and the a priori condition of classical invention. To demonstrate reasoning from the topic of "deeds done," he therefore argues that "[i]f Iulius Cesar came into England, then there was such a man called Iulius Cesar"; to illustrate the use of the topic of "contraries," he argues that "King Lud is not the same, that Iulius Cesar, or Brutus was: Kyng Lud buylded London, of whom the citee had his name, beyng called Luddes toune, and afterwarde, by alteracion of letters, called London. Ergo neither Cesar, nor Brutus, builded the same" (*Logique*, sigs. [K8ᵣ], [N6ᵣ]). Such references to ancient British history and myth skirt delicately around the fact of Wilson's own reliance on classical tradition, as he oscillates between boldly asserting England's independence from antiquity ("neither Cesar, nor Brutus, builded the same") and, more boldly still, asserting antiquity's dependence on England ("[i]f Iulius Cesar came into England, then there was such a man called Iulius Cesar"). Of course, the reverse is more properly true of England-as-*topos*: when Wilson cites "The Realm," "The Shire," and "The Toune" as primary topics of deliberative oratory in his *Arte of Rhetorique* (6ᵥ),[29] he positions England as the literal ground of rhetorical invention but also offers it as the "strange fruit" of his own foray into Greek and Latin learning.

This is not necessarily a contradiction of his *Rhetorique*'s stylistic precepts, for even at his strictest moments Wilson is no Anglo-Saxon purist. When Greek or Latin terms are required "to set forth our meaning in the English tongue, either for lacke of store, or els because we would enrich the language: it is well doen to vse them," he explains, provided that "all other are agreed to followe the same waie." Such words, "being vsed in their place," should cause no one to be "suspected for affectation," he writes, as long as they are "apt and meete . . . to set out the matter." In fact, rhetoric may describe just such a matter, for the examples Wilson cites of apt and meet borrowing are suggestively redolent of his earlier account of the art as a whole: "There is no man agreued, when he heareth (letters patentes) & yet patentes is latine, and signifieth open to all men. The Communion is a felowship, or a commyng together, rather Latine then Englishe: the Kynges prerogatiue, declareth his power royall aboue all other, and yet I knowe no man greued for these termes, beeyng vsed in their place, nor yet any one suspected for affectacion, when suche generall wordes are spoken. The folie is espied, when either we will vse suche wordes, as fewe men doo vse, or vse theim out of place, when another might serue muche better" (87$_v$). Wilson's rationale is plain enough and consistent with his reasoning throughout the *Rhetorique*: as always, his concern is with place, that words be accommodated to the place in which they are written or spoken and that they do not displace more familiar and proper terms. Nonetheless his examples are, in context, provocative: the phrase "open to all men" recalls his definition of the province of rhetoric as "all such matters, as may largely be expounded . . . for all men to heare them"; the description of communion as "a fellowship, or a coming together" echoes the myth of rhetoric's origins; the description of "power . . . aboue all other" mimics the account of the orator's supreme power in his dedicatory epistle to Dudley. These are, according to Wilson, places where English speakers either must or may turn to the classical tongues for assistance, but they map quite closely onto the central concerns of his own treatise: accessibility, community, and authority. Is rhetoric a native discourse, after all, or a place where Englishmen must agree to follow a foreign way?

The three samples of deliberative oratory placed at the center of Wilson's *Arte* introduce further notes of uncertainty. The first is devoted, unexpectedly given his loudly aired prejudices against foreign travel, to persuading young Englishmen of the virtues of travel abroad—in praise of which he cites, especially, "the swetnesse of the tongue[s]" spoken elsewhere (16$_v$). The second, urging a young man "to study the laws of England," gives way to a disquisition against the stubborn "kepyng of Commons for custome sake," even though lands fenced for private use "might gain ten tymes the value"—an argument that sits uneasily beside Wilson's vision of the vernacular as just such a common space (19$_r$). Third, he translates the entirety of an Erasmian epistle in praise of marriage, returning in the process to the figure of Orpheus, mythical orator and lawgiver. When Orpheus rescued Eurydice from Hades, he demands, "what other thinge do we thinke that the Poets meant, but only to set forthe vnto vs the loue in wedlocke the whiche euen amonge the Deuilles was compted good and Godlye?" "Emonge diuers countries, and diuers menne, there haue bene diuers lawes and customes vsed," he allows, "[y]et was there neuer anye countrey so sauage, none so farre from all humanitie, where the name of wedlocke was not counted holye, and hadde in great reuerence. This the Thracian, this the Sarmate, this the Indian, this the Grecian, this the Latine, yea, this the Britain that dwelleth in the furtheste parte of all the worlde, or if there be anye that dwell beyonde them haue euer counted to be most holy" (26_v). Suddenly, in the midst of the first English art of rhetoric, a treatise that works diligently to establish England's native claim to the strange fruits of classical civilization, Britain finds itself back on the margins, in "the furthest parte of all the worlde." Sixteenth-century English readers may have been accustomed to seeing their home cited by ancient authors as a byword for savage extremity, but the inclusion of such language in Wilson's *Arte* is particularly jarring—both because it reminds us, rather tactlessly, that Wilson has had to borrow his central example of eloquence from a non-English author and because it produces a rhetorical geography that conflates Thracian and Sarmation, Greek and Latin, Indian and British with no regard for the boundaries that Wilson elsewhere cherishes and defends.

Indeed, for all its emphasis on home, the "pattern of eloquence" on which Wilson's *Rhetorique* relies remains every bit as far-fetched as Roger Ascham's: the England that underwrites his *Arte* is an imaginary (and occasionally awkward) synthesis of classical ideals and local anecdotes. The terms in which Wilson's contemporaries received his work reflect this ambiguity. Gabriel Harvey hailed the *Rhetorique* as "the daily bread of our common pleaders and discoursers," and there is little doubt that both the dailiness of the use and the commonness of the users would have pleased Wilson.[30] At the same time, when the poet Barnabe Barnes credited *The Arte of Rhetorique* with "redress[ing] our English barbarism," he signaled how far Wilson's ideal of English remained from the ordinary speech of his day.[31] As Wilson allows, familiarity may be the basis of persuasive power, but the best orator does not blend into the crowd his eloquence assembles: "among all other, I thinke him most worthie fame," he writes, "that is among the reasonable of al most reasonable, and among the wittie, of all most wittie, and among the eloquent, of all most eloquent: him thinke I among all men, not onely to be taken for a singuler man, but rather to be coumpted for halfe a God" (*Rhetorique*, $A7_v$). The singularity and near divinity of the eloquent man—his ability to invent the place in which he speaks—derive not from his speaking commonly but his speaking extraordinarily.

Wilson's own account of this paradoxical process highlights the mixed genealogy of his supposedly English *Rhetorique*. In the opening pages of his *Arte*, Wilson, like so many other sixteenth-century humanists, turns to the origins of eloquence, but he gives the familiar narrative of communal gathering a distinctive twist, marrying the classical legend of Orpheus to a quasi-biblical saga of sin and salvation. "After the fall of our firste father," Adam, Wilson writes, the "eloquence first giuen by God" was lost, and with it the foundation of human community: "all things waxed sauage, the earth vntilled, societie neglected." Lacking a productive relation to the land, or to each other, men "grased vpon the ground" and "romed" like wild beasts, "liu[ing] brutishly in open feeldes, hauing neither house to shroude them in, nor attire to clothe their backes" (Aiii_r). Wilson's allusion to the Fall reminds his readers that linguistic degeneracy and geographic dispersal are the twin plots of the book of Genesis: Adam and Eve lose the divine speech when they are cast out of the garden; Cain becomes, in the words of the 1560 Geneva Bible, "a vagabond and a runnagate in the earth" (Gen. 4:12); Noah's sons are "deuided in their lands, euery one after his tongue; [and] after their families, in their nations" (Gen. 10:5); and, at last, at Babel, God resolves to "confound the language of all the earth" and "scatter them vpon all the earth" (Gen. 11:9). At this point in the story, however, Wilson grafts onto his biblical narrative the pagan myth of Orpheus, which contrasts the vagrancy of prerhetorical mankind with the purposeful solidarity of a people "moved" by eloquence: alienation and confusion persist, he alleges, until God's "faithfull and elect . . . called [men] together by vtteraunce of speech," persuading them "to live together in fellowship of life" and "to maintain Cities." By no "other meanes," he asserts, echoing Quintilian, could men have been brought to submit to the authority of God and his ministers (Aiii_v).

The conclusion to this curiously hybrid story is Wilson's own: man's natural vagrancy would lead him to seek to move to a higher station, he writes, "were [he] not persuaded, that it behoueth [him] to liue in his owne vocation: and not to seeke any higher roume" (Aiiii_r). Eloquence creates community, that is, but also maintains, according to degree, the natural boundaries between peoples, classes, nations, and all other entities otherwise vulnerable to motion, error, and change. It is a stirring claim with which to begin England's first full-fledged vernacular rhetoric but an odd moral to append to a narrative that thrives on an illicit mingling of Christian theology, pagan myth, and Tudor political doctrine, straying heedlessly close to heresy in its conflation of eloquence and election, and assigning to Orphic orators and poets a redemptive role the Bible reserves to Christ. Here, as in his descriptions of the topics, Wilson seems eager to test the boundaries of what may be claimed as English, asserting the virtue of native purity at the very moment he indulges in a more complicated, potentially more generative kind of cross-breeding. His *Rhetorique* testifies to the changes wrought upon a classical ideal of eloquence when it is identified with England's daily talk, but it testifies as well to the changes wrought upon sixteenth-century ideals of Englishness as they assimilate an alien theory of eloquence.

Marveling at Strangers: Ancient Rhetoric's Foreign Figures

In its boldest gesture, the preface to Sherry's *Treatise of Schemes and Tropes* construes ancient rhetoric's foreign provenance as its chief enticement for the vernacular reader. Although he worries that some readers will scan the title of his book, "marvayle," and cast it aside as "some newe fangle," he imagines "other[s], whiche moued with the noueltye thereof, wyll thynke it worthye to be looked vpon, and se what is contained therin" (A2ᵣ). In appropriating wonder as a productive response to the foreign terminology of style—schemes and tropes, metaphors, zeugmas, and antistrophes—Sherry does not simply make good on an inevitable feature of his own rhetorical project, the need to reckon with peculiar Greek and Latin terms of art; he also recovers for the vernacular a central, and puzzling, feature of what Elyot calls "the ancient rhetoric": for all its emphasis on the importance of familiarity and proximity to the genesis of plausibility, when it comes to style, classical rhetoric places a counterintuitive premium on the orator's ability to impress his audience with the *unlikelihood* of his expressions. In consequence, a particular, paradoxical glamour attaches to precisely those figures whose speech locates them outside, or on the margins, of the linguistic community. "Style contrary to the usage of well-bred Greeks," cautions Diogenes Laertes in his treatise on grammar, is "barbarism."[32] But when the historian Diodorus Siculus describes the sophist Gorgias's arrival in Athens from his home in Sicily, he attributes the power of his eloquence to its very difference from the usage of well-bred Greeks. "When [Gorgias] had arrived in Athens and had been brought before the people," Diodorus writes, "he addressed them on the subject of an alliance" and won them over "by the novelty of his style," which "amazed" them with its "extravagant figures of speech marked by deliberate art: antithesis and clauses of exactly or approximately equal length and rhythm and others of such a sort, which at the time were thought worthy of acceptance because of the strangeness of the method, but now seem tiresome and often appear ridiculous and excessively contrived."[33]

The mingled notes of admiration and of censure in Diodorus's account of Gorgias persist throughout the classical tradition: the subject of style invariably elicits, in almost equal measure, both the impulse to protect ordinary speech and the yearning to depart from it. Aristotle, for instance, reserves any mention of style to the third and final book of his *Art of Rhetoric*, which begins with the cautious concession that "the subject of expression [*lexis*] . . . has some small necessary place in all teaching; for to speak in one way rather than another does make some difference in regard to clarity, though not a great difference; but all these things are forms of outward show and intended to affect the audience."[34] In addition to his skepticism about the tendency of "outward show[s]" to distract an audience from their real task of evaluating probability, Aristotle worries about the disciplinary propriety of ornamentation. In his view the stylistic excesses of sophistic oratory improperly blur the distinction between rhetoric and poetry: "[S]ince the poets, while speaking sweet nothings, seemed to acquire their reputation through their *lexis*, a poetic style came into existence [in prose as well], for example, that of Gorgias. Even now, the majority of the uneducated think such speakers speak most beautifully. This is not the case; but the *lexis* of prose differs from that of poetry."[35] The only valid aims of rhetorical style, Aristotle insists, are "to be clear"—for "speech is a kind of sign, so if it does not make clear it will not perform its function"—and "appropriate," that is, "neither flat nor above the dignity of the subject, but appropriate." To achieve both clarity and appropriateness, the orator must adhere to the standards of ordinary speech: "The use of nouns and verbs in their prevailing [*kyrios*] meaning makes for clarity; other kinds of words, as discussed in the *Poetics*, make the style ornamented rather than flat."[36]

Thus far Aristotle's theory of style is consistent with his account of topical invention: the limits of both invention and ornamentation reflect the bounds of the place in which the orator speaks. What is familiar or prevalent in that community determines what is persuasive, clear, or appropriate, so that style, like probability, is essentially local. But if ordinary usage sets the standards of clarity and propriety, it is nonetheless true that speech is only *recognizable* as stylish insofar as it departs from the ordinary and expected. Thus, in a striking inversion of the terms of his discussion of clarity, Aristotle notes, "To deviate [from prevailing (*kyrios*) usage] makes language seem more elevated; for people feel in the same way in regard to style [*lexis*] as they do in regard to strangers compared with citizens. As a result, one should make the language unfamiliar, for people are admirers of what is far off, and what is marvelous is sweet."[37] Here stylized or figurative language is likened to a foreign traveler—and unexpectedly, the presumed response to this strange intruder is not defensiveness but *hospitality*: his very remoteness from the familiar experiences of those he encounters makes him "marvelous" and "sweet" to them.

As Aristotle admits, this effect of language, the appeal of the unfamiliar, is more often associated with poetic fictions than with arguments. "Many [kinds of words] accomplish this in verse," he observes, "for what is said [in poetry] about subjects and characters is more out of the ordinary, but in prose much less so."[38] Nevertheless and in spite of his own earlier cautions against the poeticizing of rhetoric, he directs readers interested in these "other kinds of words, [which] make the style ornamented rather than flat" to his discussion of figurative language in the *Poetics*.[39] The relevant passages further elaborate the relationship between ornamentation and strangeness. Indeed cultural and geographic distinctions form the basis of Aristotle's theory of figurative language: "By a current [*kyrion*] noun," Aristotle explains, "I mean one which is in use among a given people; by a non-standard [*glotta*] noun I mean one which is in use among other people."[40] Standard and nonstandard, strange and familiar, figurative and proper are not therefore fixed categories for Aristotle. Instead language is strange or familiar only in relation to one's place in the world: "Obviously the same noun may be both current and non-standard, but not for the same people," Aristotle notes. "*Sigunon* is current among the Cypriots, but non-standard to us; 'spear' is current among us, but non-standard to them."[41] The crucial point to be made here is that—while the terms "standard" and "non-standard" appear to make strangeness the mark of improper, and hence ineffective, usages—both the *Poetics* and the *Rhetoric* assign strange language a valuable and even necessary function in the work of persuasion. A poet or orator alters his language to achieve the effect of strangeness not primarily through the borrowing of foreign terms but through metaphor, which Aristotle defines as "the application of a noun which properly applies to something else" or "a movement [*epiphora*] of an alien [*allotrios*] name."[42] This movement from the "proper" to the "alien" transforms language from what is *kyrion*, or common, to what is *glotta*, or strange. As the term "metaphor," which literally means "carrying something from one place to another," suggests, it enacts a kind of travel within language: the stranger is brought among citizens.

Both the general requirements of *lexis*, or style, and the particular operations of metaphor require Aristotle to grant foreignness a role in the work of rhetorical persuasion that is seemingly at odds with his insistence that rhetorical style not violate the norms of clarity and common usage. Discussions of style after Aristotle run into the same apparent contradiction: the excesses and transgressions that mark barbarous speech as improper are the same gestures by which figurative speech achieves its distinction from ordinary prose. For instance, when he turns to the subject of metaphor, Quintilian admits that "in dealing with ornament, I shall occasionally speak of faults which have to be avoided, but which are hard to distinguish from virtues."[43] The difficulty of the distinction, he observes, derives from the fact that the figuration that provides rhetoric with its supreme ornament "originates from the same sources as errors of language": that is, from deviations from the common idiom and from "proper" relationships of meaning. He is reduced to the relativistic conclusion that "propriety . . . must be tested by the touchstone of the understanding, not the ear,"[44] and turns at last to intention as the only distinction between flaws and figures of speech: "every figure would be an error, if it were accidental and not deliberate."[45]

The near identity between rhetorical ornamentation and rhetorical abuse (indeed, as Quintilian notes, there is a rhetorical figure, *catachresis*, whose name literally means "abuse"[46]) produces a constant anxiety over the desirable and dangerous effects of language that departs from ordinary usage. As in Diodorus Siculus's anecdote of Gorgias, this anxiety about strange language often merges with an anxiety about the strange origins of the orator himself: geographic or cultural distance, that is, became a sign of the innate foreignness of figuration. As the debate over proper rhetorical language evolved, style was literally mapped onto the globe: rhetoric that eschewed ornate gestures and artificial phrasing, hewing closely to supposedly natural patterns of speech, was dubbed "Attic," while rhetoric adorned with elaborate figures and carefully wrought periods was dubbed "Asiatic." Initially, at least, there was some descriptive accuracy to such geographic distinctions. As the once powerful Greek Empire fragmented, cultural and political power shifted to the outlying cities of Alexandria and Pergamon, in which a more rarefied and literary mode of eloquence developed. The first orator to be dubbed "Asiatic," Hegesias of Magnesia, lived in the third century and developed a neatly epigrammatic form of address. This "Asiatic" style was perpetuated in the second century by the brothers Menecles and Hierocles of Alabanda in Asia Minor and made more ornate by Aeschines of Miletus and Aeschylus of Cnidus.[47] But what originated as a descriptive taxonomy—a way of distinguishing the new rhetoric from that which had flourished in Athens—quickly acquired a more value-laden set of connotations and a more polemical intent. As Jeffrey Walker points out, the accounts of Asiatic rhetoric written in the Hellenistic period vastly overstate the real link between eastern oratory and the emergence of a more "florid" style: "If there is a 'literaturizing' or belletristic turn in Hellenistic rhetoric," he observes, "it would seem to make its clearest appearance not in the sophistic or even 'Asianist' tradition . . . but in the Peripatetic, Aristotelian-Theophrastian tradition embodied in Demetrius' *On Style*."[48] The association between Asiaticism and an ornate style owes less to real rhetorical history, he suggests, than it does to a desire to disavow tendencies within the Greek tradition that seemed to threaten rhetoric's practical and ethical functions.

Indeed an array of later texts written after the summit of Athenian rhetorical accomplishment sought to maintain the vitality of that tradition by asserting the inherent aesthetic and moral superiority of Attic style and blaming the decline of "pure," philosophically based rhetoric on the influence of Asiatic oratory. Caecilius of Calacte, the author of a Hellenistic treatise on figuration that defined figuration pejoratively as "a turning to a form of thought and diction which is not in accordance with nature" and argued for the possibility of a purely literal mode of expression, also wrote two polemics of which only the titles survive: "How the Attic Style Differs from the Asian" and "Against the Phrygians."[49] In a similar vein, at the end of the first century B.C., Dionysius of Halicarnassus illustrated his critique of rhetorical excess, *Peri ton Archaion Rhetoron* ("On the Ancient Orators"), with an analogy likening true eloquence to an Attic wife who has been displaced by a lewdly flamboyant Asiatic mistress:

In the time before our own, the old and philosophic rhetoric was so abused and endured such terrible mistreatment that it fell into decline; after Alexander of Macedon's final breath it gradually withered away, and by our generation had come to seem almost extinct. Another stole past the guards and took its place, intolerably shameless and theatrical, and comprehending nothing either of philosophy or of any other liberal training [*eleutherios paideuma*], escaping notice and misleading the ignorance of the masses, it came to enjoy not only greater wealth, luxury and splendor than the other, but also the honors and high offices of cities, which rightfully belong to the philosophic, and it was wholly vulgar and importunate, and finally made Greece resemble the households of the profligate and evil-starred. For just as in these there sits the freeborn, sensible wife with no authority over her domain, while a senseless harlot brings

ruin upon her life and claims control of the whole estate, casting
filth upon her and putting her in terror, so too in every city and
even among the well-educated (for this was the utmost evil of them
all) the ancient and indigenous Attic muse was dishonored and
deprived of her possessions, while the new arrival, some Mysian or
Phrygian or Carian trash just recently come from some Asian pit,
claimed the right to rule over Greek cities and drove her rival from
the commons, the unlearned driving out the philosophic and the
crazed the sensible.[50]

Dionysius's account of rhetorical excess is clearly itself excessive, even, as Walker
comments, "histrionic,"[51] but it mobilizes a series of associations between
eloquence and place that become conventions of rhetorical history and theory,
conventions that sixteenth-century English writers absorb and transform. On
the one side we have the old, properly "philosophic" rhetoric—legitimate,
ancient, indigenous, honest, restrained, chaste, sensible, self-effacing, and
decorous—whose rightful (and painstakingly earned) place within the local
community is usurped by enthusiasm for a "theatrical" rhetoric of stylistic
ornamentation—alien, Eastern, novel, luxurious, vulgar, sexually profligate,
morally degenerate, deceitful, crazed, and power-hungry. The stereotype of
Asiatic eloquence thus establishes a link between metaphor's effect on plain
language and the foreign interloper's effect on the Greek *oikos* or the English
commons. The geographic, cultural, and racial prejudices that structure the
history of rhetoric bespeak discomfort with the alien allure of figuration:
foreignness, distance, and travel come to represent tensions internal to
eloquence.

"Faire and Orient": The Asiatic English Poet

Within the sixteenth-century English art of rhetoric these ancient tensions
produce a conspicuous metaphorical volatility: the imagery of estrangement
so often invoked to stigmatize awkward or affected speech proves equally
available for positive representations of a vernacular enriched and transformed
by style. In the final section of his *Arte of Rhetorique*, Thomas Wilson hails
elocution as "that part of *Rhetorique*, the which aboue all other is most
beautifull," and without which reason "walk[s] . . . both bare and naked" or,
worse, clad "in apparel . . . so homely" that its virtue goes unrecognized (85ᵥ).

Wilson represents ornamentation as the logical addendum to invention and arrangement—"when wee haue learned apte wordes, and vsuall phrases to set foorth our meaning, and can orderly place them," he writes, then "wee may boldely commende and beautifie our talke" (89ᵥ–90ᵣ)—but it adheres to a very different set of values: boldness and beauty are the marks at which the truly expert speaker aims, even if their attainment means violating the standards of apt, usual, and orderly speech. That such violations will be necessary is apparent from Wilson's account of "exornation," which he defines as "a gorgeous beautifying of the tongue with borrowed wordes, and change of sentence or speech with much varietie," so that "our speech may seeme as bright and precious, as a rich stone is faire and orient" (90ᵣ). The contrast with his earlier prohibitions on strange words grows more marked as Wilson's discussion of exornation proceeds: ornament, he writes, is most often achieved by figures of speech, which are "vsed after some newe or straunge wise, much vnlike to that which men commonly vse to speake." Without such new and strange figures, Wilson claims, "not one can attaine to be coumpted an Oratour, though his learning otherwise be neuer so great" (90ᵥ). Among the most skilled speakers, he observes, "[m]en coumpt it a point of witte, to passe ouer such words as are at hand, and to vse such as are farre fetcht and translated"—by such diversions from common use, he concludes, "[a]n Oration is wonderfullye enriched" (91ᵥ–92ᵣ).

Most English rhetorical manuals of the late sixteenth and early seventeenth centuries are more interested in the new and strange effects of figuration than they are in the invention of topics or the elaboration of commonplaces for arguments. By means of figures and tropes, as Abraham Fraunce writes in his *Arcadian Rhetorike* (1588), language is transformed: "turned" or "drawen away from his first proper signification, to another," but "so conuenientlie, as that it seem rather willingly ledd, than driuen by force."[52] The effect of such "turning" or "drawing away" is not, as with the commonplaces, an articulation or confirmation of shared experience or belief but rather the introduction of something different: "A Figure," writes Henry Peacham in *The Garden of Eloquence* (1577), "is a forme of words, oration, or sentence, made new by art, differing from the vulgar maner and custome of writing or speaking."[53] The virtues of figurative speech are thus difficult to distinguish from the vices of Wilson's far-journeyed gentleman. Indeed in sixteenth-century England as in ancient Athens and Rome, the subject of style entails a striking reversal of the relationship presumed to exist between place and eloquence: now rhetoric leads away to the alien and exotic rather than sustaining the common and usual.

George Puttenham's *Arte of English Poesie* (1589) famously provides precise geographic coordinates for proper English usage, which he locates "in London and the shires lying about London within lx. myles, and not much aboue." The best speech in any language, Puttenham writes, is not that which is spoken "in the marches or frontiers, or in port townes, where straungers haunt for traffike sake, or yet in Vniuersities where Schollers vse much peeuish affectation of wordes out of the primatiue languages, or finally, in any vplandish village or corner of a Realme, where there is no resort but of poore rusticall or vnciuill people"; rather it is strictly that dialect that is used "in the kings Court, or in the good townes and Cities within the land"—a dictum that, in sixteenth-century England, disallows "any speech vsed beyond the riuer of Trent."[54] But Puttenham also urges his readers to cultivate "a maner of utterance more eloquent and rethoricall than the ordinarie prose . . . because it is decked and set out with all maner of fresh colours and figures." This kind of speech, he claims, is eminently fit not only for the delight of one's audience but also for the task of persuasion: figurative speech "sooner inuegleth the iudgement of man, and carieth his opinion this way and that" (24). Like Aristotle's *lexis* and Wilson's "exornation," Puttenham's figuration owes its persuasive force not to familiarity or likelihood but to the luster of its "rich Orient coulours," which "delight and allure as well the mynde as the eare of the hearers with a certain noueltie and strange maner of conueyance, disguising it no little from the ordinary and accustomed" (149–50).

As figuration, rhetoric recapitulates the pleasurable effects of travel, transporting listeners from "the ordinary and accustomed" to things novel and strange. Metaphor, as all of these writers well knew, means "to carry across"—as Puttenham says, it might be dubbed "the figure of *transport*," since it entails "a kinde of wresting of a single word from his own right signification, to another not so naturall" (148). That less "naturall" signification might imply a transgression of decorum—Ben Jonson notes in his commonplace book that "*Metaphors* farfet hinder to be understood" and that a speaker should take care not to "fetcheth his translations from a wrong place"[55]—but it also opens language up to exotic delights and strange riches. "There is a greater Reverence had of things remote, or strange to us, then of much better, if they be nearer, and fall under our sense," Jonson allows, and although he pauses to wonder "why . . . men depart at all from the right, and naturall wayes of speaking," he promptly answers his own question: they do so "sometimes for necessity, [and] sometimes for pleasure, and variety, as Travailers turn out of the high way, drawne, either by the commodity of a footpath, or the delicacy or freshnesse of the fields."[56] Jonson's fields and footpaths are plausibly English, but in treatises such as Wilson's and Puttenham's, the transports of metaphor invariably lead East, to an exotic and gem-rich Orient. In part this association may reflect the persistence of the belief that the vernacular as it was commonly spoken was inadequate—too narrowly provincial—to serve as a staging ground for eloquence, but it reflects as well the conviction that eloquence demands liberal bounds. If English were to become eloquent, Englishness would need to be more expansively construed.

This, according to Puttenham, was the function of all figurative language: "As figures be the instruments of ornament in euery language, so be they also in a sorte abuses or rather trespasses in speech, because they passe the ordinarie limits of common vtterance," becoming a "manner of forraine and coloured talke" (128). Ultimately, Puttenham suggests, the effect of rhetoric on an audience is not to confirm their sense of place in the world but to provide the illusion of leaving it: figures of speech, he writes, "carieth [the listener's] opinion this way and that, whither soeuer the heart by impression of the eare shalbe most affectionately bent and directed," "drawing [the minde] from plainnesse and simplicitie to a certain doublenesse" (6, 128). This "doublenesse," the "inuersion of sense by transport" (128), serves as yet another response to the relationship understood to exist between English language and England's place. Here neither the vernacular nor the foreign is shunned, since figuration allows for the coexistence of the two in a single discourse: "euery language" has the capacity to become a "manner of forraine . . . talke."

In other words, every language is capable of poetry. Puttenham's treatise begins with the assertion that eloquence is bred only by the influence of poets upon a language. "The vtterance in prose is not of so great efficacie," he writes, "because . . . it is dayly vsed, and by that occasion the eare is ouerglutted with it" (5). Whereas Wilson cautioned orators against adopting the extravagant style of the poet, Puttenham offers poetry as the ideal model for rhetorical excellence: "the Poets were . . . from the beginning the best perswaders, and their eloquence the first Rhethoricke of the world" (6). The division between poetry and "ordinarie prose" thus becomes another boundary to be trespassed in the pursuit of eloquence.[57] How is it that poetic language accomplishes this internal estrangement of the vernacular? George Gascoigne offers one explanation in "Certayne Notes of Instruction Concerning the Making of Verse," an essay appended to his 1575 anthology *The Posies*. Gascoigne begins the essay by urging his fellow vernacular poets *not* to regard poetic diction as alienated from ordinary speech and encouraging them rather to hew to "playne Englishe" in the composition of their verses.[58] Take care, he writes, that "you wreste no woorde from his natural and vsuall sounde" and, when possible, choose short and simple words, for "the more monosyllables that you vse, the truer Englishman you shall seeme" (50–51). Gascoigne particularly urges vernacular poets to "eschew straunge words, or *obsoleta et inusitata*," and to "use your verse after theenglishe phrase, and not after the maner of other languages" (52–53).

Nevertheless it is by no means obvious to Gascoigne that poetic language always can or should adhere to the boundaries of "playne Englishe." Indeed he quickly qualifies his own ruling, allowing that archaisms and other "unnatural" words are sometimes permitted to verse by "poetic license": "Therefore even as I have advised you to place all wordes in their naturall or most common and usuall pronunciation, so would I wishe you to frame all sentences in their mother phrase and proper Idioma, and yet sometimes (as I have sayd before) the contraries may be borne, but that is rather where rime enforceth, or *per licentiam Poeticam*, than it is otherwise lawfull or commendable" (53). Gascoigne's own language at this moment ironically and playfully enacts the permeability of that supposedly lawful and commendable boundary between "theenglishe phrase" and "the maner of other languages," even in prose: "straunge words" is glossed with the Latin "*obsoleta et inusitata*"; the "mother phrase" is elaborated—gratuitously—by the Greek "Idioma"; and "*per licentiam Poeticam*" substitutes for the perfectly serviceable vernacular equivalent. Recourse to language outside of the common usage, it seems, is not simply a freedom allowed to English verse: prose stylists too may find themselves straying into foreign tongues, either where the paucity of the vernacular "enforceth" such transgressions or simply where the whim of the author makes them desirable.

As Gascoigne unfolds his theory of "*licentiam poeticam*," he further multiplies the qualifications to his own rule against "straunge words." "This poeticall license," he writes, is "a shrewde fellow," which "covereth many faults in a verse." Poetic license, he observes, has the procrustean ability to "maketh words longer, shorter, of mo syllables, of fewer, newer, older, truer, falser, and to conclude it turkeneth all things at pleasure" (53–54). Here again Gascoigne's own language partakes of the license he describes: "turkeneth," according to the *Oxford English Dictionary*, is emphatically a "newer" word in 1575, perhaps even Gascoigne's own coinage. The twofold connotation of the word preserves a sense of Gascoigne's ambivalence about poetic license: on the one hand, "to

turken" (or, to use an earlier, related form of the word, "to turkesse") means either "to transform or alter for the worse; to wrest, twist, distort, pervert" or—
much less negatively—"to alter the form or appearance of; to change, modify,
refashion (not necessarily for the worse)."[59] Which definition applies to the
"turkening" of that shrewd fellow, poetic license, is uncertain in Gascoigne's
account. Are the alterations wrought in the common language by poetic usage
"perversions" of that language, or are they simply acts of "refashioning" and
"modification"? Is poetic license an invitation to poetic licentiousness? Insofar
as it signifies a potentially illicit "turning" of language, "turken" is also a syn-
onym for "trope," the operation by which words, as Puttenham says, "haue
their sense and understanding altered and figured . . . by transport, abuse,
crosse-naming, new-naming, change of name" (189). Such conversions force
both language and listeners from their common uses: when speech is ornamented with "figures rhethoricall," Puttenham writes, it possesses, in addition
to the "ordinarie vertues" of "sententiousnes, and copious amplification," an
"instrument of conueyance for . . . carrying or transporting [meaning] farther
off or nearer" and for making the mind of the listener "yielding and flexible,"
susceptible to persuasion in any direction (207). Figuration invests language
with the power to transport listeners, both within and beyond the confines of
the mother tongue.

There is, of course, another ambiguity nested in Gascoigne's uncommon
turn of phrase, with its etymological relation to early modern England's preeminent figure for *global* difference and licentious excess: the Turk. According to the *OED*, while "turken" and "turkesse" are understood by some as
versions of the French "torquer" or the Latin "torquere," meaning "to twist,"
this etymology presents "difficulties both of form and sense." An alternative
derivation, "from Turk and Turkeys, [or] Turkish," is suggested since, as the
OED observes, "they were often associated with these words." A survey of the
citations provided in the *OED* suggests that these two etymologies converged
in the early seventeenth century, when "turken," "turkesse," and "turkize" were
used to describe the transformation or conversion of sacred language or objects or individuals from Christian truth to Islamic error. In *Purchas His Pil-
grimage* (1613), for instance, Samuel Purchas describes how "the Turkes, when
they turkeised it [St. Sophia], threw downe the Altars, [and] turned the Bells
into great Ordinance," while a citation from 1648 deplores "those . . . which
are so audacious as to turcase the revealed, and sealed Standard of our salvation . . . to the misshapen models of their intoxicated phansies." Gascoigne's
use of "turkeneth" does not explicitly invoke the presence of Islam, but his

witty phrasing invites readers to locate his discussion of poetic license within a larger conversation about the boundary between the native and the foreign, the natural and the unnatural, the lawful and the unlawful. The link between the foreign and the poetic, Gascoigne suggests, inheres in the (dangerously) transformative power of each.

In texts such as Sherry's *Treatise*, Puttenham's *Arte*, Gascoigne's *Notes*, and even Wilson's concertedly domesticated *Rhetorique*, eloquence thus finds a place within the vernacular that is as extravagant as it is English. Critics are not wrong to claim these texts as important contributions to the formulation of cultural and linguistic identity, but the versions of English and Englishness they produce resist assimilation to England itself: depending on where one looks in the corpus of vernacular rhetoric, language becomes eloquent either by reinscribing the boundaries of intimacy and familiarity or by transgressing those bounds in the pursuit of the exotic and the new. That indeterminacy is, as suggested throughout this chapter, a mark of English rhetoric's persistent classicism, its grounding in a tradition that simultaneously denigrated and romanticized the speech of strangers, positing foreignness as both the antithesis and the epitome of linguistic refinement. Because it so insistently foregrounded the distinction between native and foreign, the discourse of racial, cultural, and geographic identity internal to the classical conception of eloquence both impeded and abetted its translation into England: on the one hand, sixteenth-century England's distance and difference from classical antiquity were all too easily read as markers of barbarity; on the other hand, the ancient geography of eloquence proved surprisingly amenable to the incursions of outsiders.

Insofar as their attempts to translate classical terms and precepts into English met with resistance, then, this was not necessarily (or at least not only) cause for alarm on the part of the first vernacular rhetoricians and poetic theorists, for they could claim alienation as the signal feature of style and imagine an English language enriched and enlarged by its estrangement from both the classical past and itself. For vernacular literary writers too, the discovery that their own prose or verse would have to depart from the models of Greek and Roman eloquence engendered both self-consciousness and daring—daring to assert native custom against antique precept and daring to discard native custom in favor of eccentric alternatives. The chapters that follow assess formal strategies that arise from frustrating, even humiliating, linguistic confrontations: English sentences' inability to mimic the periodic structure of classical prose; English poets' exclusion from the breeding ground of classical poetry; English meter's failure to adhere to the rules of Greek and Roman versification. In each case linguistic necessity proves the mother of stylistic innovation, and stylistic innovation unmoors seemingly fixed categories of identity and difference.

Chapter 3

"A World to See":
Euphues's Wayward Style

Reprinted in some twenty editions in the decades following its initial publication, *Euphues: The Anatomy of Wit* (1578) made John Lyly the most influential prose writer of the late sixteenth century.[1] The richly ornamented, densely patterned style of Lyly's romance produced a popular sensation, a host of imitators, and a distinctly mixed set of critical responses: for every Francis Meres, whose litany of English authors in his 1598 *Palladis Tamia* named "eloquent and wittie Iohn Lilly" as one of "the best . . . amongst vs,"[2] there was a Gabriel Harvey, who bluntly declared, "I cannot stand . . . Euphuing."[3] The vehemence with which those early readers responded to *Euphues's* distinctive style has guaranteed its place in literary history, but the text has persisted in seeming marginal—too "peculiarly mannered," as a recent editor notes, to fit in any larger narrative of vernacular literature and culture.[4] But *Euphues*, both as a cultural phenomenon and as a literary work, has much to teach us about the encounter between ideals of eloquence and of Englishness in the late sixteenth century—and, precisely because it is so ostentatiously "peculiar," about the rivalrous impulses toward familiarity and estrangement that structure that encounter. At the heart of the heated debate over "euphuing" or euphuism, as Lyly's style came to be known, was an implicit question about the English language's own natural limits: to some readers, *Euphues's* hyperornate expressivity proved that the boundaries of English had been too narrowly fixed; to others, it fostered a perilous conflation of eloquence with excess. Lyly does not simply provide the fodder for that debate; he also helps to set its terms, crafting a narrative of errancy and promiscuity that reflects cannily on its own departure from the usual precincts of vernacular style. Anticipating and even prescribing responses to the extremity of its rhetoric, *Euphues* transforms the conventional romance plot into an ironic and insightful critique of the English pursuit of eloquence.

One Step Further

The story of *Euphues*'s reception by late sixteenth-century readers is a familiar one, but the precise texture of that response bears closer examination. Acclaim for *Euphues* tended to focus on how directly its style seemed to answer anxieties about the adequacy of English as a literary language. As Graham Tulloch observes, Lyly was no inkhornist: "For all the elaboration of his style Lyly shows very little fondness for aureate diction; his vocabulary is basically that of the vernacular."[5] Thus William Webbe's 1586 *Discourse of English Poetrie* could hail *Euphues* as a "manifest example" of "the great good grace and sweete vayne, which Eloquence hath attained in oure speech." What made *Euphues* remarkable in Webbe's eyes was its reconciliation of vernacular diction to classical rhetorical forms: here, at last, was an "English worke answerable, in respect of the glorious ornaments of gallant handling," to the greatest achievements of Greek and Latin oratory. "[S]urely," Webbe enthuses, "in respecte of his singuler eloquence and braue composition of apt words and sentences, let the learned examine and make tryall thereof thorough all the partes of Rethoricke, in fitte phrases, in pithy sentences, in gallant tropes, in flowing speeche, in plaine sence, and surely in my iudgment, I thinke he wyll yeelde him that verdict, which Quintilian giueth of bothe the best Orators Demosthenes and Tully, that from the one nothing may be taken away, to the other nothing may be added." Lyly, he concludes, "hath deserued most high commendations as hee which hath stept one steppe further then any either before or since he first began the wyttie discourse of his Euphues."[6]

But that "steppe further" could equally be perceived as a step out of bounds: Thomas Nashe, Lyly's sometime friend, accused him of having "surfetted vnawares with the sweete sacietie of eloquence, which the lauish of our copious language maie procure," surely the first time that an English author was charged with such an error. More pointedly critical is Philip Sidney's assault on euphuism in his *Apologie for Poetrie* (1595), which charged Lyly and his imitators with having "appareled, or rather disguised" that "hony-flowing Matron Eloquence . . . in a Curtisan-like painted affectation," adorning her "with so farre fetched words, that many seeme Monsters, but must seeme strangers to any poore English man." In love with "figures and phrases" gathered from arcane sources, Sidney jibed, the euphuists "cast sugar and spice upon every dish that is served to the table"; like barbarous "Indians, not content to weare eare-rings at the fit and naturall place of the eares," they "thrust jewels through their nose and lippes, because they will be sure to be fine."[7] *Astrophil and Stella* (1591), composed at the height of *Euphues's* initial fame, glances slightingly at Lyly in its mockery of those "dainty wittes" who "flaunt in their phrases fine" and "with straunge similes inrich each line, / Of hearbes and beasts, which *Inde* or *Affricke* hold"—readers should not look for such curiosities in his own verse, Sidney cautions, for "straunge things cost too deere for my poore sprites."[8]

Like Webbe's image of the "step further," Sidney's painted courtesan, the spiced and sugared dish, and the jewel-laden Indian implicate euphuism in a larger debate about the insular linguistic identity of the "poor English man"—and, especially, about the vernacular's capacity for *copia*, or rhetorical abundance. In Webbe's view euphuism extends the reach of a tongue whose constraints otherwise betray "the rudenesse [and] vnaptenesse of our Countrey" (20); in Sidney's view it nurtures a taste for strangeness more likely to bankrupt the vernacular than to enrich it. As it happens, this very tension between constraint and excess, poverty and prodigality structures Lyly's own perspective on *Euphues*. In the dedicatory epistle to the text's first edition, he announces that certain kinds of eloquence lie beyond his reach: comparing himself to a humble "butcher," "horse-leech," "shoemaker," or "hedger," he begs pardon for the "rudeness" of his "discourse" and consoles himself with the thought that "[t]hough the style nothing delight the dainty ear of the curious sifter, yet will the matter recreate the mind of the courteous reader." And yet, anticipating Sidney's equation of stylistic ornament with the costliness of "strange things," he adds, "Things of greatest profit are set forth with least price."[9]

Having made the case for rhetorical simplicity, however, Lyly promptly— and paradoxically—proceeds to enrich it:

When the wine is neat there needeth no ivy bush. The right coral needeth no colouring. Where the matter itself bringeth credit, the man with his gloss winneth small commendation. It is, therefore, me thinketh, a greater show of a pregnant wit than perfect wisdom in a thing of sufficient excellency to use superfluous eloquence. We commonly see that a black ground doth best beseem a white countenance. And Venus, according to the judgment of Mars, was then most amiable when she sat close by Vulcanus. If these things be true which experience trieth—that a naked tale doth most truly set forth the naked truth, that where the countenance is fair there need no colours, that painting is meeter for ragged walls than fine marble, that verity then shineth most bright when she is in least bravery—I shall satisfy mine own mind, though I cannot feed their humours which greatly seek after those that sift the finest meal and bear the whitest mouths. It is a world to see how Englishmen desire to hear finer speech than the language will allow, to eat finer bread than is made of wheat, to wear finer cloth than is made of wool. (5–6)

This is euphuism in a (necessarily somewhat roomy) nutshell—the relentless use of parataxis, the heaping of example upon example, the mingling of homespun proverbial wisdom and references to classical lore—but it is also a maddeningly difficult passage to interpret. Obviously, Lyly chooses a needlessly elaborate way of making a case against needless elaboration, and it is hard to take his reproof of "superfluous eloquence" or his indignation at the immoderate desires of English readers at face value when those statements are couched in prose whose only stylistic rule would seem to be that more is more. Indeed threaded through the homily on sufficiency is a pattern of rhymes and near-rhymes—read/need/feed/eat/see/seek—that tell a rather different story about the self-perpetuating nature of both desire and language. If, as Lyly charges, the English reader's desire for fine speech exceeds the reach of his homely mother tongue, his own fondness for what Sidney calls "sugar and spices"—for curious analogies, ear-catching patterns of alliteration, and rhythmically stylized phrasing—belies his professed attachment to the language of wheat and wool.

For C. S. Lewis, this disjuncture was evidence of hypocrisy: inverting Lyly's injunction to mind his matter and not his style, Lewis declared that *Euphues* could "only be read . . . for the style," for "the more seriously we take [its content] the more odious [it] will appear."[10] Judith Rice Henderson more generously assumes that the passage—in fact, the whole of *Euphues*—is a kind of joke, Lyly's way of poking fun at the moral pretensions of his age: in Lyly, she argues, we find the rare "humanist capable of laughing at himself."[11] And surely some allowance must be made for wit—the object of the "anatomy," after all—but Lyly may be in earnest when he suggests that the desire for fine speech strains the resources of the vernacular just as the desire for other foreign commodities strains the limits of the native economy, for this very tension between the virtues of home and the appeal of the far-fetched is central to the story he proposes to tell. Euphues's near-dissolution in a seductive foreign landscape provides an apt reflection of Lyly's self-consciously daring effort to extend the reach of vernacular prose, and his errant progress from Athens to Naples mimics the dilatory drift of Lyly's sentences.

Indeed, as a number of more recent critics have argued, it is impossible to read Lyly for the style without noticing its entanglement in his subject: "[I]t is not merely the extravagance but the entirety of Lyly's audacious examination of humanism that now so fixes us," writes Arthur Kinney; "humanist ideas as well as humanist rhetoric are seen from multiple view [within *Euphues*] and become the *total* matter and manner of his fiction."[12] Neither is it possible to separate his reflections on the vernacular from his concern for his wayward protagonist. For the insatiable English reader of Lyly's epistle bears an unmistakable resemblance to the figure introduced in the opening passage of the narrative: "Euphues, whose wit being like wax apt to receive any impression, and having the bridle in his own hands either to use the rein or the spur, disdaining counsel, leaving his country, loathing his old acquaintance, thought either by wit to obtain some conquest or by shame to abide some conflict and leaving the rule of reason, rashly ran into destruction; who preferring fancy before friends and his present humour before honour to come, laid reason in water, being too salt for his taste, and followed unbridled affection most pleasant for his tooth" (11). Like Lyly's superfluous sermonizing on superfluity, the strung-on clauses and convoluted conjunctions of this sentence seem designed in ironic counterpoint to its moralizing against its subject's undisciplined careering.

Indeed it is worth pausing to notice how closely Euphues's impulsive and greedy disposition corresponds to euphuism's compulsively additive syntax. As Janel Mueller observes, Lyly draws heavily on the parallel structure of biblical rhetoric, but his intricately wrought equivocations tend not to resolve into straightforward declarations; rather they "thwart closure . . . by a surplusage of contrastive elements"[13]—"one step further" is exactly the impulse that drives his style. Here the surplus of syntactical units unbalances Lyly's sentences in ways that mimic the unbalancing of Euphues's own mind: the seeming parallelism of "being," "having," "disdaining," "leaving," "loathing," "leaving," "preferring," and "being" occludes an oscillation between subjects— "Euphues," his waxen "wit," and "reason"—that Lyly eventually pinpoints as the essence of his protagonist's folly. For the reader, the indeterminacy of reference creates a niggling sense of uncertainty as to the moral of his story: does

Euphues leave the rule of reason before or after he leaves his home in Athens? Is travel abroad the cause or merely a symptom of his degradation? At a later point in the narrative, Euphues will debate these very questions with a would-be counselor; should we refer back to the narrator's own original account of things to settle the matter, we discover that the sonorous but shifty quality of Lyly's prose resists any conclusive judgment.

In its propensity to mislead the unwary reader, the euphuistic sentence foregrounds—even exaggerates—a basic distinction between English and the classical tongues; far from approximating antique oratorical style, as William Webbe alleges, the hyperextensibility of many of Lyly's sentences is the clearest mark of their vulgarity. Classical and neo-Latin prose stylists relied on the *periodos*, or "period," to reconcile the demands of rhetorical expansiveness with those of logical and syntactical coherence. The recursive structure of the periodic sentence—which, as Demetrius observes in his treatise *On Style*, takes its name from "paths traversed in a circle"[14]—enabled orators to digress and amplify without sacrificing what Sidney identifies as the "chiefe marke of Oratory," the impression of "playne sensibleness" that is "the nearest step to perswasion."[15] "I call a period an expression having a beginning and end in itself and a magnitude easily taken in at a glance," writes Aristotle in book 3 of the *Art of Rhetoric*. "This is pleasant and easily understood, pleasant because opposed to the unlimited, and because the hearer always thinks he has a hold of something, in that it is always limited by itself."[16] If, as Aristotle insists, eloquence ought to generate a sense of communal belonging, founded on the invocation of shared assumptions and ideals, the period builds this sensation into each individual utterance, so that every sentence, however amplified or digressive, resembles a collective journey home.

But the self-limiting power of the classical period depends on the syntactical flexibility of an inflected language: the artful deferral of completion of the main subject-verb clause until the sentence's end allows the orator to circumscribe his thoughts so that they arrive at what feels like a logically necessary end. Because it depends on word order to convey the relation between terms, the English sentence lacks this homeward thrust; its meaning is yoked much more closely to conventional arrangements of its component parts, and sentences that stray from those conventions flirt with unintelligibility. Sixteenth-century English writers understood this constraint as a major obstacle to the attainment of eloquence in the vernacular; paradoxically it is a constraint that betrays itself as superfluity. In the preface to his 1570 translation of three orations by Demosthenes, Thomas Wilson confesses that the chief beauty of the

Greek orator's style, "his short knitting vp of his matters together" in periodic form, is absent from his own prose, being "hard and vnable to be translated, according to the excellencie of his tongue"; at times, he admits, he has been forced to resort to "addicions in the margine" or an italicized "sentence or half a sentence . . . not in the Greeke, but added onely, for the more playne vnderstanding of the matter." Sounding a good deal like John Lyly, Wilson protests in defense of his translation that "all can not weare Veluet, or feede with the best, and therefore such are contented for necessities sake to weare our Countrie cloth, and to take themselues to harde fare, that can haue no better."[17]

Wilson's embarrassment that he has been forced to supplement Demosthenes's neat periods mirrors the embarrassment Lyly expresses at the immoderate desires of English readers, or that Sidney embodies in the figure of the barbarously bejeweled Indian: in each case excess is an outward sign of a fundamental impoverishment. But the reverse is no less true: the loosely conjunctive structure of the English sentence also aids the proliferation of illustrations, examples, similitudes, and other ornaments, and such figurative abundance—or *copia*[18]—is what sixteenth-century writers were taught to identify as the essence of rhetorical skill. It is no wonder, then, that *Euphues* aroused such conflicted responses in early readers, or that even Lyly seems ambivalent about his style: euphuism thrives on the conjunction of one of the vernacular's most glaring defects with one of its most alluring prospects for enrichment. The sweet-toothed, straying youth introduced in *Euphues*'s opening pages does not simply resemble the narrative's readers; he is also a figure for its author, whose endlessly digressive style flaunts his own capacious appetite for the wealth to be gotten from alien texts.

Words on the Move

Euphues is a story about the perils and pleasures of foreign travel, but it is also a story about the perils and pleasures of a rhetorical technique—commonplacing, or the harvesting of proverbs, sententiae, similitudes, and exempla from classical texts for reuse in one's own writing—whose kinship to travel made it at once seductive and suspect to an English audience. This latter claim requires some explication, for commonplacing is typically understood as an attempt to anchor texts in the firmest possible ground, that of ancient authority. Indeed, on the face of it, commonplacing is the least likely of all early modern rhetorical practices to arouse the fear and fascination associated with foreign travel: if travel means leaving behind the familiar and courting the unknown, commonplacing, as Walter Ong has shown, entails "an organized trafficking in what in one way or another is already known."[19] It is this recycling of knowledge, Henderson argues, that "prescribes the plot" of Lyly's romance, which "illustrates a series of 'olde sayed sawes'": "witte is the better is it bee the deerer bought"; "wit . . . deemeth no pennye good silver but his own"; "amitie grounded upon a little affection . . . shall be dissolved upon a light occasion"; the fool "thinketh all to bee golde that glistered."[20] It is not simply that such phrases, and the ideas they express, lack originality; rather, as Jeff Dolven has argued, commonplaces are "a kind of teaching antithetical to the career of accident" that romance is meant to describe, and the formulaic and familiar wit they display "is a kind of enemy of narrative." Dolven's thoughtful effort to read *Euphues*'s plot alongside its style leads him to conclude that the two are at cross-purposes: Lyly's substitution of the atemporal, fixed discourse of commonplacing for the fictive progress typical of his genre constitutes, in Dolven's view, a perverse and self-defeating experiment, as the prospect of discovery held out by Euphues's foreign travels is repeatedly frustrated by the fundamentally conservative impulses of "purely bookish, schoolmasterly authority."[21]

But *Euphues* and the excited (even alarmed) responses it aroused in its first readers point us to a rather different understanding of commonplacing, especially as it relates to the aspirations of vernacular writers. For all its modern associations with the most conservative impulses of Renaissance rhetoric and pedagogy, in the early modern imagination commonplacing was a mode of exploration and discovery, feeding as much on desires for novelty and variety as it did on admiration for the ancient and unchanging. For as Ong also points out, it was the strangeness and novelty of the classical tradition—the fact that "Latin . . . was a foreign language to all its users" and its wisdom "much newer than the products of more recent centuries"—that made commonplacing so necessary to early modern readers: the "common knowledge" presumed by classical authors required self-conscious cultivation on the part of a Renaissance schoolboy.[22] Thus Thomas Wilson, even as he obsesses over the incompatibility of Greek with English, urges his readers of his translation to appropriate Demosthenes's style for themselves by copying passages from his orations in their own hands:

For . . . who can euer come to any such excellencye that doth not acquaynte himselfe first wyth the best, yea and seeketh to followe

the chiefest that haue traueyled in those thinges, the perfection
whereof hee wysheth to gette? So did Plato traueyle from Greece
into Aegypt: Aristotell from Stagira in Macedonie, to Athens
in Greece, to heare his maister Plato: and Cicero from Rome to
Athens, and Anacharsis that barbarous Scithian to talke with Solon
that wyse law maker of Athens, seeking euerye one of them the best
abrode, when they coulde not haue them at home. ("A Preface to
the Reader," *Three Orations*, sig. [a3$_v$])

Lyly's exclamation in his dedicatory epistle that "It is a world to see how
Englishmen desire to hear finer speech than the language will allow" draws
on this same association of travel and travail, reading and seeking. "It is a
world to see" is a conventional expression of incredulity, but in this context
it also signals the expansive ambition of the humanist reader, trained (by
schoolmasters and rhetoricians alike) to regard classical literature as foreign
material awaiting conversion to his personal use.

The habit of dissecting what one read and entering it into a notebook for
reuse in one's own writing was, as Wilson suggests, a way of domesticating this
vast and alien tradition. But the condensed form of the typical commonplace-
book entry—often as brief as a sentence or phrase—also made the diversity of
the classical tradition a source of intellectual stimulation and pleasure: skip-
ping from one entry to the next, juxtaposing citations from disparate sources,
and extracting passages at will for use elsewhere, the owner of a commonplace book was in possession of an endlessly mobile form of eloquence. "The
transformation of the text into notebooks," writes Rebecca Bushnell, "converted . . . pieces of writing into counters of currency, spatially distinct, usable
and distinguishable"—commonplacing allowed readers to take possession of
texts by transporting them, bit by bit, into new places of their own. In this
regard, Bushnell points out, commonplacing plays a double role: as a means of
generating new writing, of saying more about any given topic, the commonplace book was an instrument in service of the multiplication of words and
texts; as a method of "cutting books into pieces and compressing the pieces in
a 'small compass,'" commonplacing rendered an unmanageably diverse—and
rapidly proliferating—world of books traversable.[23] Traversable and profitable:
as one early modern schoolboy observed in his commonplace book, the goal
was not to collect everything but only those things likely to prove useful to the
collector, to "note some Rhetoricall expressions, Description, or some very apt
Simile, or a very applicative story, and the most choise morrall sentences, and

here a mans sense must direct him, when he considers how aptly such a thing would fitt with an exercise of his."[24]

The literal portability of the commonplace book was, as Peter Beal has noted, crucial to its value; its suitability for "use as a *vade mecum*" guaranteed its owner's readiness for any rhetorical occasion.[25] This portability is the focus of a letter written in 1521 by the man chiefly responsible for English schoolboys' indoctrination in commonplacing, the Dutch humanist Desiderius Erasmus. Erasmus's letter congratulates its recipient, Adrianus Barlandus, on the completion of a pocket-sized version or epitome of the *Adagia*, Erasmus's massive compilation of "brilliant aphorisms, apt metaphors, proverbs, and similar figures of speech . . . from approved authors of every sort." If the personal or manuscript commonplace book was a way of distilling one's own reading to more manageable proportions, the *Adagia* represented an even more useful tool: a predigested compendium of the whole classical tradition. And yet, Erasmus confesses, his constant additions to the collection had made it "too large a volume to be within reach of those in modest circumstances, or to be read in grammar schools, or to be carried round with them by those who like strolling players are always on the move." However, thanks to Barlandus's "admirable undertaking," he writes, the *Adagia* "can be bought by anyone however ill endowed, and thumbed by schoolboys, and will add little weight to a traveler's baggage."[26]

Erasmus's concern for those readers who "are always on the move" may stem from his own ample experience of the rigors of early modern travel: as Kathy Eden recalls, the *Adagia* was born out of a spectacularly bad trip, a journey Erasmus made to England at the end of the fifteenth century. The aim of the journey was to secure the patronage of a young nobleman, Lord Mountjoy, but the money Mountjoy gave to Erasmus never made it out of England: when the Dutch humanist attempted to leave the country, he was informed by customs officials that it was illegal to export English coins and that his purse would therefore have to remain with them. Erasmus's loss was England's gain: needing cash and eager to assure his patron that he bore him no ill will, Erasmus hastily assembled his collection of commonplaces, dedicated the text to Mountjoy, and published it in 1500 as the *Adagiorum collectanea*, or *Collection of Adages*. Eden's reading of this anecdote (which Erasmus recounts in a letter he then includes as part of his 1522 treatise on letter writing, *De Conscribendis Epistolis*) highlights Erasmus's concern with the transmission and sharing of property across time, space, and cultural distance, especially between ancient and modern writers. Eden places particular emphasis on the word Erasmus uses to describe his ongoing additions to the *Adages*, the "curious compound *locupletare* from *locus-plenus* [full of places]," a term she identifies with his anxiety about the confiscation of his property and his desire to redress that loss with rhetorical abundance.[27]

"Full of places" is also, of course, an apt description of the universalizing intent of the commonplace book, which in its Latin form, as Ann Moss argues, served as "the common ground for a European culture increasingly divided by language."[28] This perception of the commonplace book as an easily traversable, shared space conforms, moreover, to Erasmus's understanding of the adage, which is, as he emphasizes in his introduction to the edition of 1508, a rhetorical form whose value rests entirely in its portability. The Greek word for "adage," *paroemia*, means "a road . . . well polished in use," while the Latin *adagium* refers to "something passed around." Thus, he explains, the adage derives its persuasive force from the fact that it "travels everywhere on the lips of men" and may be transferred from one context to another without losing its value.[29] In this sense the adage is emblematic of Erasmus's whole approach to rhetoric, which depends on the writer's ability to treat words and phrases as movable goods, appropriating language from one textual locale and transplanting it to another, all the while enlarging and enriching his private store, organized under topical headings that could themselves be conceived as "places" for visiting and inhabiting.

According to the *Adagia*'s theoretical counterpart, Erasmus's 1512 treatise *De duplici copia verborum ac rerum comentarii duo*, the transfer of phrases from source text to commonplace book serves as an engine for eloquence, the travel between rhetorical places yielding a correspondingly vigorous and mobile style. "The speech of man is a magnificent and impressive thing when it surges along like a golden river, with thoughts and words pouring out in rich abundance," *De Copia* begins. But if Erasmus promoted commonplacing as a way of evening the distribution of rhetorical wealth—securing from abroad what could not be had at home, as Wilson puts it—he also burnishes its allure by representing it as a potentially dangerous and costly adventure. "Yet the pursuit of speech like this involves considerable risk," *De Copia* continues: "As the proverb says, 'Not every man has the means to visit the city of Corinth.' "[30] Erasmus glosses the saying, which appears in the earliest edition of the *Adagia*, as an illustration of the skill and perseverance needed to master the rhetoric of abundance or *copia*: like the merchants who sought access to the ancient city of Corinth, whose position on a narrow isthmus between Europe and Asia made it both uncommonly wealthy and uncommonly difficult to approach, he explains, the student who wishes to cultivate his own abundant style faces an arduous but richly rewarding journey. The commonplace book's topical headings set the itinerary for this journey: "Anyone training with a view to acquire eloquence," Erasmus instructs, "will have to look at all the possible places—that is, topics—in turn, go knocking from door to door so to speak, to see if anything can be induced to emerge."[31] Each individual topic then becomes its own point of departure, as the student is urged to generate a variety of perspectives on his theme. It is only by entertaining all possible means of expression, Erasmus emphasizes, that an orator can adapt his speech perfectly to the demands of a given situation, choosing to perform Attic brevity, or "the exuberance of Asianism," or "the intermediate style of Rhodes."[32]

Commonplacing was not only a means of mastering the vast topical resources—"all the possible places"—of classical eloquence and its richly various stylistic geography; it was also an instrument for appropriating to the arts of eloquence all that the classical world did *not* know, precisely because its own geography was so limited. Those eager for wealth of expression, Erasmus reminds readers of *De Conscribendis Epistolis*, would do well not to restrict themselves to Homer and Cicero but to draw on what is "readily available and close to hand" and what is exotically far-fetched: "For each race," he reminds his readers, "has its own marvels, ceremonies, and institutions," and "Africans, Jews, Spaniards, French, English, or Germans" are as likely sources for an apt simile or a striking expression as the Greeks and Romans.[33] "One should therefore apply as many different illustrations as possible at each point, derived not only from the whole range of Greek and Latin literature, but also from the sayings of other nations": true *copia*, he emphasizes, derives not simply from "antiquity" but from "recent history, and things in our own lives," for "[e]ven today, sailors and traders, who rush across land and sea in their eagerness to acquire wealth," report "wonders no less extraordinary than those antiquity is thought to have invented."[34] The model of those eager sailors and traders inspired quite a few early modern commonplacers—indeed the analogy between global exploration and the labor of reading and writing functions as a kind of meta-commonplace of sixteenth-century humanism. Thus, Theodor Zwinger, compiler of the immense *Theatrum humanae vitae* (1565), repeatedly compares his work as a collector and organizer of classical quotations to that of geographers and cartographers, likening his "ranging of *exempla* under titles (*tituli*) . . . to the plotting of travels such as those of Alexander the Great and of Ulysses."[35] Another sixteenth-century collector of commonplaces, Ravisius Textor, made actual geography the foundation of his popular compendia: the *Specimen Epithetorum* (1518) contains long lists of epithets fit for various parts of the globe (Africa is "glowing, fertile, full of fords, bristling, teeming with wild beasts"; the inhabitants of Arabia are "rich in odours, palm-bearing, incense-collecting, tender, Oriental, wealthy, ardent, opulent, and so on"), while the *Cornucopia* section of Textor's *Officina* (1520) charts the natural abundance of various goods in countries around the world.[36]

For Erasmus and his contemporaries, then, commonplacing figures as the ideal and essential rhetorical strategy of a cosmopolitan age, a practice that allows writers to enfold geographic and historical diversity into a unified whole, "passing," as Erasmus says in *De Conscribendis Epistolis*, "from Egyptian and Phrygian to Persian, from Persian and Syrian to Greek, from Greek to Hebrew and thence to Roman, from Roman to barbarian, from Gentile to Christian, from foreign to those of our own country, until we reach the events of our own nation and finally our own home."[37] Stylistic abundance, like material wealth, is the function of an extraordinarily wide-ranging, even global ambition: the student desirous of this kind of eloquence must, Erasmus famously claims, "ma[ke] up [his] mind to cover the whole field of literature": "no discipline," he insists, "is so remote from rhetoric that you cannot use it to enrich your collection."[38] As evidence of "how far one can go" in this pursuit, Erasmus offers a "practical demonstration" of *copia*, concluding the introductory section of *De Copia* with a list of more than a hundred variations of a single sentence, *Tuae litterae me magnopere delectarunt*, or "Your letter greatly pleased me."[39] His modifications range from the blandly local—inserting a proper name in place of "your," using "delighted" instead of "pleased"—to the sumptuously far-fetched: "The pages of my dear Faustus were more splendid to me than Sicilian feasts"; "The lotus tastes not as sweet to any mortal man as your letters do to me"; "Your letter was to me a positive 'choice morsel' for a Persian, as the Greeks say."[40] Some of these variants may, he confesses, seem implausible—"hardly . . . tolerable in prose"[41]—but that is the beauty of the rhetoric of *copia*: its expansiveness permits experimentation and even errancy in pursuit of the perfect expression. "It is foolish to bind utterance to fixed laws," Erasmus scolds in *De Conscribendis Epistolis*, and to expect all eloquence "to conform to a single type, or to teach that [it] should, . . . is in my view at least to impose a narrow and inflexible definition on what is by nature diverse and capable of almost infinite variation."[42]

Almost infinite: although he dedicated the *Adagia* to an English patron and wrote *De Copia* for John Colet's pupils at St. Paul's School, Erasmus nowhere suggests that the promise of *copia* extends so far as English itself—his energies are directed solely to the cultivation of Latin eloquence. And yet to his sixteenth-century English readers, the method propounded in *De Copia* and exemplified by the *Adagia* offered an irresistible prospect, that of commonplacing as a means of transcending geographic and temporal alienation and transporting eloquence across textual and linguistic boundaries: "seeking . . . the best abrode, when they coulde not haue them at home," as Wilson writes. The breadth and heterogeneity of the commonplace book compensated for the narrowness and sameness of private experience: Erasmus, Gabriel Harvey wrote in the margins of his copy of the *Similia*, "will teach a man to Temporize and Localize at occasion"[43]—to find a manner of expression fit for any circumstance. Erasmus's friend William Warham, the archbishop of Canterbury, claimed to carry his copy of the *Adagia* "with him wherever he went," so as never to be without an apt means of expressing himself.[44] Thomas Elyot confessed that although a rigorous course of study in Greek and Latin authors was the ideal prerequisite for anyone seeking to write well, *De Copia* alone made a fair substitute: "in good faythe to speake boldly that I think: for him that nedeth nat, or doth nat desire to be an exquisite oratour, the litle boke made by the famous Erasmus (whom all gentill wittis are bounden to thanke and supporte) which he calleth *Copiam verborum et rerum*, that is to say, plenty of wordes and maters, shall be sufficient."[45]

Indeed, although Erasmus defines *copia* in terms of the rich potential of Latin, his methods had a particular appeal to those who wished to promote the rhetorical and poetic fortunes of a vernacular typically characterized in terms of its rudeness and rusticity. To English authors accustomed to thinking of their native tongue as homespun and coarse grained, commonplacing offered the opportunity to introduce into the language a new world of ideas and expressions: the habit of scouring texts for bits and pieces of quotable material, as Steven Zwicker notes, "focused the mind . . . on what was translatable and transportable."[46] Not surprisingly, then, the sixteenth century witnessed more than one attempt to import the wealth of Erasmian eloquence into the vernacular, beginning with Richard Taverner's 1539 *Proverbes or Adagies*, an English version of the *Adagia* dedicated "to the furtheraunce . . . of my natiue country."[47] And yet Erasmian commonplaces did not necessarily or easily accommodate the aims of the English translator: the preface to Thomas Chaloner's 1549 translation of Erasmus's *Moriae encomium* notes that Erasmus's fondness for proverbial expressions made him—like Demosthenes—an especially *difficult* subject for translation, since the ideas that commonplaces express may have universal appeal, but their phrasing is often explicitly local. "[I]n my translacion I haue not peined my selfe to render worde for woorde," Chaloner confesses, "nor prouerbe for prouerbe, werof many be . . . such as haue no grace in our tounge: but rather markyng the sense, I applied it to the phrase of our englishe. And where the prouerbes would take no englishe, I aduentured to put englisshe prouerbes of like waight in their places, whiche maie be thought by some cunnyng translatours a deadly sinne."[48] Gabriel Harvey certainly thought so, accusing Taverner, Chaloner, and their ilk of having "turkissed" Erasmus's Latin eloquence—a charge that equates vernacularization with sacrilege and English translators with the specter of encroaching Islam.[49] Some, such as Sir Henry Wotton, regarded the dissemination of printed commonplace books, whether English or Latin, as a dubious endeavor, however well done: Wotton complains that such collections, by relieving readers not only of the effort of reading classical texts in their original form but even of learning Latin at all, "show a short course to those who are contented to know a little, and a sure way to such whose care is not to understand much."[50]

It is in this context that we might best understand both the appeal and the danger of *Euphues*, for no English author made more diligent use of the many versions of Erasmus available to the early modern English reader than John Lyly. *Euphues* is written in what Ann Moss calls "the language of the commonplace book"[51] and is organized, as Arthur Kinney observes, as "a series of exercises in copia."[52] Both the moralizing frame and the hyperstylized diction are, Judith Rice Henderson argues, "most easily explained as Elizabethan schoolboy rhetoric"[53]—as a carefully wrought tribute to the principles and the pattern of Erasmus's own eloquence. The hundreds of proverbs, illustrations, similitudes, and sententiae with which Lyly fleshes out the skeleton of his plot are nearly all derived not from primary sources but from the pages of the *Adagia* and its companion texts, the *Similia* and the *Apophthegmata*, while the epistles collected at the end of the narrative are structured according to the instructions provided in *De Conscribendis Epistolis*.[54] "Reading through the *De Copia*," Joel Altman observes, "one can recapture momentarily the excitement that a man like John Lyly must have experienced"—excitement at the prospect of an eloquence limited only by its author's willingness to amass textual fragments and compound them into something new.[55]

Wandering in Study

It was the spectacle of those glittering fragments that distinguished Lyly from his predecessors and peers, earning him his place in Thomas Lodge's canon of England's "divine wits, in many things as sufficient as all Antiquity": "*Lilly*, the famous for facility in discourse," is the first vernacular author to achieve something like Erasmian abundance.[56] But *Euphues* also deliberately confronts readers with the ethical and rhetorical hazards of commonplacing, with the allure of the short cut and the risk of the false turn: "Lyly," Andrew Hadfield observes, "appears to . . . enjoy the copiousness of his style and simultaneously to be suspicious of it."[57] For if commonplacing encourages writers to regard language as eminently portable, transferable across temporal, linguistic, and textual boundaries, it is this portability of language that Lyly's prose both exploits and critiques, turning a story of geographic errancy, in which travel functions as an impetus to morally wayward behavior, into a far more complicated meditation on the waywardness of rhetoric itself. Euphues's copious expressivity permits him a kind of cosmopolitan ease, but it threatens to leave him morally and socially unmoored.

Here we would do well to recall the influence of the text from which Lyly derived not only his title but also the geographic lineaments of his plot—the course of Euphues's ill-fated journey from virtuous Athens to decadent Naples and (not quite) back—and his suspicion of rhetorical errancy: Roger Ascham's *The Scholemaster*, in which *euphues* appears as the first of seven qualities requisite in the ideal pupil, describing "he that is apte by goodnes of witte, and appliable by readines of will, to learning."[58] The kind of learning that interests Ascham, of course, is the learning of Latin, and one of *The Scholemaster*'s primary aims is to propose a course of study that would allow English youths to master that tongue without being exposed to "the inchantmentes of Circes, the vanitie of licencious pleasure, [and] the inticements of all sinne" (24v)—in other words, to Italy. Ascham identifies Italian decadence with the devaluation of eloquence, falsely claimed by those who are "common discourser[s] of all matters" and "faire speaker[s]" with "talkatiue tonge[s]" but are not, emphatically, the kind of orators England so desperately needs (30r). But when it comes to the devaluation of eloquence, Ascham, it is worth noting, is equally suspicious of the commonplace book. Compiling one's own collection of wise and witty sayings is, he allows, a potentially worthwhile pursuit: "In deede bookes of common places be verie necessarie, to induce a man, into an orderlie generall knowledge," that he might "not wander in studie." But to rely exclusively on the collections of others—on Erasmus, for instance, or on the truncated versions of Erasmus produced by Barlandus, Taverner, and others—promotes the opposite fault, a kind of intellectual and textual tourism: "to dwell in *Epitomes* and in bookes of common places, and not to binde himselfe dailie by orderlie studie," Ascham warns, "maketh so many seeming, and sonburnt ministers as we haue, whose learning is gotten in a sommer heat, and washed away, with a Christmas snow againe" (43r).

This sounds very much like the language that John Lyly uses, rather less seriously, to characterize the fruits of his own learning, *Euphues* itself, which, he writes in his preface, "I am content this winter to have read . . . for a toy that in summer [it] may be ready for trash" (8). In fact, the whole of Lyly's plot may be read as, in R. W. Maslen's words, "an impudent response" to *The Scholemaster.*[59] *Euphues* takes Ascham's ideal pupil, furnishes him with an endless supply of commonplaces, and then exposes him to the very Circean enchantments, vanities, and enticements against which Ascham inveighs. Lyly's Naples is certainly faithful to the anti-Italian prejudices of Ascham's treatise: "a place of more pleasure than profit, and yet of more profit than piety," it is replete with "all things necessary and in readiness that might either allure the mind to lust or entice the heart to folly" (11–12). And Euphues's reaction to those enticements more than confirms Ascham's suspicions about the nefarious effects of travel on youthful minds and morals: he promptly falls in with a fast crowd, squanders his wealth, neglects his studies, and becomes the sort of "common discourser" and "faire speaker" whose glibness Ascham deplores. If Erasmus taught Gabriel Harvey to "localize at occasion," his methods seem to have taught Euphues to mimic the worst in any locale: "Being demanded of one what countryman he was," Euphues blithely responds, " 'What countryman am I not? If I be in Crete I can lie, if in Greece I can shift, if in Italy I can court it' " (13).

Witnessing his folly, Eubulus, an elderly resident of the city, confronts Euphues and attempts to persuade him of the error of his ways. Eubulus echoes Ascham in wondering at the folly of Euphues's parents in permitting their young son to embark on a life of travel: did they fail to remember, he asks Euphues, "that which no man ought to forget, that the tender youth of a child is like the tempering of new wax apt to receive any form," that "the potter fashioneth his clay when it is soft," and that "the iron being hot receiveth any form with the stroke of the hammer" (14)? Such commonplaces, he argues, bespeak a general truth about the dangerous malleability of youth, which is most vulnerable to the allurements of novelty and change. Likening Euphues's moral danger to the perils of Odysseus, he cautions, "Thou art here amidst the pikes between Scylla and Charybdis. . . . If thou do but hearken to the Sirens thou wilt be enamoured, if thou haunt their houses and places thou wilt be enchanted" (16–17).

But Euphues, in his turn, contends that Eubulus's argument is of no force, since his own rhetorical artillery is as well stocked as his adversary's—"as you have ensamples to confirm your pretence, so I have most evident and infallible arguments to serve for my purpose" (19)—and he proceeds to mount a case that the places one haunts are in no way determinative of moral character. "[S]uppose that, which I will never believe," he states, "that Naples is a cankered store-house of all strife, a common stews for all strumpets, the sink of shame, and the very nurse of sin. Shall it therefore follow of necessity that . . . whosoever arriveth here shall be enticed to folly and, being enticed, of force shall be entangled" (22)? In a fine display of rhetorical virtuosity, Euphues demonstrates that the raw materials of Eubulus's own commonplaces—the new wax, the soft clay, the hot iron—are themselves subject to sudden transmutations: "The similitude you rehearse of the wax argueth your waxing and melting brain, and your example of the hot and hard iron showeth in you but cold and weak disposition," he retorts, for although "the sun doth . . . melt the wax," making it "apt to receive any impression," it also "harden[s] the dirt." "Do you not know that which every man doth affirm and know," he rudely demands, that "there is framed of the self-same clay as well the tile to keep out water as the pot to contain liquor," and "though iron be made soft with fire it returneth to its hardness" (20)?

Euphues's argument is not a refutation of Eubulus's premises; rather it is a devastatingly effective manipulation of the forms those premises take, of the endless iterability of the commonplace. It is because the similitude of the wax is, like all similitudes, waxen—apt to receive any impression—that it may be pressed as easily into service on one side of an argument as to another; [60] conversely it is because the proverb of the iron is, like all proverbs, ironlike in its formal durability, that it may be used and reused without losing its force. Of course, Elizabethan schoolboys were trained to value such adaptability and durability as the chief signs of aptitude, not only in a rhetorical figure but also in the orator: arguing on both sides of a question, *sic et non*, was the essence of early modern rhetorical pedagogy, the foundation of what Joel Altman calls "the Tudor play of mind."[61] According to Erasmus, commonplaces are uniquely useful tools in this enterprise, precisely because of their lack of contextual grounding. In *De Copia* he urges his readers, when distributing proverbs, similitudes, and sententiae into the topics of their commonplace books, to remember that "[s]ome material can serve diverse uses, and for that reason must be recorded in different places," that "[i]t is easy to modify related ideas and adapt them to neighbouring concepts," and that "[o]ne can even twist material to serve the opposite purpose."[62]

This conceit of the "neighbouring concept" raises the possibility of an argument founded not on a strict progression of logical claims but on similitude and adjacency: on the sort of witty but spurious associations Euphues uses to craft his response to Eubulus. And yet, as Euphues perceives, the very copiousness such wit engenders makes similitudes and proverbs and all the other sayings a clever and diligent schoolboy might amass in his book curiously self-defeating, indeed static. As he points out to Eubulus, they might remain at the same literal and rhetorical crossroads for the rest of their lives, should the twisting, turning, and trading of commonplaces be their only means of moving one another: "Infinite and innumerable were the examples I could allege and declare . . . were not the repetition of them needless, having showed sufficient, or bootless, seeing those alleged will not persuade you," he observes (20). "Seeing therefore it is labour lost for me to persuade you, and wind vainly wasted for you to exhort me," he concludes, "here I found you and here I leave you, having neither bought nor sold with you but exchanged ware for ware" (24).[63]

Euphues's departure from the scene of the debate prompts a pained interjection from the narrator, who blames "too much study," by which he seems to mean too much commonplacing, for his protagonist's intractability. More than travel itself, it is the sophistical inhabitation of *rhetorical* places—what Ascham calls "dwell[ing] in commonplace books"—that "doth intoxicate the brains" of witty young men, according to Lyly's narrator: " 'For,' say they, 'although iron the more it is used the brighter it is, yet silver with much wearing doth waste to nothing; though the cammock' "—or crooked stick—" 'the more it is bowed, the better it serveth, yet the bow the more it is bent the weker it waxeth; though the camomile the more it is trodden and pressed down the more it spreadeth, yet the violet the oftener it is handled and touched the sooner it withereth and decayeth. For neither is there anything but that hath his contraries' " (26–27). Once again the figures can be read reflexively; the oppositions they embody—between currency and devaluation, flexibility and laxity, commonness and corruption—are tensions built into the practice of commonplacing. This passage is perhaps the most famous in all of *Euphues,* for it is the one that Falstaff mocks in his parody of euphuism in *Henry IV, Part 1*, when pretending to be the king, he playfully chides Hal for his youthful errancy. What Falstaff fails to remark, however, is that the passage is already parodic in tone—even critiques of Lyly's style end up sounding redundant. For *Euphues*, here and elsewhere, is a peculiarly and powerfully self-critical text: Lyly seems bent on eviscerating the rhetoric on which his own style depends, exposing commonplacing as a kind of anti-*copia*, the profitless changing of "ware for ware," and *copia* itself not as a golden torrent but as an aimless overflow of speech, capable of setting men and morals adrift.

It is this peculiar rhetorical drift that structures Lyly's plot, which is, as Dolven remarks, devoid of the "pointless narrative wandering" typical of its genre.[64] Instead what *Euphues* indulges in is a series of pointless arguments: "It hath been a question often disputed, but never determined . . ." begins a typical episode (35). Nor is it Euphues's ambition to put periods to such questions: for all his reputation for eloquence—traditionally understood as the power to produce conviction—undecidability is the essence of his appeal. The opening line of *Euphues* introduces the title character as "a young man of great patrimony and of so comely a personage that it was doubted whether he was more bound to Nature for the lineaments of his person or to Fortune for the increase of his possessions" (10). It is such doubt—the potentially ceaseless oscillation between equally plausible contraries—that Lyly's narrative increasingly identifies, paradoxically, as the real mechanism of persuasion: discourse moves its audience not by leading them to a conclusion but rather by refusing to settle on any single point of view, putting them, as Lyly often says, in "a quandary" or "a maze." The setting of the romance itself is a kind of quandary or maze: Euphues "determine[s] to make his abode in Naples" not because that is where he intends to go when he leaves Athens, but rather because "for weariness he could not or wantonness would not go any further" (12). That indecisive "or"—and its syntactical cousins "but" and "but yet"—is the engine driving his progress: as long as another alternative can be imagined, no journey or argument can reach any definitive end. Erasmus warns of this possibility in *De Copia* when, several pages into his variations on the theme of receiving a letter, he abruptly breaks off, saying, "But let us make an end, as it is not our purpose to demonstrate how far we can go in inventing alternatives," since "pursuing every possible [variant of thought and expression] would involve endless work" and "an attempt to pursue the infinite would be madness."[65] It is to the lure of such infinite alternation that Euphues falls prey, when "disdaining counsel, leaving his country, [and] loathing his old acquaintance," he "follows unbridled affection" and makes his commonplace book his guide.

Visiting Corinth

Where, then, does commonplacing lead Euphues, and where does it lead the English language? In one sense, Euphues's mastery of the abundant style takes him exactly where Erasmus promises it will, to a remote city stocked with pleasures and the promise of wealth. "[N]ot every man has the means to visit the city of Corinth," observes the opening paragraph of *De Copia*, but the journey to Corinth is one for which Euphues, to borrow Ascham's phrase, is both apt and appliable. Erasmus, as noted earlier, uses this proverb to establish at the outset of his treatise the value of commonplacing, the riches of invention and expression it makes accessible to those willing to conduct the arduous journey through the whole field of literature. But this is not the only way to read the proverb—in fact, it is not the only way Erasmus reads it. Although the 1500 edition of the *Adagia*, in which the proverb first appears, notes simply that it applies to "things which are not to be attempted by all and sundry," subsequent editions add a less innocuous interpretation, glossing the expression as a reference "to the luxury of Corinth and its courtesans." "In this city," Erasmus writes, "there was a temple dedicated to Venus, so rich that it had over a thousand girls whom the Corinthians had consecrated to Venus as prostitutes in her honour. And so for their sake a large multitude crowded into the city, with the result that the public funds became enriched on a vast scale; but the traders, visitors and sailors were drained of resources by the extravagance to which the city's luxury and voluptuousness led them."[66] In other words, Erasmus's commonplace, when pressed to yield its own copious significations, offers not a promise of wealth and abundance but a warning against the depletion of meaning and abandonment of sense that haunt the orator's quest for stylistic abundance: this Corinth is populated not by that "hony-flowing Matron Eloquence" but by her monstrous twin, the painted courtesan who, according to Philip Sidney, is the true source of euphuism.

But if Sidney finds a painted courtesan in the pages of Lyly's narrative, that is surely because Lyly puts her there. For as Euphues's journey proceeds, both the pleasures and the perils of *copia* are increasing aligned not with Lyly's hero but with the woman he briefly takes as his lover, his best friend's fiancée, Lucilla. Lucilla first appears as the rare Neapolitan unimpressed by the agility

of Euphues's mind or the fluency of his speech: indeed in her presence he
is uncharacteristically tongue-tied, breaking off a lengthy discourse in praise
of women's love with the apology that "I feel in myself such alteration that
I can scarcely utter one word" (39). Ironically, Euphues's abrupt silence accomplishes what his "filed speech" does not: "struck into . . . a quandary with
this sudden change," Lucilla, we are told, "began to fry in the flames of love"
(39). Alone in her chamber, she compulsively picks up the dropped threads
of his argument, "enter[ing] into . . . terms and contrarieties" whose dizzying
rhetorical heights and hairpin logical turns sway her more effectively than any
of Euphues's own words (39). She moves rapidly from the moral dilemma of
which man she ought to love ("Why Euphues perhaps doth desire my love,
but Philautus hath deserved it. . . . Aye, but the latter love is most fervent;
aye, but the first ought to be most faithful" [40]) to the more immediate uncertainty of whether or not Euphues will return her love ("Dost thou think
Euphues will deem thee constant to him, when thou hast been unconstant to
his friend? . . . But can Euphues convince me of fleeting, seeing for his sake I
break my fidelity?"[40]) and finally to the baldly pragmatic question of how
to dissemble her infidelity ("I hope so to behave myself, as Euphues shall think
me his own and Philautus persuade himself I am none but his" [42]).

In keeping with this resolution, when Lucilla finds herself alone at last
with Euphues, she pretends to doubt his sincerity, protesting, "But alas, Euphues, what truth can there be found in a traveler, what stay in a stranger;
whose words and bodies both watch but for a wind, whose feet are ever fleeting, whose faith plighted on the shore is turned to perjury when they hoist
sail" (61)? Drawing on the same rich array of classical allusions as Euphues
typically does, she summons a host of examples to confirm her suspicions:
"Who more traitorous to Phyllis than Demophon?" she asks, "Yet he a traveler. Who more perjured to Dido than Aeneas? And he a stranger. . . . Who
more fals than Ariadne to Theseus? Yet he a sailor. Who more fickle than
Medea to Jason? Yet he a starter." "Is it then likely," she demands, "that Euphues will be faithful to Lucilla being in Naples but a sojourner" (62)? She
does not, of course, pause to give Euphues time to answer these questions;
instead she moves quickly to her next point: Euphues has met his match. But
the love that begins in discourse never actually proceeds any further: aside
from several minutes spent "pleasantly conferring one with the other" (67),
the time Lucilla and Euphues waste in debating whether or not to pursue one
another occupies the whole of their affair. Hardly does Euphues have time to
boast of his success to the jilted Philautus—"Dost thou not know that far fet

and dear bought is good for ladies?" he mockingly asks (79)—before his own commonplace justification rebounds on him. Lucilla, he learns, has deserted him for a man whose name, Curio, suggests that he is the embodiment of all strangeness and novelty, and yet whose utter unlikelihood as a candidate for Lucilla's affections—he is poor, stupid, and lame to boot—seems to be his chief attraction. Curio is the far-fetched demystified and devalued, the trash only a savage would mistake for treasure.

The reader is given to understand that Curio is simply a placeholder for the next man, and the next: what Lucilla ultimately falls in love with is change—rhetorically speaking, with the freedom she discovers in the endless succession of positions that commonplacing allows her to inhabit. Progressing from one plausible point to another, equally plausible, from "but" to "but yet" and back again, she learns to regard no conclusion as conclusive: "I am not to be led by their persuasions," she announces; "I will follow my own lust" (42). In support of this aim, she even rewrites what Roger Chartier and Peter Stallybrass have dubbed "the commonplace of commonplacing,"[67] Seneca's image of the industrious bee who flits through the garden of literature sucking nectar from each text and compounding it into the honey of his own inventions: for Lucilla, however, the bee's search for nectar is an image of the careening and self-serving course of desire, which will "gathereth honey out of the weed, [but] when she espieth the fairest flower flieth to the sweetest." Lucilla uses proverbs and similitudes as she does men, changing one for the next as her needs demand, and it falls to her to point out the unsettling resemblance between the rhetoric of commonplacing and the exercise of sexual promiscuity. When her father urges her to accept Philautus as her husband, just as she welcomed him as a friend, she retorts, "I fear I shall be challenged of as many as I have used to company with, and be a common wife to all those that have commonly resorted hither" (70). As Kathy Eden has shown, Erasmus promoted commonplacing as a mode of intimacy with antiquity and with other readers—"Friends hold all things in common" is the watchword of the *Adagia*[68]—and Lucilla follows this premise to its least savory conclusion.

She is guided throughout by the "infinite and innumerable . . . ensamples" that she, like Euphues, can marshal in support of whatever argument or man most pleases her at the moment: "Myrrha was enamoured of her natural father, Biblis of her brother, Phaedra of her son-in-law," she recalls when her affection for Euphues is challenged (73); "Venus was content to take the blacksmith with his polt-foot," she notes in defense of Curio's lameness (82). And when Euphues reproaches her for her infidelity, she is ready with a litany of fickle women from the pages of history and literature, from Venus to Helen of Troy, and concludes that she is determined to join their ranks, becoming "an ensample to all women of lightness" (82). Euphues belatedly—and rather hypocritically—protests that this is not the purpose to which exempla are meant to be put: "These are set down that we should fly the like impudency, not follow the like excess," he exclaims. "Shall the lewdness of others animate thee in thy lightness? Why then dost thou not haunt the stews because Lais frequented them" (83)? Euphues's own example is inadvertently revealing, for Lais is the most famous of the Corinthian prostitutes: it is her rapacity that inspires Erasmus's adage, and her insatiable appetites that impinge most closely on the history of eloquence. "It was notorious," Erasmus writes in the *Adagia*, that "the great [orator] Demosthenes went to her in private and asked for her bounty. But Lais demanded ten thousand drachmas. Demosthenes, much struck and alarmed by the woman's impudence and the amount of money, withdrew, and said as he departed, 'I'm not spending ten thousand drachmas on something I should be sorry for.'"[69] Of course, Demosthenes is not only famous as the man canny enough to resist Lais's charms; more important, he is the classical orator whose brevity becomes a byword for the virtues of rhetorical restraint—it is Demosthenes whose compact periods defy Thomas Wilson's efforts at translation, Demosthenes from whose eloquence, as William Webbe recalls, "nothing may be taken away" (sig. $C1_v$). Webbe is surely the only critic ever to contend that such praise could reasonably be applied to *Euphues*, for if Euphues fails to follow Demosthenes's course in avoiding the enticements of Lais, he certainly fails to follow him in avoiding the enticements of *copia*.

Superfluous Ends

In this regard he is not so different from Lyly, who dispenses—or tries to dispense—with Lucilla by informing the reader that her "end, seeing as it is nothing incident to the history of Euphues, it were superfluous to insert it, and being so strange, I should be in a maze in telling what it was" (89). But superfluity and strangeness are the hallmarks of Lyly's style, and Lucilla's very impertinence makes her all the more irresistible: although the "history" ostensibly concludes with Euphues's return to Athens and his abjuration of idle women and idle words, the text is further drawn out—in a maze, as it were—by a series of letters Euphues sends back to Naples, many of which concern Lucilla's strange end: after losing her inheritance to Curio, she takes up harlotry, gains "great credit" with the local gentlemen, is stricken by a sudden illness, and dies "in great beggary in the streets" (170). Although Lucilla is gone—consumed by her lust—her immoderate discourse lives on, for no one, it seems, can stop talking about her: "It is a world to see how commonly we are blinded with the collusions of women, and more enticed by their ornaments being artificial than their proportions being natural," complains Euphues. "[T]he nature of women is grounded only upon extremities" (102–3). He seems utterly blind to the degree to which his own attachment to extremities and opposition has led him astray, enticed by the ornaments of rhetorical artifice to depart from the natural proportions of truth. Of course, Lyly's readers are likely to hear in Euphues's protest an echo of Lyly's own, in his dedicatory epistle, that "It is a world to see how Englishmen desire to hear finer speech than the language will allow." Ultimately, Lucilla's "superfluous end" and the "superfluous eloquence" with which she is identified are integral to Lyly's narrative because they are emblems of an England and an English tired of wheat and wool but wary of sugar and spice, addicted to the far-fetched and dear-bought but unnerved by its implications for what Sidney calls "the poor Englishman."

For all Euphues's misogynist ranting, Lucilla does not bear the burden of superfluity and strangeness on her own. The final sentences of *Euphues* leave its hero "ready to cross the seas to England," and a 1580 sequel entitled *Euphues and His England* describes his adventures in what is presented—in a witty reversal of the usual relationship between English readers and the Italianate settings of romance—as an exotic foreign land: Euphues presents his account of England as one might show off "little dogs from Malta or strange stones from India or fine carpets from Turkey" (415). Indeed, England first appears, like Naples in the *Anatomy*, as a dangerously exotic foreign land: hardly has his ship set sail before Euphues is declaiming against the folly of his journey, recalling (in a peculiar conflation of his own narrative with Erasmus's *Adagia*) the story of "the young scholar in Athens" who "went to hear Demosthenes' eloquence at Corinth and was entangled with Lais' beauty," and inveighing (like Roger Ascham) against "our travellers which pretend to get a smack of strange language to sharpen their wits" but "are infected with vanity by following their wills" (206). For Lyly's English readers, who are imagined as foreigners in their own land, the joke resides in the identification of provincial England with cosmopolitan Corinth and of homely English with "strange language." But stock associations between strange tongues and moral disorder are not the true concern of *Euphues and His England*—unlike his time in Naples, Euphues's visit to England never threatens to corrupt him with foreign influence. On the contrary, Lyly's melancholy sequel is more preoccupied by a vision of its protagonist as somehow existentially strange, insular, and peripheral wherever he goes. For in a cruel trick, Euphues is summoned out of Athens only to be forced, repeatedly, to the margins of his own story, the odd man out in a narrative overflowing with more or less happy couples.

Although he proclaims that being in England fills him with delight in society—"In sooth . . . if I should tarry a year in England, I could not abide an hour in my chamber" (299)—that proclamation accords ill with Euphues's actual behavior. Having quarreled with Philautus soon after his arrival, he spends much of his visit huddled in his chamber, "determined . . . to lie aloof" (369). "You have been so great a stranger," his English host rebukes him when he does emerge (383), and even Philautus treats him with "much strange courtesy, . . . being almost for the time but strangers because of [his] long absence" (375). Eventually, we are told, Euphues "with all became so familiar that he was of all earnestly beloved" (410), but before we can see him in this comfortable position, he is called back to Athens, alone, on unspecified urgent business: "England," he says sadly, is "not for Euphues to dwell in" (412). Once home, however, he is more isolated than ever before, for his yearning for England unfits him for life anywhere else: "I know not how it fareth me," he writes pitifully to a friend in Naples, "for I cannot as yet brook mine own country, I am so delighted with another" (414). Finally, the narrator reports, he "gave himself to solitariness, determining to sojourn in some uncouth place." "And so I leave him," Lyly concludes, "neither in Athens nor elsewhere that I know" (462).

As Leah Scragg observes, this ending is largely inscrutable: "the precise cause of [Euphues's] 'cruelly martyred condition' remains . . . uncertain."[70] But like Lucilla's superfluous end, Euphues's sad end hints at Lyly's suspicion of the claims made on behalf of rhetoric by its most eager humanist advocates— promises not simply of ever-increasing abundance but also of intimacy and community. It is no coincidence that the sentence Erasmus chose for his first "practical demonstration" of *copia* is a profession of delight at a letter from a friend, or that *De Conscribendis Epistolis* promotes the exercise of letter writing as the ideal path to rhetorical mastery: the genre of the friendly epistle epitomizes the Erasmian faith in the power of eloquence to overcome the distance between men, turning strangers into friends and friends into "other selves." For Erasmus, both the letter and the commonplace are emblems of eloquence's social function: a letter is "a mutual conversation between absent friends,"[71] while the commonplace facilitates such conversation across centuries and cultures. The abundant style testifies to the pleasures of human companionship: the object of the other "practical demonstration" of *copia* is a sentence professing Erasmus's undying affection for his friend Thomas More. And yet for Euphues, the rhetoric of *copia* yields only solitude and strangeness—and so it proves for euphuism as well. If commonplacing confers upon the vernacular what at first seems like a Corinthian abundance, that very abundance tends toward extravagance, prodigality, and impoverishment: to a language so alienated from its natural proportions that it must be cast off.

By the turn of the seventeenth century, John Hoskins's *Directions for Speech and Style* (c. 1600) interpreted euphuism's success not as evidence of how far English eloquence had come, but of how narrow its limits remained: referring to Lyly's copious similitudes, he mocks, "See to what preferment a figure may aspire if it once get credit in a world that hath not much true rhetoric!"[72] Twenty years after Lyly's death, his publisher Edward Blount offered a more generous but in its own way equally damning assessment of *Euphues's* legacy. In the preface to his 1632 edition of six of Lyly's dramatic works, Blount reminds readers that the now obscure author was once hailed as England's chief literary talent, the savior of the vernacular, the "onely rare poet of that time": "Our nation are in his debt for a new English which hee taught them," he urges; "Euphues began first that language, and that Beautie in Courte, who could not Parley euphuism was as little regarded as shee there now who speaks not French."[73] Blount means to revive Lyly's literary fortunes, but in the very act of praising Lyly, he may well bury him: euphuism, Blount makes clear, is no longer new, and its closest analogue is not even English but an affected foreign tongue. Whatever euphuism did bring to the vernacular in the way of eloquence has already come to seem the relic of a distant time and place, a world without much rhetoric.

It remained to another writer, Edmund Spenser, to show how exile might be productive of eloquence: published just a year after *Euphues's* debut, *The Shepheardes Calender* turns the identification of England as "a world without much rhetoric" into the ground of its stylistic and generic innovation. As for Lyly, his real legacy may reside not in the way English was spoken or written but in the way it was read. "Before the final years of the sixteenth century," Ann Moss has observed, "there is little evidence that vernacular literature (as distinct from vernacular translations, proverbs, and the sayings of important historical figures) had acquired sufficient status to be excerpted for commonplace-books, at least in print."[74] In England, as Roger Chartier and

Peter Stallybrass have shown, that changed with the publication of Nicholas Ling's *Politeuphuia: Wit's Commonwealth* (1597) and Francis Meres's *Palladis Tamia: Wit's Treasury* (1598), both of which mingle quotations from classical sources with those from contemporary vernacular texts.[75] The prominence of *Euphues* in each collection—Ling's title nods in the direction of Lyly's protagonist, while Meres relies extensively on quotations from the text[76]—bespeaks the ease with which it was disassembled and returned to its component parts. This fragmentary quality may to us seem symptomatic of *Euphues*'s defects: its scanty and inconsistent characterization, the cursory development of its plot, the awkward joinery of its many segments. To its early modern audience, however, dispersal into commonplaces was the lot of even the most distinguished texts—*especially* the most distinguished texts—and the generous contribution *Euphues* made to the common stock of tropes and figures, sentences and similitudes may well have seemed its great and enduring achievement. Not long exemplary in its own right, *Euphues* nevertheless made exemplarity something to which English prose might aspire.

Chapter 4

Pastoral in Exile: Colin Clout and the Poetics of English Alienation

No writer labors more conspicuously to claim the mantle of exemplarity than the "new poete" of *The Shepheardes Calender*, who presents himself to readers as the latest to walk a hallowed and well-trod path to literary glory. As E. K.'s introduction to the 1579 poem reminds us, pastoral is the time-honored birthplace of poetic excellence, the "nest" of literary ambition: "So flew Theocritus, as you may percieue he was all ready full fledged. So flew Virgile, as not yet well feeling his winges. So flew Mantuane, as being not full somd. So Petrarque. So Boccace; So Marot, Sanazarus, and also diuers other excellent both Italian and French Poetes, whose foting this Author euery where followeth, yet so as few, but they be well sented can trace him out."[1] Because the *Calender* was quickly recognized as a signal achievement not only for the then-anonymous "new poete" Edmund Spenser but also for the hitherto undistinguished canon of English poetry, E. K.'s analysis of its generic orientation has remained persuasive. It has become, as Anne Lake Prescott observes, "a scholarly commonplace" that by "mask[ing] in lowly shepherds' weeds . . . Spenser was gesturing at a laureate Virgilian career."[2] Pastoral is the "inaugural phase" in what Patrick Cheney dubs "the New Poet's flight pattern";[3] it serves, in Louis Montrose's words, as "a vehicle for the highest personal aspirations and public significance a poet can claim" and "demonstrate[s] the capacity of the vernacular to produce a poetry 'well grounded, finely framed, and strongly trussed up together.'"[4] But if pastoral is a logical generic locus for the expression of literary ambition, it is a rather more vexed starting point for an *English* poet—or for an English poetic renaissance—than E. K. and most subsequent critics acknowledge.[5] After all, the most influential poems in the tradition, Virgil's eclogues, establish their vision of the genre on the assumption that

Britain is no place for pastoral. Indeed, as the first English translation of the eclogues makes clear, only a few years before *The Shepheardes Calender*, England may have been no place for poetry at all.

Certainly such a dismal conclusion is not the intended message of Abraham Fleming's *The Bucoliks of Publius Virgil* (1575). Rather, Fleming undertook his translation in order to remove the barriers between English readers and what he regarded as an unnecessarily remote poetic tradition. By rendering Virgil's elegant Latin into "ye vulgar and common phrase of speache," amplified by an abundance of marginal notes and glosses, Fleming hoped to foster a new sense of "familiaritie and acquaintance with Virgils verse": to guarantee "readie and speedie passage" across the distances imposed by geographic, historical, and linguistic difference.[6] This desire to domesticate Virgilian pastoral takes its most literal form in the compilation of marginal glosses defining all place names and geographical features cited in the poems. Like a map of a foreign country, Fleming writes, his glosses will prevent "the ignorant" from "wander[ing] wyde" by erroneously "applying . . . the name of a mountaine to a man, the name of a fountaine to a towne, the name of a village to a floud, the name of a citie to a riuer" (sig. A3ᵥ).[7] Thus freed from all "stoppes and impediments" to understanding, the reader may use Fleming's translation as a stile or bridge "to passe ouer into the plaine fields of the Poets meaning" (sig. A2ᵥ).

But if Fleming's translation, and especially his glossary, is meant to help readers traverse an unfamiliar poetic landscape, it also exposes England's own place in—or displacement from—that landscape. It is not only that the glosses highlight precisely those aspects of Virgil's diction—namely the "proper names of gods, goddesses, men, women, hilles, flouddes, cities, townes, and villages &c." (sig. A1ᵣ)—least amenable to vernacular translation, since by definition proper names cannot be rendered "plaine and familiar Englishe" (sig. A1ᵣ). More important, the focus on strange place names and geographic features foregrounds the fact that Virgilian pastoral is emphatically—and literally—*topical*, rooted in the particular place and time of its composition. Critics of the genre rarely identify pastoral with a language of geographic and historical specificity; indeed, its landscape is associated with an allegorical conventionality that would seem to exclude proper names. As one critic asserts, contingencies of time and place are precisely what the pastoral poet must eschew in his pursuit of "a world of his own, a cleared space counterfeited from tradition and his own inventive wit," a "green world" crucially and definitively "distant from our own."[8] But Fleming's readers do not have the luxury of subsuming Virgil's landscape into such amorphous generalities: the challenges of translation, and the compensatory labor of Fleming's assiduous glosses, force attention to the fact that pastoral abounds in local particularity.

The problem is more pointed—and painful—than this. Virgil's eclogues locate pastoral existence firmly within the world of Augustan Rome in order to make a claim about the interdependence of poetry and place.[9] The eclogues begin by contrasting the circumstances of two pastoral poets: Tityrus, a figure, Fleming informs us, "represent[ing] *Virgilles* person" (C1r); and his neighbor, Meliboeus. Tityrus attributes his poetic success to his happy proximity to "the Citye . . . call'd Rome," whose "God . . . hath graunted these my beastes to grase, and eake my selfe with glee / To playe vpon my homelye pipe such songes as liked mee" (C1v). He laments the fate of less fortunate foreigners— the "Parthian banisht man" and the "German stranger"—who, if they would seek Rome, are condemned to "wandring others ground" (C2r). Meliboeus concurs in praising Rome: although "in fieldes abroade such troubles bee," in Roman pastures a shepherd "lying at [his] ease, vnder the broad beeche shade, / A countrye song does tune right well" (C1r–v).

But Meliboeus's associations with the city and its ruler have proved less fortunate: his land has just been confiscated to pay one of Caesar's mercenaries, and he therefore faces an imminent departure from Rome: "Our country borders wee doe leaue, and Medowes swete forsake" (C1r). Anticipating an end to his pastoral contentment, Meliboeus bids his sheep "[d]epart . . . a[nd] Cattell once full happye goe and flytt, / I shall not see you after this, in greene caue where I sytt" (C2r). He and his fellow exiles must seek refuge on the outskirts of the Roman Empire, whose territories he enumerates in a grim litany: "[S]ome of vs to droughte Affrike land hence wyll go, / To Scythia and to Candy, where Oaxis scarce doth flowe" (C2r). But he saves the worst for last: some, perhaps he himself, will be sent "[a]s farre as Britan Ile, cut of from the wide world" (C2r).[10] Just in case any of his English readers should have missed the point, Fleming drives it mercilessly home: "Britan," he notes, "is an Ilande, compassed about with the sea, . . . called also Anglia because it standeth in a corner of the world alone" (C2r–v, note n). In such a place, Meliboeus glumly concludes, "no sonnets will I syng" (C2r).[11]

This assumption—that to go to Britain is to abandon poetry—poses serious difficulties for Fleming and his readers. After all, what kind of "familiaritie" or "speedie passage" can be fashioned in relation to a poem that locates England—and English readers—on the far side of an apparently unbridgeable divide? Tityrus's response to Meliboeus in the eclogue's final lines, the offer of a final night's rest in his cottage, tacks on a consolatory ending and temporarily forestalls the threat of exile.[12] But for the English reader, there is no reprieve: in the poem that inaugurates the career of Rome's greatest poet, Britain remains the sign of all that is antithetical to poetry. The somewhat fanciful claim Fleming makes on behalf of his translation, that it carries Virgilian pastoral out of Rome and into England, turns out, on the poem's own terms, to be impossible.

I have dwelled at some length on Fleming's translation—admittedly a very minor entry in the canons of late sixteenth-century classical scholarship and vernacular poetry—because it provides an especially concrete demonstration of the challenges facing all those who sought to use classical texts and forms as vehicles for importing poetic excellence into England. "[I]n the process of retrieving from Antiquity the terms and concepts that introduced new distinctions to the field of English writing," Sean Keilen has argued, "vernacular writers were obliged to confront the radical alterity of England to the ancient world, and of English to the languages and aesthetic canons they wanted to assimilate."[13] Of course, the challenge of bridging the gap created by this "radical alterity" was not unique to English poets: vernacular authors on the Continent struggled under similar burdens of belatedness and distance from the classical world, and as E. K. points out, Spenser's efforts are inspired by the successes of such poets as Marot and Sannazaro.[14] And yet, as my reading of Fleming's translation suggests, would-be authors of English pastoral encounter the difficulties—and perhaps the opportunities—of alienation from antiquity in their most stringent guise, for no other form insists so strongly on the interdependence of poet and place, song and setting. It is therefore crucial that we not forget what E. K.'s survey of pastoral poets and poetry conveniently overlooks: that in the form's preeminent incarnation, the Virgilian eclogue, English readers find their own native place located beyond poetry's pale. This inescapable fact invites us to reconsider Spenser's choice of pastoral as the generic locus of his own ambitious foray into vernacular poetics: "the best and most Auncient Poetes" may, as E. K. claims, have valued pastoral for its "homely" qualities, but for Spenser, the pastoral tradition has more to say about the "unhomely"—about alienation, exclusion, and the paradoxical virtues of exile.

The ironies and incongruities of Fleming's English Virgil may therefore help us to appreciate in a new way how and why Spenser's vernacular pastoral embraces linguistic estrangement and geographic dislocation as the emblems, and engines, of English poetry.[15] For if alienation is the defining characteristic of Colin Clout, with his neglected flocks and his shattered pipe, it is also the central strategy of Spenser's poetry, which forces his readers to reencounter their native tongue through a process of occlusion and defamiliarization. In the world of Virgilian pastoral, exile to Britain marks the limits of geographic and poetic possibility; in the world of *The Shepheardes Calender*, distance and disability become the necessary conditions of writing and reading English verse. "Cut off from the wide world"—by virtue of its Englishness but also by virtue of its willfully difficult language—Spenser's *Calender* finds in the rudeness and rusticity of the mother tongue the materials of its own peculiar eloquence.

A Familiar Acquaintance Far Estranged

The reader's experience of estrangement begins on the *Calender*'s title page, which, although it names the poem, offers a brief description of its contents, and announces its dedication to Philip Sidney, makes no mention of an author. Turning the page, one learns that this omission is deliberate: a verse *envoi* instructs the poem to present itself "[a]s child whose parent is vnkent" and cautions, "if that any aske thy name, / Say thou wert base begot with blame, / For thy thereof thou takest shame."[16] The poem is famously signed "*Immeritô*" (24), which translates as "the unworthy one." The following page introduces a new character, the equally mysterious E. K.,[17] whose introductory epistle claims as its goal to "commendeth the good lyking . . . and the patronage of the new Poete" (25) but who proves a rather jealous guard of the privileges of his own "familiar acquaintance" (29) with both poet and poem. He boasts, for instance, of having been "made priuie to [*Immeritô*'s] counsel and secret meaning" in writing the *Calender* but unhelpfully adds that, "[t]ouching the generall dryft and purpose of his Aeglogues, I mind not to say much, him selfe labouring to conceale it" (29). As Lynn Staley Johnson observes, E. K.'s remarks frequently afford *Immeritô* an "opaque cover" not unlike the pseudonym itself, as the commentator "interposes himself between *Immeritô*" and his public.[18] In his epistle's final paragraph, therefore, when E. K. addresses the mystery of *Immeritô*'s identity, he does so simply to declare himself an accessory to the poet's desire to keep himself, for the time being, "furre estraunged": "worthy of many, yet . . . knowen to few" (30).

The peculiarities of E. K.'s relation to the poem sharpen when he turns to the issue of *Immeritô*'s language. As he acknowledges, his own "maner of glosing and commenting" must "seeme straunge and rare" (29) when applied to a poem ostensibly written in the reader's "own country and natural speech," his very "mother tongue" (27). In fact, these glosses and commentary seem more suited to an edition of classical verse—such as Fleming's translation of Virgil—or the work of a celebrated modern poet such as Petrarch or Sannazaro. Both Fleming and E. K. offer prefatory essays on the history of pastoral and the etymology of the word "eclogue," provide prose "arguments" summarizing each eclogue, and surround the poems with an abundance of editorial notes and glosses. Fleming can justify such an elaborate apparatus by appealing to the distance separating his English readers from the language and landscape of Virgil's poetry. As E. K. confesses, his own interventions are less easily accounted for: why should an English reader require a gloss or commentary to assist his comprehension of a work set in his own time, place, and native tongue? Rather, such commentary as E. K. does provide seems calculated to *intensify* the reader's sense of remove from the poem he is about to read—to function, that is, as the very sort of "stoppes and impediments" (sig. A2) Fleming is so eager to remove from his own reader's path.

Certainly a scholarly apparatus would have seemed out of place in earlier English pastorals, whose authors tend to apologize for the straightforward and uncomplicated nature of their verses rather than offer any aid in understanding them. Indeed poets such as Alexander Barclay and George Turbervile worry that the language of their pastorals will seem all too familiar to the average reader. Urging readers of his *Egloges* (c. 1530) "not to be grieved with any playne sentence / Rudely conuayed for lacke of eloquence," Barclay reminds them that "[i]t were not fitting a heard or man rurall / To speak in termes gay and rhetoricall."[19] Turbervile, whose *Eglogs* (1567) mimic those of Mantuan, apologizes for "forcing" that poet's Latin-speaking shepherds "to speake with an English mouthe" and cautions that "as ye conference betwixt Shepherds is familiar stuffe and homely: so haue I shapt my stile and tempred it with suche common and ordinarie phrase of speech as Countrymen do vse in their affaires."[20]

E. K. mentions the homely style of pastoral verse, but he also declares that *Immeritô*'s "words" are "the straungest" of "many thinges which in him be straunge" (25). When he insists on the need for a gloss for those words or feels constrained to point out that they are "both English, and also vsed of most excellent Authors and most famous Poetes" (25–26), he redefines the limits of both pastoral and the vernacular: neither will be confined to the familiar or homely. Although he begins by asserting an equivalence, or at least a dependence, between familiarity and admiration, he ultimately advances a more complicated understanding of that relationship. Just as his avowed long-ing to make *Immeritô* familiar to all conflicts with his wish to protect his own "familiar acquaintance" with the poet's "secret meanings," his observations on Spenser's language seem poised between the impulse to demystify and a desire to highlight its peculiarities. His glosses, for instance, serve a double purpose: added "for thexposition of old wordes and harder phrases," they are necessary lest the "excellent and proper devises" of Spenser's verse "passe in the speedy course of reading, *either as vnknowen, or as not marked*" (29, emphasis added). The gloss is a corrective, that is, against two equal and opposite dangers: that Spenser's language will strike readers as so remote as to be incomprehensible, or that it will fail to strike them at all. Where Fleming sought a "readie and speedie passage" into Virgil's poem, E. K. aimed to slow his readers down—to function, in Fleming's terms, as both pathway *and* impediment, both stop *and* stile, champion of the poem's "seemely simplicity" *and* gatekeeper of its "graue . . . straungenesse" (25).[21]

The seemingly paradoxical claims that E. K. makes on behalf of Spenser's poetic diction—that it is a function of both "custome" and "choyse" (26), that its archaisms are both a source of "great grace and . . . auctoritie" and a "rough and harsh" foil to more "glorious words" (26–27), and that it generates a style both "straunge" (25) and "homely" (29)—are hard to reconcile with the straightforward equation of pastoral and plainness found in the prefaces to so many other vernacular poems, but they do reflect the complicated and at times contradictory interpretive practices of another important literary genre of sixteenth-century England: biblical translation. That Spenser's *Cal-ender* is a profoundly Protestant text is a familiar claim, but most accounts of the poem's religious affiliations restrict themselves to questions of content, to analyses of the eclogues' satirical and allegorical engagements with doctrinal and ecclesiastical controversies.[22] I suggest that Protestantism also provides a matrix for understanding the poem's language and the way that language is represented and mediated by E. K. Among the translators of scripture, we find an approach to the vernacular that is, like that of E. K., precariously poised between the values of simplicity and strangeness—and here, as in *The Shepheardes Calender*, the practice most likely to disturb this equilibrium is glossing.

As Lynne Long has established, glossing was the original point of contact between the vernacular and sacred writing, an essential and often controversial precursor to full-fledged biblical translation.[23] The vernacular notes that ap-peared, as early as the eighth century, in the margins and between the lines of

English biblical texts served as important aids to readers whose Latin was weak or nonexistent, but they also forced translators and editors to think carefully about the relative values of accessibility and difficulty. Of his vernacular edition of the *Lives of the Saints*, the Anglo-Saxon translator Aelfric writes that his desire to render his text "into the usual English speech [ad usitatem Anglicam sermocinationem]" conflicted at times with his wish to preserve the challenges and mysteries of his source-text as guards against an unfit readership: "I do not promise however to write very many in this tongue, . . . lest peradventure the pearls of Christ be had in disrespect."[24]

The sixteenth century, and especially the decades preceding the publication of *The Shepherd's Calender*, witnessed an explosion of English translations of the Bible and a corresponding rise in both the estimation of the vernacular and the anxiety about its adequacy as a vehicle for divine wisdom and eloquence. Like Aelfric, the translators and editors of these texts often seem to have been torn between a desire to promote the plain and homely virtues of their vernacular scriptures and to insist upon the salutary challenges posed by correct interpretation. Thus, although the title page to the 1560 Geneva Bible promises readers "the holy Scriptures faithfully and playnely translated" into their own native tongue, the translators later note that "we moste reuerently kept the proprietie of the [original Greek and Hebrew] wordes" and "in many places reserued the Ebrewe phrases, notwithstanding that thei may seme somewhat hard in their eares that are not well practiced" because the preservation of such interpretive challenges accords with the practice of the Apostles, "who spake and wrote to the Gentiles in the Greke tongue, [but] rather constrained them to the liuely phrase of the Ebrewe, then enterprised farre by mollifying their langage to speake as the Gentils did."[25] The English of the Bible, it appears, must seem both familiar and strange in order to elicit the proper readerly response—like E. K., these commentators are eager both to assist and to impede the "speedy course" of their readers' understanding, to engender a sense of connection and proximity to the text even as they retain a sense of its distance and difficulty.

The English Bible translators also anticipate E. K. in that they must justify the deployment of often elaborate explanatory apparatuses alongside texts ostensibly written in plain English. Indeed the desire to eliminate obtrusive and potentially misleading glosses was a primary impetus for translating scripture into the vernacular in the first place: in the preface to his 1534 *New Testament*, William Tyndale assails the obscurantism and elitism of the Catholic Church, whose mystique depends on the labor of those "false prophets and malicious hypocrites, whose perpetual study is to leaven the scripture with glosses." But Tyndale's concern for the proper reception of his own translation prompts him "in many places" to "set light in the margin to understand the text by": as he admits, due to allegorical figuration or theological complexity, "the scripture and word of God, may be so locked up, that he which readeth or heareth it, cannot understand it" unless it is "dress[ed]" and "season[ed]" for "weak stomachs."[26] So too the Geneva translators, who chastise those (Catholic) scholars who "pretend" that ordinary readers "can not atteine to the true and simple meaning" of the scriptures even as they admit "how hard a thing it is to vnderstand the holy Scriptures."[27] Indeed it is precisely because such understanding is so elusive that their translation comes equipped with a complex apparatus of "brief annotations," "figures and notes," and even "mappes of Cosmographie" to guide the reader through scriptures' "hard" and "darke . . . places" and their "diuers . . . countries."[28]

Is the vernacular Bible easy or difficult to read? Are its "places," whether textual or geographic, accessible to or remote from the understanding and experiences of the English reader? The translators of the English Bible leave such questions largely unresolved, and they resonate with E. K.'s contradictory descriptions of the "new Poet's" simple yet strange verses. Indeed the similarities between the presentation of the Geneva Bible and that of *The Shepheardes Calender*—the prefatory essays, prose arguments, marginal annotations and glosses, and woodcut illustrations—suggest that Spenser's pastoral is designed to elicit a reading practice like that promoted by the authors of the English Bibles, in which the value of accessibility is in constant, productive tension with the value of alienation. We might further note that the *Calender*'s affinity with England's vernacular Bibles affords the poem and its readers a very different view of Rome, and of classical antiquity, than that associated with the pastoral tradition. If, for Virgil's shepherds and their English heirs, eloquence must be anchored in Rome and Britain remain forever beyond the pale, within the context of the Protestant Reformation, this geography could be wholly reversed.[29]

When the Geneva Bible translators proclaim in their dedication to Queen Elizabeth I that "the eyes of all that feare God in all places beholde your countreyes as an example to all that beleue,"[30] they are, of course, making a calculated appeal to the vanity of a monarch whose support was crucial to the success, indeed the survival, of their text. But they also invoke England's historic importance to the Protestant cause in general and Bible translation in particular. In this one area, thanks to a long tradition of vernacular homiletics and scriptural translation—from Aelfric through Wycliffe—England could position itself in the vanguard of linguistic progress and cultural achievement, even as it anchored itself to a past more authentically antique than that of Rome: as the title page to the Geneva Bible states, it was "[t]ranslated according to the Ebrue and Greke," "the languages wherein [the scriptures] were first written by the holy Gost," and not, pointedly, according to the Latin Vulgate edition used by the Church of Rome. Far from being the sign of a privileged antiquity, as it is in Virgil's pastorals and in the rest of the secular literary tradition, for the translators of English scriptures Latin is the language of a belated and debased tradition, itself remote from the true origins of divine wisdom and Christian eloquence. The distance between the vernacular and Latin is thus touted as an advantage by Tyndale, who defends his own early sixteenth-century scriptural translations on the grounds that English is closer to the truly biblical languages: "For the Greek tongue agreeth more with the English than with the Latin. And the properties of the Hebrew tongu agreeth a thousand times more with the English than with the Latin."[31] Tyndale's rationale upends the linguistic hierarchy assumed by secular translators such as Abraham Fleming and brings the vernacular into desirable proximity with a religious history and geography in which Rome (and Latin) is more peripheral than privileged.[32]

The complex, even contradictory, attitudes toward the vernacular evinced by E. K.'s epistle to *The Shepheardes Calender* produce a similarly radical reworking of linguistic and literary values. E. K.'s epistle does more than simply characterize *Immeritô's* peculiar poetic voice; like the prefaces to English Bibles, it also reflects upon the peculiar position of the English language at the end of the sixteenth century. That is, if E. K. seeks to characterize *Immeritô's* voice as simultaneously rare and unremarkable, he also seeks to characterize English as a paradoxical blend of the foreign and the familiar—a language that may appear most alien and inaccessible precisely when it hits closest to home. As the epistle draws to a close, E. K.'s argument thus shifts from the particular case of *The Shepheardes Calender* to that of the vernacular as a whole. Those who "will rashly blame [*Immeritô's*] purpose in choyce of old and vnwonted words," he writes, are themselves to be "more iustly blame[d] and condemne[d]" for failing to appreciate one of the chief beauties of his poetry, which aims "to restore, as to theyr rightfull heritage, such good and naturall English words as haue ben long time out of vse and almost cleane disherited" (27). This disregard for the origins of the language has deprived the vernacular of its own best resources and "is the onely cause, that our Mother tonge, truely of it self is both ful enough for prose and stately enough for verse, hath long time ben counted most bare and barrein of both" (27). Even worse than those who neglect English's roots are those who, "endeuour[ing] to salue and recure" the language's perceived deficits, have "patched vp the holes with peces and rags of other languages, borrowing here of the French, there of the Italian, euery where of the Latine, not weighing how il those tongues accord with themselues, but much worse with ours" (27). Over time, E. K. argues, the very concepts of foreign and familiar have been so confused that, while the adoption of alien terms has "made our English tongue, a gallimaufray or hodgepodge of al other speeches," the "very naturall and significant" words on which the tongue was founded are rejected as "no English, but gibberish" (27). Thanks to such linguistic promiscuity,[33] England has become estranged from itself, a nation "whose first shame is, that [its inhabitants] are not ashamed, in their owne mother tonge strangers to be counted and alienes" (27). If it is "straunge and rare" for a vernacular author to require the mediation of an editor in order to be understood by a native readership, that very peculiarity is, in E. K.'s view, what marks *Immeritô*'s work as truly and properly English.

In Virgil's first eclogue, and in Fleming's translation, distance is inimical to poetry: Meliboeus's exile threatens to end his song, and the unguided reader, "wander[ing] wyde" of Virgil's meaning, loses both the pleasure and the profit of his labor. Familiarity—whether it appears in the guise of a fellow shepherd's hospitality or a helpful translator's marginal glosses—becomes the only defense against an alienation that threatens to dissolve the pastoral landscape into a foreign wasteland, to turn eloquent Rome into mute and barren Britain. In pre-Spenserian English pastorals, by contrast, familiarity and proximity—"homeliness"—are qualities that threatened to deny the vernacular poet his bid to participate in a more elevated literary tradition—without the sponsorship of remote authorities, English verse has no value. E. K.'s epistle reformulates these dilemmas—and offers *Immeritô* a way out of the impasse—by refusing to admit an opposition between familiarity and strangeness. Instead he makes familiarity (such as that he claims between himself and Spenser) an excuse for secrecy and identifies the strangeness of Spenser's language with its most native and homely virtues.

The Unrestful Shepherd

Spenser's pastoral narrative performs a similarly complex rereading of the literary significance of exile. For most sixteenth-century English rhetorical and poetic theorists, exile functions as a metaphor for the exclusion of the vernacular from the company of learned and eloquent tongues, and for the hardships vernacular speakers endure as a result of this exclusion. In *The Pastime of Pleasure*, Stephen Hawes identifies "elocucyon" with a process of purification that consigns the homely vernacular "to exyle": separating "the dulcet speech / from the langage rude," "the barbary tongue / it doth ferre exclude."[34] In *The Boke named the Governour*, Thomas Elyot makes the more literal point that if they wish to master the most rarefied arts, eloquence included, Englishmen must often endure exile, being "constrained . . . to leave our owne countraymen and resorte vs vnto strangers."[35]

But for England's Bible translators, who endured unpredictable and often violent reversals of fortune under the Tudors, exile bore a more complicated relation to eloquence, as it was often the necessary condition of writerly survival. William Tyndale concluded as a young man that "there was no place . . . in all England" for someone who believed as strongly as he did in the virtues of an English Bible, and the very name of the Geneva Bible betrays the fact that well into the sixteenth century this continued to be the case.[36] Striking too is that Bible's curious gloss of Psalm 137, whose well-known opening lines recall the Israelites' refusal to sing during their exile from the promised land: "By the rivers of Babylon, there we sat down, yea, we wept, when we remembered Zion. / We hanged our harps upon the willows in the midst thereof. / For there they that carried us away captive required of us a song; and they that wasted us [required of us] mirth, [saying], Sing us [one] of the songs of Zion." The Israelites' insistence that "the songs of Zion" belong to Zion alone would seem to make Psalm 137 a kind of sacred precursor to the lament of Meliboeus in Virgil's first eclogue, with the same melancholy alignment of poetry and place, exile and silence; but the Geneva translators interpret it rather differently, as a mournful comment on the necessity of self-imposed exile from a people who have lost their way. Its opening plaint is glossed as a response not to the insults of foreign captivity but to the disappointments of home: "Even though the country [of Babylon] was pleasant," the translators remark, "yet it could not stay [the Israelites'] tears" when they recalled "[t]he decay of God's religion in their country," which "was so grievous that no joy could make them glad, unless it was restored."[37] In other words, the roots of the Israelites' silence lie not in Babylon but in Zion; exile is simply the literal expression of—or even a consolation for—a more profound and painful internal alienation. There is little in the psalm to support such a reading—on the contrary, the psalmist emphatically identifies his own ability to sing with his attachment to his native land, vowing, "let my tongue cleave to the roof of my mouth, if I prefer not Jerusalem above my chief joy"[38]—but much, perhaps, in the translators' own experiences, as writers whose preference for English meant leaving England behind.

Spenser's poem both invokes and recasts these associations: while acknowledging the loneliness of the poet severed from his native land, it also embraces alienation as the paradoxically enabling condition of a truly native eloquence. Like Tyndale and the Geneva translators, Spenser follows the "barbary tongue" and "langage rude" into exile, finding there the materials for renovating and replenishing an impoverished tradition. *The Shepheardes Calender* thus transforms Meliboeus, Virgil's unwilling victim of exile, into Colin Clout, a poet whose exile from the pastoral community is both self-imposed and strangely productive. Like Meliboeus, Colin enters the pastoral world on the verge of departing from it, breaking his pipes at the end of the "Januarye" eclogue and quitting himself of the "rurall musick" to which his "vnlucky Muse" has called him (ll. 64, 69). His break with pastoral poetry, we learn, is the consequence of infidelity to the pastoral landscape, a fatal "long[ing]" to see "the neighbour towne" (l. 50). This wanderlust leads to an unrequited passion for Rosalind, a town-dwelling lady who loathes "shepheards devise" (l. 65), "laughes" (l. 66) at shepherds' songs, and infects Colin with a similar disdain. Although he returns to his flocks and farm, he remains alienated from the pleasures they once provided: neither his own verses nor the "clownish giftes and curtsies," "kiddes," "cracknelles," and "early fruits" of his rustic companion Hobbinol please Colin any longer.

In his gloss of this passage, E. K. observes that "[n]eighbour town . . . express[es] the Latine *Vicina*" (38n50), a clarification many critics have cited as characteristically egregious—why bother to translate a perfectly clear English phrase into its Latin equivalent? But if the note violates the usual function of a gloss, its estranging effect captures perfectly the paradox inherent in both E. K.'s apparatus and Spenser's diction. Indeed the very word *vicina* is suggestively apt, as it denotes a locale that is at once elsewhere and close at hand, remote and proximate. And when Hobbinol appears in the "Aprill" eclogue, he characterizes Colin's defection in similar terms: "now his frend is changed

for a frenne" (l. 28). The latter word, E. K. informs us, is a term "first poeti-
cally put, and afterward vsed in commen custome of speech for forenne" (66–
67n28). Colin's rejection of his familiar friend in favor of Rosalind—who,
like the "neighbour towne" or *vicina* in which she dwells, is both "forenne"
and familiar—casts him into a state of self-division that, as Hobbinol reports,
alienates him from the sources of his poetic inspiration:

> Shepheards delights he doth them all forsweare,
> Hys pleasaunt Pipe, which made vs merriment,
> Hy wylfully hath broke, and doth forbear
> His wonted songs, wherein he all outwent. (ll. 13–16)

The measure of this loss to the pastoral community becomes clear when, at
his companion's request, Hobbinol recites one of the songs Colin composed in
happier days, when "by a spring he laye" and "tuned" his music to the rhythm
of "the Waters fall" (ll. 35–36). The reader is invited to compare such domestic
harmony to the frigid sympathy between poet and place that Colin expresses
in "Januarye," when the frozen barrenness of the wintry fields merely encourages the poet to forsake his pipes and regard his own youth as similarly wasted.
The song presents Colin as master of both a local and a classical poetics—he
invokes the "dayntye Nymphes" of his own "blessed Brooke" (l. 37) to join the
Muses "that on Parnasse dwell" (l. 41) and help in the fashioning of his praise
for Elisa, whose glory is likened to that of "*Phoebus*" (l. 73) and "*Cynthia*" (l.
82). The two-part Latin tag with which the eclogue concludes—Aeneas's "*O
quam te memorem virgo*," "*O dea certe*"—casts Spenser as a second Virgil, even
as it presents Elisa, England's queen, as "no whit inferiour to the Maiestie" of
the goddess Venus and England, perhaps, as the fertile ground of a new poetic
and political imperium.

Such sympathetic affinities—between poet and place, local and classical, vernacular and Latin, England and Rome—are, however, the stuff of
the past, as Hobbinol regretfully notes: "But nowe from me hys madding
minde is starte" (l. 25). The breach between Colin and his "clownish" friend
signals a more pervasive state of alienation. A disinclination to sing, in fact,
is the inauspicious starting point of nearly all of the *Calender*'s eclogues—
whether it be the consequence of cold or age ("Februarie"), the afflictions of
love ("March," "August"), the disapproval of one's fellow shepherds ("Maye,"
"Julye"), or the lack of a patron to support the poet's efforts ("October"). This
last circumstance leads the shepherd Cuddie to despair of the future of English

pastoral: Virgil, "the Romish *Tityrus*" ("October," l. 55), had both matter and means for his art, but now "Tom Piper" (l. 78) with his "rymes of rybaudrye" (l. 78) is the only poet who thrives. Once inspiration, like the Roman Empire itself, seemed boundless; the muse "stretch[ed] her selfe at large from East to West" (l. 44). Now, with neither empire nor Caesar to sustain it, it lies "pend in shamefull coupe" (l. 72). "O pierlesse Poesye," Piers exclaims, "where then is thy place?" (l. 79). Its place, Cuddie replies, is with Colin Clout—with his departure, poetry too has been "expell[ed]" (l. 99).

The apparent solution, then, is to woo Colin back to the place (and time) in which his poetry flourished, to the domesticity and community represented and advocated by homely, humble Hobbinol, who becomes the voice of what Harry Berger has dubbed the poem's "paradisal" imperative: the call to a kind of "literary withdrawal" that is also "characteristically a 'return to' . . . a set of *topoi*, of 'places' as well as conventions, authenticated by their durability."[39] Reunited with Colin in the "June" eclogue, Hobbinol does his best to woo his friend from his errant existence:

> Lo *Colin*, here the place, whose pleasaunt syte
> From other shades hath weand my wandring mynde.
> Tell me, what wants me here, to worke delyte?
> The simple ayre, the gentle warbling wynde,
> So calme, so coole, as no where else I fynde. (ll. 1–5)

Colin concurs with Hobbinol's evaluation of his own happy lot but insists that such domestic bliss is not for him:

> O happy *Hobbinoll*, I blesse thy state,
> That Paradise hast found, whych *Adam* lost . . .
> But I unhappy man, whom cruell fate,
> And angry Gods pursue from coste to coste,
> Can nowhere fynd, to shroude my lucklesse pate.[40] (ll. 9–10, 14–16)

Hobbinol responds with an obvious solution—Colin must come home:

> Forsake the soyle, that so doth the bewitch:
> Leaue me those hilles, where harbrough nis to see,
> Nor holybush, nor brere, nor winding witche:
> And to the dales resort, where shepheards ritch,

And fuictfull flocks bene every where to see.

. . . .

Such pierlesse pleasures haue we in these places. (ll. 18–22, 32)

Colin counters that his dilemma is not situational but existential: "since I am not, as I wish I were" (l. 105)— that is, since he is exiled from Rosalind's affections—no place, "[w]hether on hylls, or dales, or other where" (l. 107), can do more than "[b]eare witnesse" (l. 108) to his suffering.

The aptness of Hobbinol's advice is cast into further doubt by his encounter with Diggon Davie in the "September" eclogue. In many ways Diggon is a clear surrogate for Colin, another wayward prodigal, "a shepheard," as E. K. describes him, "that in hope of more gayne, droue his sheepe into a farre countrye" (116). Like Colin, who "curse[s]" the "carefull hower" of his departure from his pastoral home ("Januarye," l. 49), Diggon comes to regret his waywardness, "curs[ing] the stounde / That euer I caste to haue lorne this grounde" (ll. 56–57). He eventually makes his way back home, but errancy has marked his speech, which Hobbinol professes not to understand: "speake not so dirke" (l. 102), he urges. Diggon acknowledges that "this English is flatt" (l. 105), and E. K. comments that the peculiar "Dialecte and phrase of speache in this Dialogue," which "seemeth somewhat to differ from the comen," reflects Diggon's travels: having "bene long in foraine countries, and there seene many disorders," his very speech has become alien and disordered (125).

Diggon would appear to represent an extreme case of the dangers facing Colin Clout, whose defection from the pastoral world also threatens to divorce him from its poetry. But the "September" eclogue takes on a more ambiguous meaning in light of the *Calender*'s own departures from linguistic and pastoral convention. After all, one of the expressions that E. K. singles out as foreign and disorderly is the word "uncouthe" (l. 60), which Diggon uses to disparage his decision to leave home—but which E. K. himself used in his epistle to describe the poem's author and which he attributed to England's own "olde" and "famous" poet Chaucer (25). The moral of the "September" eclogue is further complicated by Diggon's choice of a Latin tag, *Inopem me copia fecit* (l. 261), a phrase drawn, as E. K. observes, from Ovid's version of the tale of Narcissus. Diggon uses it, he hypothesizes, to show that "by tryall of many wayes, [he] founde the worst," but this is, he admits, "to other purpose" than "fyrste Narcissus spake it" (127). And indeed Narcissus is an odd figure for Diggon: while Diggon's desire for "chaunge" (l. 69) displaces him, leading him to abandon the "grounde" (l. 57) he knows best, Narcissus's self-love engrafts him in one place—if anyone could be said to be "[c]ontent [to] liue with tried state" (l. 70), as Hobbinol urges Diggon to be, it is Narcissus. If both Narcissus and Diggon ultimately find cause to mourn that "plenty has made me poor," they seek for plenty in very different places: one in the too-close circuit formed by his own person and its reflection; and the other by "measur[ing] much grownd, . . . wandr[ing] the world rounde" (ll. 21–22). They are linked, perhaps, by their inability to judge distances rightly: for Narcissus, distance from the object of his desire is both unattainable and inescapable; for Diggon, whose very name proclaims his homely, earth-bound calling, distance is a false lure, an invitation to riches that vanish when seen up close.

Ultimately, Narcissus is perhaps a less apt figure for Diggon (of whom he is, at best, an inverted or mirror image) than he is for Colin Clout—not as he is, but as Hobbinol wishes him to be. The self-love and stasis that waste Narcissus are not so different from the paradisal pleasures Hobbinol urges upon Colin in the "June" eclogue, pleasures of proximity, familiarity, and sameness. And indeed when the reader first encounters Colin, in "Januarye," his condition is perilously Narcissus-like. The icy sheen of the frozen ground, he claims, had been "made a myrrhour, to behold my plight" (l. 20), and his own self-absorbed reflection threatens to consume him. The very syntax of his verse seems governed by a logic of reflexivity, replete with chiastic echoes, parallel structures, and insistent repetitions.[41] When he falls to the ground after breaking his pipe, it seems possible that he, like Narcissus, will never get up again.

It is only by rousing himself to abandon the pastoral place, rejecting home and its comforts, that Colin rediscovers his poetic voice—although it is no longer the same voice that once delighted his fellow shepherds with its sweetness. Thus when Hobbinol pleads "to heare thy rymes and roundelays, / Which thou were wont on wastfull hylls to singe" (ll. 49–51), Colin announces that "such delights . . . amongst my peeres" no longer entice him (l. 35). His exile has taught him "newe delightes" (l. 40), "play[ing] to please my selfe, all be it ill" (l. 72). These new songs, he says, do not imitate or emulate the songs of others, "to winne renowne, or passe the rest" (l. 74); instead they are fitted to the peculiar demands of his situation: "I wote my rhymes bene rough, and rudely drest," but "[t]he fitter they, my carefull case to frame, / Enough is me to paint out my vnrest" (ll. 77–79).

In making the case for his songs of "vnrest," Colin does not claim to have abandoned his roots altogether. Instead, he argues, he follows the example of his master, "[t]he God of shepheards *Tityrus* . . . / Who taught me homely, as

I can to make" (ll. 81–82). This "homely" art is, nevertheless, as remote and inaccessible as any of the prospects Hobbinol has described: "*Tityrus* . . . is dead" (l. 81), and "all hys passing skil with him is fledde" (l. 91). Colin's own song is thus defined by relationships of proximity and likeness—to Chaucer, to Virgil—that perpetually fall away into distance and alienation, just as his "place in [Rosalind's] heart" ("Argvment" to "June," 87) turns out to be no place at all—indeed turns out to spoil and evacuate all places.

Chaucer and Virgil share the role of Tityrus, Colin's poetic mentor, with an unacknowledged third poet: Ovid, the "poet . . . of exile and complaint," who, as Syrithe Pugh argues, through "an accumulation of mostly covert allusions" becomes the *Calender*'s silent "presiding genius."[42] One such allusion may be found in the song Colin sings in the "Nouember" eclogue, a dirge in honor of Dido, "dead alas and drent" (l. 37)—a passage which long puzzled Spenser's readers since the Virgilian Dido dies a famously fiery death.[43] Donald Cheney solves the conundrum by pointing to the "March" section of the *Fasti*, Ovid's never-completed calendrical poem celebrating Rome's mythic and imperial history, which recounts the fate of Dido's lesser-known sister, Anna. Exiled from Carthage after her sister's death, Anna is driven across the sea to Italy, where she seeks help from Aeneas and then, fearing his wife's jealousy, casts herself into the river Numicius.[44] In fact, the parallels between this sister of Dido and the figure mourned by Colin are even more striking than Cheney suggests: like Ovid's Anna, Colin's Dido is remembered for her generosity to the rustic poor (*Fasti* 3.670–71; "Nouember," ll. 95–96), memorialized in the bawdy songs of young girls (*Fasti* 3.675–6; "Nouember," ll. 77–79), and transcends her watery death to achieve immortality (*Fasti* 3.653–54; "Nouember," l. 175). Ultimately, however, Colin's Dido surpasses her Ovidian model; "raign[ing] a goddesse now among the saintes" (l. 175), she achieves a glory inaccessible to the pagan Anna.[45]

The Spenserian Dido's supersession of her classical predecessor reflects her creator's supersession of his own classical predecessor, for Ovid's calendrical poem has no "November" section—indeed nothing at all past "June." *The Shepheardes Calender* may follow "the ensample of . . . Ovid," as E. K.'s final note observes (156), but it also succeeds where Ovid failed, simply in arriving at an end.[46] The significance of this implicit contest with Ovid deepens if we recall the reason Ovid's calendar lacks an ending: his banishment from Rome. The fate of the *Fasti*'s author recalls that of Virgil's Meliboeus: Ovid abandoned the poem when Auguistus ordered him to abandon Rome and take up residence in Tomis, on the Black Sea—like Britain, a desolate colonial outpost on the frontier of the Roman Empire.[47] Instead of completing his calendar—a project he now regarded with bitterness—Ovid began the series of poems known as the *Tristia*, in which he bemoans the cultural and linguistic impoverishment of his new home "at the world's end."[48] The *Tristia* are haunted by Ovid's fear that, cut off from other native speakers of Latin, he will lose his poetic voice, descending to the barbarous accents of those around him. He obsessively charts the decline of his once-eloquent tongue, complaining that, surrounded by "Thracian and Scythian voices, I've unlearned the art of speech" (3.14.46). "If some phrases sound un-Latin," he apologizes, "remember / They were penned on barbarian soil" (3.1.17–18). His poetry has become a mass of "barbarous solecisms," for which, he insists, "you must blame the place, not the author" (5.7.60–61).

Ovid's mournful insistence that it is "the place," the non-Roman North, which stops his once eloquent tongue resonates with many sixteenth-century accounts of the English language: for instance, Thomas Elyot's argument that the "infelicitie of our time and countray . . . compelleth"[49] the English to labor in the study of classical tongues; and Gabriel Harvey's claim that a "revolution of the heavens" was needed to bring eloquence "to these remote parts of the world."[50] By completing the poetic project left unfinished by Ovid in his *Fasti*, and by rooting it in the seemingly unpromising locale of the rude vernacular, Spenser challenges, yet again, the classical tradition's equation of exile, especially exile to the barbarous North, with poetic impotence. The rocks on which Ovid's calendar founders become the ground in which Spenser's *Calender* thrives. Thus, when begged by Hobbinol to "forsake the soyle" that stifles his once fluent song—soil identified by E. K. as "the Northparts" ("Glosse" to "June," 91)—Colin Clout refuses to do so, embracing alienation and distance as inspirations for his "rough, and rudely drest" verses ("June," l. 77): he is, as Colin Burrow has noted, the "poet of loss, exile, and solitude."[51]

In the epilogue to the *Calender*, Spenser embraces the distance between himself and other poets, claiming that his poem has earned "a free passeporte" to "followe" from "farre off" the works of earlier authors ("Epilogue," ll. 7, 11). The claim sustains a conventional gesture of modesty—he "dare[s] not match [his] pipe" (l. 9) with those greater—but it also identifies distance, whether linguistic, temporal, cultural, or geographic, with an expansion of literary possibility and with a challenge to the hierarchies that had kept vernacular poets in their place. The strangeness that, for E. K., makes *Immeritô*'s English truly and virtuously homely works its way through the narrative of Colin Clout's poetic development, which emerges out of the same paradoxical play of distance and proximity, foreignness and familiarity, exile and return.

Poetry Beyond the Pale

For all the admiration that *The Shepheardes Calender* garnered from contemporary readers, not all of Spenser's peers appreciated the poem's embrace of strangeness.[52] William Webbe, author of *A Discourse of English Poetrie* (1586), proclaims Spenser "the rightest English Poet, that euer I read," but his praise of *The Shepheardes Calender* betrays a certain unease. Spenser's "trauell in that peece of English Poetrie," he writes, "I think verily is so commendable, as none of equall iudgement can yeelde him lesse prayse for hys excellent skyll, and skyllful excellency shewed foorth in the same, then they would to eyther *Theocritus* or *Virgill*, whom in mine opinion, if the coursenes of our speeche (I meane the course of custome which he woulde not infringe) had beene no more let vnto him, then theyr pure natiue tongues were vnto them, he would haue (if it might be) surpassed them." High praise, undoubtedly—the highest, for a critic who longs to see English poetry converted to quantitative measures "in imitation of the Greekes and Latines"—but Webbe's punning admission that "the coursenes of our speeche" or "the course of custome which he woulde not infringe" has prevented Spenser from surpassing his classical models introduces a rather serious qualification, especially since, earlier in the treatise, he identifies "the canckred enmitie of curious custome" as the single most pernicious influence on modern vernacular poets, the chief cause of England's persistent linguistic and poetic backwardness.[53] Moreover, as readers of *The Shepheardes Calender* know, far from being unwilling to "infringe" upon the "course of custome," according to E. K., Spenser's diction is the result of a *deliberately* "curious" poetic practice, his "choyce of old and vnwonted words" (27).

Sidney, the poem's dedicatee, expresses distaste for this choice in his *Apologie for Poetrie* (1595), granting that Spenser "hath much *Poetrie* in his Egloges, indeed worthie the reading," but insisting that he "dare not allow" the "framing of his style to an olde rusticke language."[54] It is difficult to understand how one might commend the pastoral conceit of Spenser's *Calender*— what Sidney calls its "*Poetrie*"—while disapproving of the rustic language that seems so central to that conceit, and the strain the *Calender* placed on its early modern readers is plain: in Sidney's treatise, as in Webbe's, admiration for the *Calender's* unmistakable genius wars with the perception that there is something flawed, even self-defeating, at work in the poem. Such ambivalent responses reproduce, almost uncannily, the tensions within the poem between the admiration expressed for Colin Clout and the irritation at his refusal to occupy a place commensurate with his talents: like Colin, Spenser is hailed by peers such as Sidney and Webbe as an exemplary genius even as he is reproached for what seems to be a posture of willful self-estrangement. Certainly Ben Jonson sounds rather Hobbinol-like when he warns readers of medieval poetry against "falling too much in love with antiquity" lest "they grow rough and barren in language only" and holds up Spenser as an example of one overcome with an unwise and immoderate affection for things remote from his experience. If antiquity—specifically, England's antiquity—is Spenser's Rosalind in this allegory of misplaced affection, his archaic diction is an instrument as fractured and self-indulgent as Colin's shattered pipe: "Spenser, in affecting the ancients," Jonson famously concludes, "writ no language."[55]

The judgments of Webbe, Sidney, and Jonson have shaped many later accounts of the poem, but it is possible that they exaggerate the strangeness and difficulty of Spenser's diction. The eighteenth-century critic Thomas Warton sounded an early note of skepticism: "The censure of Jonson, upon our author's style, is perhaps unreasonable. . . . The groundwork and substance of his style is the language of his age. This indeed is seasoned with various expressions, adopted from the elder poets; but . . . the affectation of Spenser in this point, is by no means so striking and visible, as Jonson has insinuated; nor is his phraseology so difficult and obsolete, as it is generally supposed to be."[56] Warton's argument has encouraged a few twentieth-century critics to reconsider the prevailing view of the language of *The Shepheardes Calender*, especially when it is placed alongside lesser-known works of the mid-sixteenth century. Certainly Spenser embraces an array of archaic and dialect terms to ornament his shepherds' speech, but so too, as Roscoe Parker points out, did most earlier writers of English pastoral, and Spenser's antiquated, rustic-sounding shepherds are not so different from those found in the eclogues of Barclay, Turbervile, and Barnabe Googe.[57] Veré Rubel adds that "it is interesting to note how many of the archaisms, poetic borrowings, and poetic constructions which distinguish the language of *The Shepheardes Calender* are to be found in *Tottel's Miscellany* as well."[58]

To argue, as W. L. Renwick does, that "[t]he solemn Introduction and Notes contributed by E. K. are evidence that the [linguistic] innovation was acutely felt and required explanation; further, that it claimed serious consideration; and again, that it was deliberate,"[59] may be to acquiesce too much to E. K.'s own commentary, which, as I have argued, is at least as invested in emphasizing the innovative strangeness of Spenser's language as it is in dispelling that strangeness.[60] Perhaps most intriguing in this regard is Megan Cook's observation that sixteenth-century editions of Chaucer were not glossed for "hard words" until *after* the publication of *The Shepheardes Calender*; until Thomas Speght's 1598 edition of Chaucer's poems, readers apparently were not expected to require assistance in decoding Chaucer's English or to experience that English as substantially different from their own.[61] Speght's claim that his edition has "restored [Chaucer] to his owne Antiquitie"[62] makes plain the double impulse behind his gloss—at once to facilitate the reader's encounter with poetry deemed too remote for easy comprehension and to guarantee that this remoteness is recognized and appreciated. It is a mode of annotation Speght might well have learned from E. K.

Such observations help to contextualize Spenser's language and encourage us to adopt a more skeptical view of E. K.'s claims on its behalf. They also allow us to conceive of Spenser's collaboration with E. K. as an attempt—bolstered by the mystery surrounding *Immeritô*'s identity and by the archaizing effect of the blackletter type in which the poem was printed[63]—to generate a kind of "alienation effect" for *The Shepheardes Calender*, to cultivate remoteness as a deliberate mode of relation to readers. Readers of *The Shepheardes Calender* have observed that Colin Clout's gestures of alienation and abandonment—his broken pipes, his exile to the North, his refusal to sing—are rarely permanent or wholehearted. Colin and his songs are, in fact, everywhere in the world of the *Calender*, if often at a remove, present only through the mediating influence of his fellow shepherds. The same might be said of Spenser's language, which, if it is "the straungest" of "many things which in him be straunge," is also the aspect of the poem most insistently present to its readers, thanks to the mediating influence of E. K.

This chapter began by noting that the pastoral tradition, especially Virgil's eclogues, posed difficulties for English authors and readers who wished to assert a greater affinity between their own language and culture and that of Rome. Because Virgilian pastoral acknowledges Britain only as an emblem of distance, deprivation, and barbarism, it frustrated, or at least complicated, the efforts of English translators and imitators to use pastoral as a vehicle for overcoming their geographic, temporal, and linguistic remoteness from classical Latinity. *The Shepheardes Calender* seems to have frustrated readers such as Webbe, Sidney, and Jonson—all equally, although differently, invested in the project of classicizing English poetry—for a similar reason, by both appealing to and resisting their desire for proximity to the classical world. The very aspects of the *Calender* that most clearly advertise its affiliation to the classical tradition—its genre and its scholarly apparatus—are also precisely the elements that most challenge that affiliation. E. K.'s epistle and notes habitually conflate foreignness with familiarity and estrangement with identification, insisting on such paradoxes as the necessary attributes of a truly English poetics; likewise Spenser's pastoral plot fashions itself around a figure whose perpetual departures and returns challenge any effort to fix the place of pastoral and so lay claim to it for England. To write (or read) vernacular poetry may mean estrangement from one's native tongue; to locate pastoral in Britain, "cut of[f] from the wide world," may mean leaving the community of shepherd-poets behind.

From 1580 on, of course, Spenser spent virtually his entire life in a state of literal proximity to and alienation from his native land and fellow English poets: as a functionary of Ireland's colonial administration, he watched from afar the dissolution of his hopes for a reform-minded Protestant court, a court that would nurture the kind of poetic community the language deserved. Ireland is thus a crucial figure for Spenser's ambivalent engagement with English vernacular poetry; it is the site of his own unwilling but productive displacement, the barren and rude prospect from which he, like Meliboeus or Ovid, must reenvision his native land. It is also, as Willy Maley and Andrew Hadfield have argued, the place where Spenser encountered a version of the vernacular, that spoken by members of the "Old English" colonial community, purified of modern corruptions by virtue of having been "preserved in the colonial margins rather than the cosmopolitan center."[64] Finally, Ireland is where Colin Clout reappears in Spenser's poetry, in a 1595 pastoral whose title, *Colin Clouts Come Home Againe,* invokes a "home" that turns out to be preserved in these same colonial margins.

This late work both intensifies and seeks to resolve the dynamics of displacement and estrangement that Spenser and E. K. negotiate in *The Shepheardes Calender.* It begins in what is for readers of the *Calender* a familiar vein, with Hobbinol hailing Colin's return from recent wanderings and begging him not to leave again: "*Colin* my liefe, my life, How great a losse / Had all the shepheards nation by the lacke?"[65] For the moment it appears that we are right back in the "June" eclogue and that the intervening years have been occupied with more unhappy departures from and fretful returns to the place of pastoral. The discourse of departure and return is given an unexpected twist, however, when Colin's "late voyage" (l. 34) abroad turns out to have taken him, of all places, to England: the shepherd's nation has been trans-planted, like Spenser himself, beyond the Irish pale.

The rest of the poem elaborates this ironic inversion of home and abroad, what Julia Reinhardt Lupton refers to as "the *unheimlich* contradictions and displacements implicit in the pastoral foundations of the Spenserian home."[66] When his fellow shepherds ask him to describe his exotic journey, ascribing their interest to a love of "forreine thing[s]" (l. 162), Colin obliges by describ-ing a country "farre away, / so farre that land our mother vs did leaue, / and nought but sea and heauen to vs appeare" (ll. 225–27). At first this England appears as an ideal home for poets, where "shepheards abroad . . . may safely lie" (l. 316), where "learned arts do florish in great honor, / And Poets wits are had in peerlesse price" (ll. 320–21), and where a gracious queen "enclin[es] her eare" to "take delight" in the "rude and roughly dight" music of Colin's pipe (ll. 360–63). As Colin enumerates the fortunate poets who enjoy this happy place, however, his descriptions betray a darker view: Harpalus is "woxen aged / In faithfull service" (ll. 380–81); Corydon is "meanly waged" (l. 382); "sad *Alcyon*" is "bent to mourne" (l. 384); Palin is "worthie of great praise" but consumed by "envie" (ll. 392–93); Alcon requires "matter of more skill" (l. 395); Palemon "himself may be rewed, / That sung so long vntill quite hoarse he grew" (ll. 398–99); Alabaster is "throughly taught" but "knowen yet to few" and not "knowne . . . as he ought" (ll. 400–402); Amyntas "quite is gone and lies full low" (l. 435); and the best of them all, Astrofell, "is dead and gone" (l. 449). By the time the litany ends, Colin's remark that "[a]ll these do florish in their sundry kind" (l. 452) can be read only as bitter irony, and when Thestylis asks, "Why didst thou euer leaue that happie place?" (l. 654), the answer seems self-evident: "[S]ooth to say, it is no sort of life, / For shepheard fit to lead in that same place" (ll. 688–89).

There is more at stake here than the usual pastoral satire of courtly life. Colin redefines the terms of his own apparent alienation so that exile becomes the nec-essary condition of poetic excellence and the paradoxical guarantee of a higher home. He and his fellow Irish swains may live on "barrein soyle / Where cold and care and penury do dwell" (ll. 656–57), but he anticipates a final reckoning at which the poets whose cunning has earned them proximity to power will suffer a worse fate: "Ne mongst true louers will they place inherit / But as exuls out of [Love's] court be thrust" (ll. 893–94). For Colin—and perhaps for Spenser—the very extremity of Irish colonial existence becomes an ideal, and bracingly mate-rial, figure for the displacement and alienation that have always characterized, indeed made possible, his peculiar inhabitation of the pastoral world.

Chapter 5

"Conquering Feet":
Tamburlaine and the Measure of English

The Plain Show of a Manifest Maim

Part 1 of *Tamburlaine the Great* (1587–88) forcefully inverts Spenser's vision of the English poet as exile, recasting him as a violent intruder. Christopher Marlowe, a recent arrival to the professional London theater, invited audiences to see in the audacious progress of his barbarian hero the image of his own poetic daring, claiming Tamburlaine's legendary conquest of the East as a vehicle for his campaign to enlarge the boundaries of English verse: "From jigging veins of rhyming mother-wits, / And such conceits as clownage keeps in pay, / We'll lead you to the stately tent of War," promises his prologue, "Where you shall hear the Scythian Tamburlaine / Threat'ning the world with high astounding terms / And scourging kingdoms with his conquering sword."[1] This announcement of a newly elevated voice and kingly measure for the English stage now seems as prophetic as any of Tamburlaine's boasts: "will" and "shall" befit the mighty Marlovian line as well as they do its Scythian champion. Londoners swarmed to see the outrageous and eloquent Tamburlaine make his bloody way across the vast imaginary terrain of Marlowe's play, and an inevitable host of lesser playwrights sought to capitalize on *Tamburlaine*'s success with their own spectacles of exotic savagery and their own blank verse tragedies.[2] Together with its sequel, *Tamburlaine* launched Marlowe's theatrical career and altered the course of English literary history, establishing blank verse as the keynote of vernacular heroics.

Marlowe dramatizes this conquest at the climax of part 1, when his ruthlessly ambitious hero mounts his imperial throne by stepping on the kneeling form of Bajazeth, "treading him," as the Turkish sultan's wife laments, "beneath [his] loathsome feet" (4.2.64). Critics promptly seized upon the punning analogy between Tamburlaine's martial feet and Marlowe's insistent iambs, and they have not let it go. In the sixteenth century the satirist Joseph Hall lampooned the "Turkish *Tamberlaine*," whose "huf-cap termes and thundring threats" echo "the stalking steps of his great personage"; in a less mocking vein, the twentieth-century scholar Alvin Kernan identifies "the steady, heavy beat of 'Marlowe's mighty line,' carrying authority, determination, and steady onward movement" as the most novel and distinctive feature of the poet's verse.[3] The spectacle of Bajazeth's humiliation also reminds us that, like Tamburlaine's military conquest, Marlowe's literary historical triumph is a drama of usurpation: the deposed Turk whom Tamburlaine makes his "footstool" has a double in the person of Henry Howard, Earl of Surrey, a sixteenth-century poet whose blank-verse translation of books 2 and 4 of Virgil's *Aeneid*, published several decades before *Tamburlaine*, is now regularly cast as a footnote to the arrival and ascent of Marlowe's mighty line.

But the analogy is not quite apt: strangely there is no particular arrogance—or "tamberlaine contempt,"[4] to borrow Gabriel Harvey's phrase—in Marlowe's identification of blank verse as a bold and self-authorized departure from established usage. For by the 1580s English poets and critics had largely concurred in writing off the unrhymed, accented line of Surrey's translation as an interesting but misbegotten experiment in vernacular prosody. Roger Ascham, for instance—one of the most vocal and eager proponents of unrhymed English verse in the mid-sixteenth century—treats Surrey's *Aeneid* with condescension: although he praises its author as the "first of all English men" to "haue . . . by good iudgement, auoyded the fault of Ryming," he dismisses the poem as a well-intentioned failure, saying that it does not "fullie hite perfite and trew versifying." Contrasted to Virgil's quantitative measures, he declares, Surrey's iambic feet are "feete without ioyntes, that is to say, not distinct by trew quantitie of sillables: And . . . soch feete, be but numme feete: and be, euen as vnfitte for a verse to turne and runne roundly withall, as feete of brasse or wood be vnweeldie to go well withall. And as a foote of wood, is a plaine shew of a manifest maime, euen so feete, in our English versifying, without quantitie and ioyntes, be sure signes, that the verse is either, borne deformed, vnnaturall and lame, and so verie vnseemlie to looke vpon, except to men that be gogle eyed them selues."[5] This damning assessment of blank verse was enough to obscure Surrey's achievement from view for decades to come: in *Palladis Tamia* (1598) Francis Meres praises Surrey as a love poet but repeats Ascham's criticism of his *Aeneid* verbatim,[6] while William Webbe, despite the fact that his *Discourse of English Poetry* (1586) works hard to revive the cause of metrical versification, classes the "olde Earl of Surrey" among those native poets whose praise, for all their modest talents, would make his "discourse much more tedious."[7] So total is the neglect of Surrey's poem that O. B. Hardison concludes that "there is no reason to doubt Milton's sincerity" when, in his prefatory note to *Paradise Lost*, he claimed his own epic poem to be "the first [example] in English" of heroic verse freed from the fetters of rhyme.[8]

Tamburlaine thus presents us with a peculiar literary historical phenomenon: the triumph of a formal choice that had proved an utter failure just decades earlier, when it appeared in a guise far more likely to appeal to the prejudices and preconceptions of its readers. Derek Attridge has written extensively on the question of why sixteenth-century English poets and critics found it so difficult to recognize, much less appreciate, the accentual patterns of their own verse; here, he suggests, in an especially direct and pervasive way, their formation in the classics estranged those writers from their mother tongue, whose native accents were muffled by antique precepts.[9] Confounded by the differences between classical "quantities" and English "accents," they were liable to conclude, as Paula Blank writes, "that English poetry had no meter, no 'true' numbers at all, and moreover that the English language itself was intrinsically unfit for true measure."[10] Even so, the tepid reception of Surrey's achievement by his contemporaries and successors remains "one of the curiosities of the history of English poetry."[11] For if we attend to the metaphorical terms of the debate over rhyme and quantitative measure in the sixteenth century, Surrey's *Aeneid* seems perfectly positioned to satisfy anxieties about the legitimacy of English as a literary language.

More than any other attribute of the language, the vernacular's supposed lack of measure was perceived as the tell-tale sign of England's barbarous, nonimperial past. Thus Ascham calls upon readers of *The Scholemaster* to "acknowledge and vnderstand rightfully our rude beggerly ryming" as the legacy of barbarian conquest, "brought first into Italie by *Gothes* and *Hunnes,* whan all good verses and all good learning . . . were destroyd by them: and after caryed into France and Germanie: and at last, receyued into England" (60ᵣ). Ascham's "at last" ruefully acknowledges England's perpetual belatedness: isolated on the periphery of ancient civilization, it is the last to hear even the unwelcome news of barbaric overthrow. But it also stakes out a place for England as the last standing outpost of that civilization, a lone preserve of once-widespread values and practices of eloquence, and in the efforts of his own generation of humanist scholars and pedagogues to overthrow barbaric rhyme and reinstate classical versification, Ascham sees signs that the trajectory of gothic decline might be reversed: "I rejoyce," he writes, "that euen poore England preuented *Italie,* first in spying out, than in seekyng to amend this fault in learning" (62ᵣ).

Were it not for his dismissive treatment of the blank-verse *Aeneid,* we might reasonably suppose that Ascham's joy had something to do with the Earl of Surrey: given the Virgilian ambitions that inspired the quest for vernacular metrics, the arrival of an English Aeneas who speaks in unrhymed iambic pentameter seems like an occasion for celebration—or at least for something more urgent than the general shrug that Surrey's poem receives. As Margaret Tudeau-Clayton observes, translating Virgil was a "high stakes" literary enterprise in sixteenth-century England, offering an occasion both for authorial self-promotion and "for the promotion of cultural forms, . . . national equivalents to the unifying model furnished for the Roman people" by Virgil himself, "the 'columen linguae latinae' ('the pillar of the Latin language')."[12] By anchoring blank verse in the great classical poem of the founding of civilization and the translation of empire, Surrey's *Aeneid* speaks directly to the twin desires for poetic measure and imperial stature.[13] Indeed rarely has a literary text been better positioned for success: Surrey's translation appears in print (in Richard Tottel's widely read "Miscellany" of 1557) just as the quest for an alternative to rhyme becomes the centerpiece of English humanist efforts to achieve parity with ancient Greece and Rome. To perpetuate rhyme "now, when men know the difference, and haue the examples, both of the best and the worst," Ascham famously declares, would be to embrace marginality and exclusion, to affirm one's own place outside the boundaries of civilization: "to follow rather the *Gothes* in rhyming than the *Greekes* in trew versifying were euen to eate ackornes with swine, when we may freely eate wheate bread emonges men" (60ᵣ). Ascham's metaphor echoes the opening lines of Virgil's *Georgics,* the great classical poem of civilization and culture, which hymns the dawn of human society as the moment when "earth . . . exchanged wild acorns for plump grains of wheat." The allusion invites English readers to imagine themselves as potential heirs to the empire envisioned in the *Georgics,* which hails Octavian as lord of "the great circling world," "god of the great sea," and master of "more than a fair share of heaven," while effacing—or at least downplaying—the labor and toil that are the poem's unceasing theme.[14] "I am sure," Ascham reassures his audience, "our English tong will receiue *carmen Iambicum* as naturallie, as either *Greke* or *Latin.*" If no English iambic verse has yet succeeded, he concludes, only "ignorance" is to blame (60ᵥ).

What Ascham calls "ignorance"—a culpable but passive defect of knowledge and education—may seem to us like a more active failure of recognition, but it is possible that Surrey's affiliation of his formal innovation with Virgil's great epic did English blank verse no favors. Ascham, for one, seems to feel that he has been subjected to a shoddy sleight-of-foot: where Virgil's dactylic hexameters obey the classical laws of quantity—which measure syllables according to duration in time—Surrey accommodates his iambic pentameter to the vernacular's own patterns of accentual stress. To a classicist's ear, the substitution of accent for quantity makes the English feet seem to stumble haltingly behind Virgil's own: blank verse exposes the language's native defects, making a "plaine shew of a manifest maime." English poets who tried, as Ascham urges them, to subject the vernacular to the principles of quantitative measure fared still worse: Surrey's blank verse may seem to have been "borne deformed," but according to Edmund Spenser, the imposition of classical quantities crippled even the strongest English feet. Subjected to the alien rule of duration in time, Spenser confesses in a 1580 letter to Gabriel Harvey that "the Accente" of his English hexameters "sometime gapeth, and as it were yawneth ilfauouredly, comming shorte of that it should, and sometime exceeding the measure of the Number, . . . seemeth like a lame Gosling, that draweth one legge after hir . . . [or] like a lame Dogge that holds vp one legge."[15] Ascham may present the quest for English measure as a wholly natural turn from humiliation, deprivation, and hardship to abundance and ease—trading in wild acorns for plump grains of wheat, the company of pigs for the company of men—but Spenser's experience suggests that escaping the barnyard was not so simple: quantitative versification entailed hardships, deprivations, and humiliations of its own. Harvey, who initially responded with encouragement to Spenser's efforts at quantitative verse, wrote back urging him to leave off. Spenser's insistence that "rough words must be subdued with Vse," so that English poets "might . . . as else the Greekes, haue the kingdome of our owne Language," arouses his particular indignation: what Spenser dubs a "kingdome of . . . language" Harvey regards as closer to a military occupation. Objecting to his friend's heavy-handed manipulation of a familiar English noun, he warns, "[Y]ou shall never have my subscription or consent to make your *Carpēnter* our *Carpênter* an inche longer or bigger than God and his Englishe people have made him." "Is there no other pollicie to pull downe Ryming and set vppe Versifying," he demands, "but you must needes . . . forcibly vsurpe and tyrannize vppon a quiet companie of wordes?"[16]

As Richard Helgerson has shown, the debate between Spenser and Harvey over the future of vernacular versification turns not on the question of whether English accents are compatible with classical numbers—Harvey hears the same strain and stress in Spenser's hexameters that Spenser does—but on the question of how to interpret that mismatch metaphorically. The contest between rhyme and quantitative meter in late sixteenth-century vernacular criticism serves as a surrogate for arguments about the kind of rule fit for England, about the ideal balance between centralized authority and the rule of custom.[17] But it also precipitates anxieties about the terms of Britain's relationship with the empires of antiquity. Poems written in English approximations of quantitative meter might be claimed as emblems of cultural parity, poetic fulfillment of the longing—encoded in the myth of Brutus—for a genealogical bond with antiquity. But they were also vulnerable to charges of ongoing cultural subjection, extensions of an ancient dependency. Was the application of classical prosody to English akin to the domestication of a savage and bestial herd, or was it an instance of tyrannical violence inflicted on innocent humanity?[18]

That question, which accounts for the urgency with which English humanists treated the arcana of classical prosody, points the way toward a deeper understanding of Marlowe's otherwise astonishing success with *Tamburlaine*. For the two rival narratives of the debate about metrical versification—civilizing order versus intolerable tyranny—coexist within sixteenth-century accounts of the career of the fourteenth-century Scythian warlord known variously as Timur Khan, Timur Cutlu, and Timur-i-Lenk. Timur was a popular subject for European and English moralists, who offered his life both as an exemplary instance of spectacular self-improvement—the rude shepherd becomes master of an empire—and as a cautionary tale about violent excess and unbridled ambition—the savage conqueror who is himself cut down by death, leaving his hard-won throne prey to a series of squabbling successors. As most of these narratives also note, the historical Timur walked with a limp: hence the title *Tamburlaine*—Timur-i-Lenk, or Timur the Lame. Calling upon Tamburlaine as the champion of his blank verse, Christopher Marlowe thus foregrounds the very anxieties—barbarity and cultural degeneracy, tyranny and lameness—that plagued figures such as Ascham, Spenser, and Harvey in their efforts to rehabilitate English quantitative measure.

By doing so he eludes the unfortunate comparisons that condemned Surrey's *Aeneid* to the margins of literary history. When Ascham read Surrey's *Aeneid*, its hero's imperial progress seems to have contrasted unfavorably with the effortful pacing of the poet's own feet; Tamburlaine, by contrast, was already "the plaine shewe of a manifest maime": English poetry could only look more refined, more humane by comparison. Mary Floyd-Wilson calls Marlowe's adoption of Tamburlaine "a clever joke," the reverse of type-casting,"[19] but it is possible that Tamburlaine's Scythian rudeness made him a better advocate for a novel-seeming poetic form than the Trojan Aeneas. After all, as Attridge makes plain, what sixteenth-century poetic theorists needed (and often failed) to reckon with were the fundamental differences between the classical tongues and English, differences that Timur, with his strangeness and his striving, cast in a fresh light. Not everyone welcomed the sound of *Tamburlaine*'s voice, to be sure, but even the criticisms leveled at Marlowe's verse by rivals such as Joseph Hall testify to its imperious effect, its "big-sounding sentences, and words of state."[20] Indeed critics such as Hall seem to take their cues from Marlowe himself, who crafts an overtly self-serving analogy between his own poetic ambitions and Tamburlaine's triumphs: Marlowe's "base-born hero," observes David Riggs, "is an extemporaneous oral poet whose verses . . . are his passport to wealth and dominion," a "fable [that] transforms the cycle of poverty, poetry, and social mobility that had cast Marlowe on the margins of Elizabethan society into an unexampled success story."[21]

In a more complicated fashion, I suggest, the Scythian Timur also serves the needs of sixteenth-century English rhetorical and poetic theorists, not as "an unexampled success story" but as a figure for the contradictory values ascribed to prosodic form as an index of cultural achievement. Ascham, for instance, presents quantitative measure as the antithesis of native brutality, a necessary submission to civilizing order, but he also covets classical meter as an emblem of England's capacity to resist invasion and conquest. As the exchanges between Spenser and Harvey demonstrate, efforts to adapt quantitative measures into English tend to get caught between the twin perils of barbaric marginality and tyrannical coercion: either way subjection lies. By yoking the future of the unrhymed iambic line to the rise of a notoriously violent barbarian, confounding eloquent measure with vulgar excess and outlandish extremity, Marlowe points an unlikely way out of the doomed contest between vernacular and classical prosody, suggesting that English poetry stake its legitimacy precisely on its disregard for the decorums of more civilized tongues.

He is not the only one to do so: at least two of Marlowe's contemporaries found in the legend of the lawless Timur Khan a possible solution to the question of vernacular prosody. For Marlowe, Tamburlaine serves as the avatar of English poetry freed from the petty constraints of rhyme, but for the rhetorician George Puttenham, a figure dubbed Temir Cutzclewe—Timur Cutlu, or Timur the Lucky—models a form of poetic measure that excels the classical quantities in its rigor. Meanwhile for the poet and critic Samuel Daniel, a staunch proponent of vulgar rhyme, Tamburlaine is the figure for a literary tradition that exceeds the narrow worldview of antiquity and an eloquence that is its own law. Marlowe, Puttenham, and Daniel take very different stances when it comes to defining what English measure ought to look and sound like, but they each recognize in the debate over versification an opportunity to reexamine the most basic terms of rhetorical and poetic judgment, exposing the violence within eloquence, the transgressions on which the rules of restraint depend, and the willfulness with which lines of verse and the boundaries of linguistic community are drawn.

Such internal contradictions expose the inadequacy of Ascham's binary of Greeks and Goths, humans and beasts: both Englishness and eloquence are found to inhabit a terrain where brutality is the handmaid of *humanitas*, and Scythians are the progenitors of civilization. Noticing Tamburlaine's odd prominence within the late sixteenth- and early seventeenth-century history of prosody means noticing as well that the paradoxes he comes to embody— violence married to sweetness, measure to excess, barbarity to civility, and license to restraint—are embedded in the foundation of vernacular literary theory and practice. But foundation may be the wrong term altogether, for the strikingly diverse solutions offered by Marlowe, Puttenham, and Daniel (not to mention Ascham, Spenser, and Harvey) to the nagging problem of measure suggest how very unstable and contested that theory and practice remained. More forcefully than even Euphues or Colin Clout, the Scythian Timur resists domestication as a figure of Orphic communion—which seems to have made him the ideal figure for English poetry.

Temir Cutzclewe's Arte of Poesie

"[W]hat is unrhythmical is unlimited," Aristotle writes of metrical prose and verse in book 3 of the *Art of Rhetoric*, "and there should be a limit, . . . for the unlimited is unpleasant and unknowable."[22] In the opening lines of book 2 of his 1589 *Arte of English Poesie*, Puttenham echoes Aristotle, observing that "all things stand by proportion, and that without it nothing could stand to be good or beautiful"(53). What was at stake, then, in the seemingly picayune debate over rhyme, quantities, and other forms of measure was the viability both of English eloquence and of English theories of English eloquence: without fixed formal standards, English poetry risked condemnation as unpleasant and unknowable, artless in every sense of the word. Marlowe's Tamburlaine understands the problem precisely; his quest for global dominion is propelled by his desire to know the outermost limits of his power: "Since they measure our deserts so mean . . . / They shall be kept our forcèd followers / Till with their eyes they view us emperors," he informs an early set of captives (*One* 1.2.63, 66–67), and on the point of death he will beg for a map to "see how much / Is left for me to conquer all the world" (*Two* 5.3.123–24). More pointedly than any other literary critical issue, prosody forced vernacular authors to recognize the interdependence of theory and practice: the question of whether or not the vernacular was eloquent could not, finally, be distinguished from the question of whether and how its eloquence could be measured.

Marlowe's Tamburlaine dies before he reaches that outermost bound, leaving a pair of inept sons "to finish all [his] wants" (*Two* 5.3.125), but in book 2 of Puttenham's *Arte,* the Scythian Timur helps to rescue the author from his own unbounded—perhaps unhinged—attempt to measure English verse. Puttenham dedicates his second book, "Of Proportion Poeticall," to fulfilling the bold pronouncement he makes in the *Arte's* opening pages, which claim that the vernacular's lack of quantitative feet is not a defect but a sign of superabundance. Even if English poetry does not obey the strict laws of classical versification, "the nature of our language and wordes not permitting it," he declares, it possesses "in stead thereof twentie other curious points in that skill more then they euer had, by reason of our rime and tunable concords or simphonie, which they neuer obserued" (4). Puttenham is assisted in making good on his boast because of his willingness to play fast and loose with the etymologies of terms such as *rithmos, arithmos* and rhyme, "arithmeticall" and *ars metrica*:[23] as the first ten chapters of book 2 demonstrate, a motivated rhetorician can invent meaningful ratios for every possible dimension of a poem, from the arrangement of accents within a line of verse to the number of syllables in each line, the number of lines in a stanza, the ratio of internal rhyme to end-rhyme, the distances between end-rhymes, and the degree of latitude to be granted poets in orthographical and accentual variation.

And yet for all its pretensions to mathematical precision, Puttenhamian proportion (like Puttenhamian ornament) is a contingent, not an absolute value: a function not simply of a poem's internal workings—of the length of a line relative to its fellows or to the length of the poem as a whole—but also of its relation to an unpredictable outside world. As Lawrence Manley has written, this paradox of rigidity and flexibility defines all literary—indeed, all human—conventions, which "behave as both timeless forms of objective order and temporal expressions of changing values."[24] Book 2 encounters this paradox in terms of place as well as time: Puttenham aims to fix proportion and measure on English terms, but he retains a sense of skepticism about any overly rigid boundary. "[S]hort distaunces [between end-rhymes] and short measures pleas[e] onely the popular eare," Puttenham declares at one point: "we banish them vtterly" (69). Nonetheless, he adds, it "can be obiected against this wide distance . . . that the eare by loosing his concord is not satisfied," and "therefore the Poet must know to whose eare he maketh his rime, and accommodate himselfe thereto, and not giue such musicke to the rude and barbarous, as he would to the learned and delicate eare" (71–72). This willingness to accommodate oneself, to be obedient to both the laws of proportion and the tastes of one's audience, is the paradoxical precondition of poetic supremacy. The "rhymer that will be tied to no rules at all, but range as he list, may easily utter what he will," Puttenham allows (62), but the true poet thrives on limitation: what makes verse proportionate is not the absence or presence of rhyme or quantitative feet but responsiveness to the demands and desires of a locally specific set of listeners.

But this locally specific audience is not easily defined or limited: indeed Puttenham's *Arte of English Poesie* establishes a conspicuously broad range of reference for courtly English poets, a geography of eloquence extending well past Ascham's world of Greeks and Goths. According to Puttenham, in fact, rhyme was not the compensatory innovation of barbarous, late-antique poets unable to master quantitative verse but rather an ancient poetic device literally beyond the ken of Homer and Virgil. Citing the testimony of sixteenth-century England's "marchants and trauellers, [whose] late nauigations haue surueyed the whole world, and discouered large countries and strange peoples wild and sauage," he "affirm[s] that the American, the Perusine, and the very Canniball do sing and also say their highest and holiest matters in certaine riming versicles, and not in prose." The correspondence between New World verses and English poetry "proues also that our maner of vulgar Poesie is *more ancient* than the artificiall of the Greeks and Latines, ours coming by instinct of nature, which was before Art or obseruation, and vsed with the sauage and vnciuill, who were before all science and ciuilitie." The values enshrined in classical poetic theory are, Puttenham implies, the product of an overly narrow frame of cultural reference. The global perspective afforded by England's new commercial and colonial ventures allows him to upend the ancient hierarchy of poetic virtues, as the wildness, savagery, and strangeness of rhyme—the very qualities that alienate it from the classical models of poetic excellence—become points of proud commonality with all other tongues. "[I]t appeareth that our vulgar running Poesie was common to all the nations of the world besides, whom the Latines and greekes in speciall called barbarous," he concludes. Rhyme is not only "the first and most ancient poesie"; it is also "the most vniuersall" (7).[25]

This investment in poetry as an art whose values are at once local and universal produces a noticeably wayward treatise on measure. "I could not forbeare to adde this forraine example," Puttenham apologizes after a digression into the uniforms worn by members of the Chinese court ([89]).[26] "One other pretie conceit we will impart vnto you and then trouble you with no more," begins a section on anagrams devised from the titles of various foreign monarchs ([90]). "Thus farre . . . we will aduenture and not beyond," he promises in a section exploring possible adaptation of classical feet into English—an approach he earlier dismissed as far-fetched (86); then, a bit further on, "I intend not to proceed any further in this curiositie" (91); and again, a number of pages later,[27] still on the same subject, announcing that it "nothing at all furthers the pleasant melody of our English meeter," "I leaue to speake any more of them" (107). Indeed the whole of book 2, with its haphazard juxtaposition of diagrams, digressions, anecdotes, and pseudo-learned disquisitions on the habits of exotic cultures, seems to constitute a metadiscourse on the difficulty of assessing and maintaining the proportions of its own argument.

But book 2's willingness to entertain diverse and even contradictory conceptions of measure also transforms the virtue of measure from an attribute of language to an attribute of poets. Thus, at the close of the tenth chapter of book 2, Puttenham condenses all of his rules and precepts into a single exercise, which discerns whether or not a poet is "of a plentiful discourse," "copious in his language," and "his crafts maister" by subjecting him to a stringently limited and wholly arbitrary system of measure:

Make me . . . so many strokes or lines with your pen as ye would haue your song containe verses: and let euery line beare his seuerall length, euen as ye would haue your verse of measure. . . . Then where you will haue your time or concord to fall, marke it with a compass stroke or semicircle passing ouer those lines, be they farre or neare in distance. . . . [Finally,] bycause ye shall not thinke the maker hath

premeditated beforehand any such fashioned ditty, do ye your selfe
make one verse whether it be of perfect or imperfect sense, and giue
it him for a theame to make all the rest vpon: if ye shall perceiue the
maker do keepe the measures and rime as ye haue appointed him,
and besides do make his dittie sensible and ensuant to the first verse
in good reason, then may ye say he is his crafts maister. (74)

In this test poetic mastery is recognized through obedience to conditions
that are at once contingent and inflexible, subject to change but nonetheless
binding at any given moment. The extraordinary influence and power
Puttenham bestows on his poet in book 1—his ability to "mollify . . . hard
and stonie hearts by his sweete and eloquent perswasion," to bring "rude and
sauage people to a more ciuill and orderly life," to "redresse and edifie the cruell
and sturdie courage of man" (4)—is the consequence of his own willingness
to "keep the measures and rime as ye haue appointed him," "follow[ing] the
rule of . . . restraint."

Puttenham's exercise shifts the burden of measure off the English language
and onto English poets, but it also cannily redefines measure so as to put it
within reach of the vernacular. The measure set by "you" is not a fixed pattern
of long and short syllables but an actual line drawn on the page: a line might
be a meter, or a foot, in length, but it need not contain any metrical feet. In
the following chapter Puttenham sets aside the entire question of how a poem
ought to sound, proposing instead that English poets try to achieve what he
calls "proportion in figure"—poems set "in forme of a *Lozange* or square, or
such other figure." He claims to have learned the technique from "a certaine
gentleman, who had long trauailed the Orientall parts of the world, and seene
the courts of the great Princes of China and Tartarie": chief among them the
court of the "great Emperor in Tartary whom they call *Can*," and who "for his
good fortune in the wars & many notable conquests he had made, was sur-
named *Temir Cutzclewe*" (77). This Temir's oriental pattern-poem, he argues,
both epitomizes and transcends the virtue of classical metrical proportion:
even more than the strict laws of quantitative measure, "the restraint of the
figure" fixes a limit "from which ye may not digresse." Because "the maker is
restrained to keep him within [the shape's] bounds," Temir's pattern-poem
"sheweth not onely more art, but serueth also much better for briefenesse and
subtilitie of deuice" than either English accentual rhymes or classical meters.

Why Temir Cutzclewe, famed for his fortune in war and his notable conquests? In part Puttenham is once again drawn to a position outside the arena

in which English faces off against the classical tongues. Proportion in figure is, he emphasizes, "not . . . vsed by any of the Greeke or Latine Poets" nor found "in any vulgar writer." As A. L. Korn points out, this insistence on the alien origin of "proportion in figure" is either an uncharacteristic error or a patent falsehood: Greek, Latin, continental, and even English poets had experimented amply with shape- or pattern-poems well before the late sixteenth century. It is, Korn notes,

> a curiositie of Puttenham's discourse that this otherwise erudite author gives the impression of having known almost nothing at all of the earlier pattern-poems composed by his numerous European predecessors. Puttenham's role as the naïve discoverer of an Oriental type of pattern-poetry, a literary genre he believed to be alien to the European tradition, has therefore a certain historic interest. In *The Arte of English Poesie* we find perhaps for the first time an English critic drawing upon Eastern materials, or what he conceives to be such, in the routine practice of his profession.[28]

Or maybe not so naive: after all, the far-fetched pedigree of his shape-poems constitutes much of their appeal for Puttenham, and perhaps for his readers as well. The English critic had no need of yet one more classical or continental form for the vernacular poet to emulate, but to claim the shape-poem as an exotic import from the Far East invokes a much more appealing cultural narrative: not the Englishman as laggard but the Englishman as adventurer, scouring the globe in search of foreign treasures. And indeed Puttenham's admiration for the pattern-poem's obvious formal restraint is coupled with fascination with its conspicuous material extravagance. Typically "engraven in gold, silver or ivory, and sometimes with letters of amethyst, ruby, emerald, or topaz curiously cemented and pieced together," the Tartarian or Chinese shape-poem becomes a sign of fabulous wealth and power. For Puttenham, moreover, the visuality of the pattern-poem is of a piece with its supposed exoticism: both elements make the pattern-poem a useful addition to a debate stuck on the aural incompatibilities of English accents and classical quantities.[29] Read aloud, Temir's pattern-poems would not register as poetry at all: the rhymes fall at the ends of unevenly matched lines, and accentual stresses are distributed at random. Puttenham cautions that "[a]t the beginning they wil seeme nothing pleasant to an English eare" (76), but his intent may be to bypass the troublesome English ear altogether.

By choosing Temir Cutzclewe as the patron and master of this most excellent form of proportion, Puttenham also underlines the central claim of his treatise on measure: namely that proportion is in the eye of the beholder. Like cannibal rhyme, the "great Emperor in Tartary" and his poems may be barbarous from the perspective of Homer or Virgil, but that judgment is a mark of antiquity's own provinciality, contrasted implicitly and unfavorably to the more expansive awareness of the sixteenth-century English reader: Temir is "known" to the reader both by virtue of his vast empire and thanks to Puttenham's own cosmopolitan adventures. The poems Puttenham offers as examples of Temir's art testify vividly to the splendors of global conquest but also to the tyrannical excesses by which it proceeds. The first, composed by Temir's lover, was set as a brooch "in letters of rubies and diamonds" and describes Temir's "sharp / Trenching blade of bright steel . . . cleaving hard down unto the eyes / the raw skulls of his enemies." The reply, written by Temir and fashioned "with letters of emeralds and amethysts artificially cut and intermingled," heralds "Five / Sore battles / Manfully fought / In bloody field," whereby Temir has "forced . . . many a king his crown to vail, / Conquering large countries and land" (77).

As a figure for Puttenham's own rhetorical project, Temir Cutzclewe embodies the simultaneity of ambition and insecurity within sixteenth-century vernacular poetic theory. He offers Puttenham a way out of the prolonged, perhaps irresolvable, contest between rhyme and classical quantities, but his poems present a conspicuously brutal model of poetic self-assertion. The analogy is not merely metaphorical: the violent deeds celebrated within the poems have a formal analog in the typographical devices used to achieve the desired shape. The outer edges of each poem may manifest the virtues of restraint, but the field within is marked by forcings and cleavings within words, as each line is stretched or compressed to fit the boundaries of the imposed shape. In chapter 8 of book 2, Puttenham sternly reprimands the "licentious maker" who twists a word's natural spelling of pronunciation "to serue his cadence" (67), but in these poems he grants the Scythian Temir license not simply to alter the spelling of words but to sever them into fragments and force them together, leaving gaping holes in some lines and scant room in others, syllables as "artificially cut and entermingled" (78) as the gemstones with which they are set.

Those internal gaps and forcings work to Puttenham's advantage, however, insofar as they provide a foil for the English pattern-poems that follow—two obelisk-shaped verses, two pillars, and two "roundels," composed by Puttenham and dedicated to Elizabeth I. Contrasted with Temir's bloody and

& twentie meetres,& the longeſt furniſheth the middle angle , the
reſt paſſe vpward and downward , ſtill abating their lengthes by
one or two ſillables till they come to the point : the Fuzie is of the
ſame nature but that he is ſharper and ſlenderer. I will giue you an
example or two of thoſe which my Italian friend beſtowed vpon
me,which as neare as I could I tranſlated into the ſame figure ob-
ſeruing the phraſe of the Orientall ſpeach word for word.

 A great Emperor in Tartary whõ they cal *Can*,for his good fortune in the wars & many notable conqueſts he had made, was ſur-
named *Temir Cutzclewe*, this mã loued the Lady *Kermeſine*,who
preſented him returning frõ the cõqueſt of *Coraſoon*(a great kingdom adioyning)with this *Lozange* made in letters of rubies & dia-
mants entermingled thus

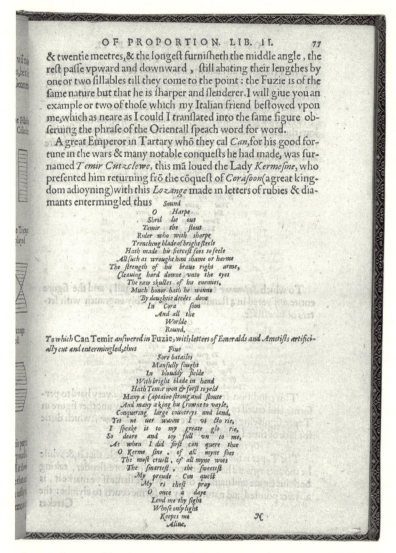

Sound
O   Harpe
Shril   lie   out
Temir   the   ſtout
Rider   who with ſharpe
Trenching blade of bright ſteele
Hath made his fierceſt foes to feele
All ſuch as wrought him ſhame or harme
The ſtrength of   his braue right   arme,
Cleauing hard downe vnto the eyes
The raw ſkulles of his enemies,
Much honor hath he wonne
By doughtie deedes done
In   Cora   ſoon
And all the
Worlde
Round,

To which Can Temir *anſwered in* Fuzie, *with letters of Emeralds and Ametiſts artificially cut and entermingled,thus*

Fiue
Sore batailes
Manfully fought
In   bloudely   fielde
With bright blade in hand
Hath Temir won & forſt to yeld
Many a Captaine ſtrong and ſtoute
And many a king his crowne to vayle,
Conquering large countreys and land,
Yet ne uer wonne I vi Eto rie,
I ſpeake it to my greate glo rie,
So deare and ioy full vn to me,
As when I did firſt con quere thee
O Kerme ſine , of all myne foes
The moſt cruell , of all myne woes
The ſmarteſt , the ſweeteſt
My proude Con queſt
My ri cheſt pray
O once a daye
Lend me thy ſight
Whoſe only light
Keepes me
Aline,

N

spangled verses, Puttenham's poems adopt a more measured tone and less ostentatious visual effects. This formal conservatism mirrors a shift in thematic
content: unlike the bloodthirsty, land-hungry Temir Cutzclewe, the English
queen is celebrated as a monarch wise enough to be content with the limits of
her domain. Her tireless quest "to mount on high," mimicked by the obelisk-
poem's upward climb, aims at a heavenly reward: hers is "an higher / Crown
and empire / Much greater, / And richer, / And better" than any merely
earthly conquest (79). The Temir Cutzclewe of the first poem may have won
"honor . . . all the / World / Round" (77), but Elizabeth's honor is "assured /
In the / Azured / Sky" (79): at its pinnacle the English pattern-poem reverts
to assonance, to the unostentatious pleasures of the ear. In fact the two "roundels" are not even round—whatever hint they contain of a desire for global
mastery is sublimated into praise for Elizabeth's chaste self-containment and
her preservation of "the dominion great and large / Which God hath given to
her charge": England's own "most spacious bound" (83).

This decorous sublimation contrasts, in the following chapter, with the
too-obvious ambition of Elizabeth's rival Philip of Spain, who adopts as his
emblem the copper figure of "a king sitting on horsebacke vpon a *monde* or
world, the horse prauncing forward with his forelegges as if he would leape of,
with this inscription, *Non sufficit orbis*, meaning, as it is to be conceaued, that
one whole world could not content him" (118). The motto's boast has come
to naught, Puttenham observes, since "[t]his immeasurable ambition of the
Spaniards" was, by "her Maiestie [and] by God's prouidence, . . . prouidently
stayed and retranched," to the gratification of "all the Princes and common
wealthes in Christendome, who haue found themselues long annoyed with his
excessiue greatnesse." Within the roundels Puttenham fashions for his queen,
greatness is the antidote to excess and measure the key to perfection. Puttenham's pattern-poems present English insularity—its lack of vast territories and
dazzling sources of wealth—as the product of a sophisticated aesthetic and political sensibility: like the maker of the pattern-poem, who displays his genius
by severely restricting its expression, Elizabeth's imperial might is best manifested by the modest proportions of her empire. Elizabeth is the protagonist of
the *Arte of English Poesie*, then, precisely because she is not the ruler of a vast
empire; rather in her power resides her talent for keeping measure in all things.

Is equally both farre and neare.
So doth none other figure fare.
Where natures chattels closed are:
And beyond his wide compasse,
There is no body nor no place,
Nor any wit that comprehends,
Where it begins, or where it ends:
And therefore all men doe agree,
That it purports eternitie.
God aboue the heauens so hie
Is this Roundell, in world the skie,
Vpon earth shoe, who beares the bell
Of maydes and Queenes, is this Roundell:
All and whole and euer alone,
Single, sans peere simple, and one.

A speciall and particular resemblance of her Maiestie
to the Roundell.

Irst her authoritie regall
Is the circle compassing all:
The dominion great and large
Which God hath geuen to her charge:
Within which most spatious bound
She enuirons her people round,
Retaining them by oth and liegeance.
Within the pale of true obeysance:
Holding imparked as it were,
Her people like to heards of deere.
Sitting among them in the middes
Where shoe allowes and bannes and bids
In what fashion shee list and when,
The seruices of all her men.
Out of her breast as from an eye,
Issue the rayes incessantly
Of her iustice, bountie and might
Spreading abroad their beames so bright,
And reflect not, till they attaine

The

Figure 2. "A special and particular resemblance of her Maiestie to the Roundell," in George Puttenham, *The Arte of English Poesie* (1589). Image courtesy of the Beinecke Library, Yale University.

The fardest part of her domaine.
And makes eche subiect clearely see,
What he is bounden for to be
To God his Prince and common wealth,
His neighbour, kinred and to himselfe.
The same centre and middle pricke,
Whereto our deedes are drest so thicke,
From all the parts and outmost side
Of her Monarchie large and wide,
Also fro whence reflect these rayes,
Twentie hundred maner of wayes
Where her will is them to conuey
Within the circle of her suruey.
So is the Queene of Briton ground,
Beame, circle, center of all my round.

Of the square or quadrangle equilater.

The square is of all other accompted the figure of most sollidi-
tie and stedfastnesse, and for his owne stay and firmitie requireth
none other base then himselfe, and therefore as the roundell or
Spheare is appropriat to the heauens, the Spire to the element of
the fire: the Triangle to the ayre, and the Lozange to the water:
so is the square for his inconcussable steadinesse likened to the
earth, which perchaunce might be the reason that the Prince of
Philosophers in his first booke of the *Ethicks*, termeth a constant
minded man, euen egal and direct on all sides, and not easily ouer-
throwne by euery litle aduersitie, *hominem quadratū*, a square man.
Into this figure may ye reduce your ditties by vsing no moe verses
then your verse is of sillables, which will make him fall out
square, if ye go aboue it wil grow into the figure *Trapezion*, which
is some portion longer then square. I neede not giue you any example, bycause in good arte all your ditties, Odes & Epigrammes
should keepe & not exceede the nomber of twelue verses, and the
longest verse to be of twelue sillables & not aboue, but vnder that
number as much as ye will.

The figure Ouall.

This figure taketh his name of an egge, and also as it is thought

Marlowe's Violent Measures

Of course vast empires, whether poetic or real, have an undeniable appeal, and despite Puttenham's stated commitment to the virtues of modesty and measure, his discussion of proportion is repeatedly pulled off course by his fascination with disproportion, excess, prodigality, extremity, and even loss of control. In this he resembles Marlowe: both *Tamburlaine the Great* and Puttenham's *Arte* invite comparisons between the state of English verse and the state of the English polity. That the playwright and the rhetorician should independently and virtually simultaneously turn to Timur, reimagining the fourteenth-century Scythian warlord as a late sixteenth-century English poet-conqueror, is more than an interesting coincidence. It accentuates the proximity of politics and prosody in the early modern English imagination, and the interplay of boundaries and transgression on which both national and poetic identities depended. When Puttenham, in the opening section of his *Arte*, names Elizabeth as England's "most excellent poet" (95), he is not only deploying flattery; he is also suggesting that the contours of English verse correspond to the contours of English empire. Book 2 complicates this equation, however, with its far-flung quest for poetic models: the task of defining the vernacular's limits gives way to the pursuit of extravagant curiosities.

As Emily Bartels, Richmond Barbour, Stephen Greenblatt, John Gillies, and others have argued, *Tamburlaine the Great* speaks to a similarly complex sense of English identity, as Marlowe's expansive approach to vernacular drama captured the enthusiasms and ideals of an increasingly mobile and outward-looking society. Tamburlaine, especially, with his habit of cataloging his conquests in rich detail, has been claimed as a figure for the "emergence of imperialist ideologies and propaganda,"[30] for "England's desire to encompass and enjoy the world,"[31] and for "the acquisitive energies of English merchants, entrepreneurs, and adventurers."[32] As it happens, Marlowe scholars are indebted to Puttenham's *Arte* for this reading of the Marlovian aesthetic: Puttenham's Englishing of *hyperbole* as "the overreacher" in book 3's catalog of tropes and figures supplied Harry Levin with both a title and a guiding conceit for his seminal study of Marlowe's dramatic career. Puttenham's epithet, Levin argues, "could not have been more happily inspired to throw its illumination upon Marlowe—upon his style, which is so emphatically himself, and on his protagonists, overreachers all." It is not simply that Marlowe's protagonists are prone to hyperbolic utterances; rather, for Levin and his successors, it is

Puttenham's notion of *hyperbole* as a figure that flirts with infinity, threatening to pass "beyond all measure" (276), as Puttenham cautions his readers, that so perfectly captures both the material and the rhetorical excesses of the Marlovian hero. And it is the empire-hungry hero of *Tamburlaine* who, with his imperial conquests and soaring rhetoric, provides the "barbaric prototype" for a newly extravagant and frankly imperial vernacular poetics.[33]

There is, however, an implicit irony to Levin's conception of Tamburlaine as the paradigmatic Marlovian "overreacher": the Scythian's "conquering feet" (*One* 3.3.230), as Marlowe punningly calls them, do not merely trample down his foes and march across vast expanses of territory; they also regulate and sustain the precisely measured and neatly contained blank verse that the play's prologue identifies as its foremost achievement. Whatever one might say about its hero, *Tamburlaine* does not pass beyond all measure so much as it *defines* English measure. Thus although *Tamburlaine* has been read as the expression of explicitly far-fetched ambitions, "the Renaissance wish-dream of global empire,"[34] it also makes a compelling case for the pleasure and discipline of confinement. The power of "Marlowe's dramatic poetry," writes Russ McDonald, "proceeds from his unique combination of the transgressive and the conventional": "The 'mighty line' . . . is marked by irrepressible energy, thrilling sonorities, and dazzling verbal pictures, but it is still a *line*, an ordering system, an invariable and comforting rhythmic standard that organizes words and ideas."[35] Levin acknowledges this tension, noting that "[m]ore than a third" of the exotic place names that litter Tamburlaine's speech and signal his imperial ambitions "gain peculiar stress by coming at the end of a line," so that the very geographic sweep of the plot helps to cement the impression of metrical containment.

It is tempting, therefore, to read Marlowe's play as reconciling the rivalrous demands that eloquence has imposed on its practitioners from the beginning: to confine and regulate wayward impulses, while satisfying the longing for estrangement. But what McDonald identifies as *Tamburlaine's* distinctive contribution to the history of English eloquence—its novel juxtaposition of high astounding terms and distant locales with rhythmic regularity and metrical restraint—seems to have been lost on Marlowe's earliest auditors, who are as often critical of the immoderation of Marlowe's verse as they are outraged by his protagonists' rhetorical and moral trespasses. Absent the audible boundary inscribed by end-rhyme, the measure of Marlowe's line proved disconcertingly elusive to the English ear: Thomas Nashe heard in Marlowe's verse both ill-disguised insufficiency—"the swelling bombast of a bragging blanke verse"—and blatant excess—the "ingrafted ouerflow" and "spacious volubility of a drumming decasillabon"; while Joseph Hall dismissed Marlowe's "pure Iambick verse" as a far-fetched concoction "patch[ed] . . . up" with "termes Italianate."[36] What Harvey called Marlowe's "tamberlaine contempt" was not countered but exemplified by his formal innovation: the "English blancke verse" of "that Atheist Tamburlan" might be rich and sonorous, wrote Robert Greene in 1588, "euerie word filling the mouth like the faburden of Bo-Bell," but it is "intolerable poetrie."[37] Even Ben Jonson, admiring heir to what he christens "Marlowe's mighty line,"[38] betrays in his commonplace book a more skeptical view of his predecessor's influence on English theater and English ears: "The True Artificer will not run away from nature, as hee were afraid of her, or depart from life and the likenesse of Truth, but speake to the capacity of his hearers. And though his language differ from the vulgar somewhat, it shall not fly from all humanity, with the *Tamerlanes* and *Tamer-Chams* of the late Age, which had nothing in them but the *scenicall* strutting, and furious vociferation to warrant them to the ignorant gapers."[39] Like Levin, Jonson credits Marlowe with the invention of a "barbaric prototype," but that prototype is here imagined as an agent of degeneracy, the begetter of a Scythian horde whose language is neither vulgar nor humane, neither common nor classical.

Vested as they are in their own notions of English eloquence, Nashe, Harvey, Greene, and Jonson are hardly disinterested auditors of Marlowe's verse, but their skeptical, even scathing, commentary provides a useful corrective to the appreciative responses of many modern scholars. For although the critical tradition has long identified blank verse as Marlowe's "most meaningful contribution" to English drama, the meaning of that contribution, as McDonald also notes, resides in its unlikelihood: however much unrhymed iambic pentameter now sounds like the natural voice of English drama, making it so entailed the "renovation and development of a hitherto undistinguished poetic form," a "strange tongue" fit for the strange figures with which his plays are peopled.[40] Marlowe himself suggests that comfort, order, and regularity were not the governing principles of his new poetic form; in fact Jonson's accusation of reckless departure is more in keeping with the playwright's own claims for blank verse. According to the prologue to part 1 of *Tamburlaine*, vernacular verse suffered from needless constraint, from the limited talents and provincial tastes of "rhyming mother wits"; what English poetry requires above all, Marlowe declares, is freedom from end-rhyme's petty bounds and access to the rhetorical terrain of "high astounding terms." The prologue thus "invites English auditors away," "throwing off [the] domestic confinements [of] comedy, rhyme, location" in pursuit of what Richmond Barbour calls "an eloquence of nomadism."[41]

To put it in Jonson's terms, if this Scythian struts, it is because we are meant to notice his feet. According to most early modern histories, the real Tamerlane walked with a limp—hence his name, Timur the Lame—but George Whetstone's *English Myrrour* (1586) rejects this bit of the legend, claiming that "the strength and comeliness of [Tamburlaine's] body, aunswered the haughtiness of his hart."[42] Marlowe takes full advantage of his source, imagining a Tamburlaine whose gait is as steady as the stressed and unstressed beats of an iambic pentameter line. In case we should miss the pun, Marlowe's play is full of references to feet: "A thousand horsemen! We, five hundred foot! / An odds too great for us to stand against!" Tamburlaine exclaims on the verge of an encounter with the Persian monarch's host (*One* 1.2.121–²2). But stand they do: Tamburlaine's forceful eloquence persuades the Persian general to join forces with him against the rest of the Persian army. Later, when he seizes the Turkish sultan's crown and the title of emperor of the East, Tamburlaine exults that "[t]he pillars that have bolstered up those terms / Are fall'n in clusters at my conquering feet," and to drive the point home, he uses the former sultan, Bajazeth, as his footstool, "treading him beneath [his] loathsome feet"(*One* 3.3.229–30, 4.2.64). Such self-conscious jokes invite us to see Tamburlaine's imperial progress as the perfect and perhaps necessary analog to his creator's literary innovation: "repeatedly in the play," observes J. S. Cunningham, "metre and syntax . . . become analogues of other kinds of capability."[43] But Zabina's revulsion at Tamburlaine's "loathsome feet" anticipates the resentment Marlowe's supposedly orderly and comforting standard occasioned in some auditors. It is not simply that Marlowe's verse sounded strange in the ears of early modern English audiences; it also seemed to manifest a particularly willful, even violent disregard for the proper limits of poetic expression. If we take those reactions seriously, what can appear as distinct, even opposed qualities of the play[44]—on the one hand, its disregard for geographic and moral boundaries and, on the other, its investment in the apparent regularity and order of the blank-verse line—may better be read as complimentary dimensions of its interest in the often problematic relationship between eloquence and abuse, measure and trespass.

Indeed Marlowe makes it difficult for us to distinguish his protagonist's extreme strategies for global dominion from his own poetic tactics. Initially, to be sure, the contrast between eloquence and abuse is externalized in the contrast between the smooth-spoken Tamburlaine and his ham-fisted, spluttering rivals. Having promised audiences an outsize spectacle, the prologue to part 1 gives way to a startling anticlimax: instead of the Scythian Tamburlaine with his high astounding terms and conquering sword, the audience is confronted with the Persian Mycetes, feeble and tongue-tied master of a "maimed empery" (*One* 1.1.126). "Brother Cosroe, I find myself aggrieved, / Yet insufficient to express the same, / For it requires a great and thund'ring speech," he whines (1–3). Cosroe's withering response establishes Mycetes's rhetorical ineptitude as the sign of a more profound unfitness for the task of empire: "Unhappy Persia, that in former age / hast been the seat of mighty conquerors/ that in their prowess and their policies / Have triumphed over Afric, and the bounds / Of Europe," he laments, while "Now Turks and Tartars shake their swords at thee, / meaning to mangle all thy provinces" (6–10, 16–17). Mycetes protests at the insubordination—"I might command you to be slain for this!"—but the pretense of imperiousness is undercut by his childish appeal for confirmation: "Meander, might I not?" "Not for so small a fault, my sovereign lord," comes the humiliating reply. "I mean it not, but yet I know I might," the embarrassed king insists, and then, in a last-ditch effort to save face, "Yet live, yea, live, Mycetes wills it so" (23–24, 25, 26–27). The inability to maintain order within his own throne room is tied to the impoverishment of Mycetes's speech. Cosroe has at least a rudimentary grasp of rhetorical effect, evident in the aggressive alliteration of "Turks and Tartars . . . meaning to mangle," but his brother's retort degenerates into a mumble, while his sole attempt at wordplay sounds more like a stutter: "I refer me to my noblemen, / That know my wit and can be witnesses" (21–22).

Such incompetence effectively sets the stage for Tamburlaine's vastly more eloquent and effective sovereignty. The Tamburlaine who appears onstage in the first act of part 1 not only satisfies the expectations aroused by Marlowe's prologue but also fulfills the fantasy on which the English rhetorical tradition is founded: that eloquence offers a bloodless path to imperial might. "[W]hat worthier thing can there bee, then with a word to winne Cities and whole Countries?" Thomas Wilson asks in the dedicatory epistle to his *Arte of Rhetorique* (1560). "[W]hat greater gaine can we haue, then without bloudshed achiue to a Conquest? [And] what greater delite doe wee knowe, then to see a whole multitude, with the onely talke of man, rauished and drawne which way he liketh best to haue them?" Rhetoric, Wilson urges, is the key to such profit and pleasure, for "such force hath the tongue, and such is the power of Eloquence and reason, that most men are forced, euen to yeeld in that which most standeth against their will." Wilson substantiates his claim by invoking the figure of the Gallic Hercules, described by the Greek sophist Lucian as having "all men lincked together by the eares in a chaine" attached to his tongue, "to drawe them and leade them euen as he lusted." For, Wilson explains, "his witte was so great, his tongue so eloquent, and his experience such, that no man was able to withstande his reason, but eueryone was rather driven to doe that which he would, and to will that which he did, agreeing to his aduise both in word and worke in all that euer they were able."[45] But as Sean Keilen observes, the Gallic Hercules is an ambivalent figure for the civilizing power of eloquence, "a half-divine, half-bestial man," towering over his captives but swathed in animal skins.[46] In the numerous sixteenth-century editions of Andrea Alciato's popular *Emblematum Liber*, the figure of the Gallic Hercules appears under the motto *Eloquentia fortitudine praestantior* but rests his weight on a stout club (or, in the image reproduced here, from a 1584 Paris edition, lofts it menacingly in the air): physical force is eloquence's silent partner.[47] "The addressees of [Hercules's] eloquence," observes Wolfgang G. Müller, "appear as a kind of rhetorical chain gang, with no choice but to listen and accept the wisdom which the orator instills into them."[48]

In the first act of *Tamburlaine*, Marlowe provides his audience with a similarly equivocal spectacle of bloodless conquest, in which the eloquence of the Scythian warlord triumphs over the far greater military might of the Persian army. Faced with "a thousand horsemen" against his own "five hundred foot," Tamburlaine "play[s] the orator": "Forsake thy king and do but join with me," he invites his opponent, the Persian captain Theridamas, "And we will triumph over all the world" (*One* 1.2.121, 129, 171–72). It is a patently ludicrous claim—as Tamburlaine admits, the "odds" of a battle between his own force and the Persian army are "too great for us to stand against" (122)—but one Tamburlaine buttresses with impressive argumentative skill. Improvising as he goes, he builds credibility from hints and shreds of evidence—a hastily assembled display of booty becomes proof that Jove favors Tamburlaine's prospects, "rain[ing] down heaps of gold in showers, / As if he meant to give my soldiers pay," while a recent captive, the daughter of the Egyptian sultan, is trotted out "as a sure and grounded argument / That I shall be the monarch of the East" (181–84). Tamburlaine's bravado succeeds; almost in spite of himself, Theridamas is convinced. "Not Hermes, prolocutor to the gods, / Could use persuasions more pathetical," he marvels (209–10). In a touch that would have been especially gratifying to an English audience, Theridamas claims that Tamburlaine's rude origins only make his eloquence the more potent: "What strong enchantments 'tice my yielding soul? / Are these resolved,

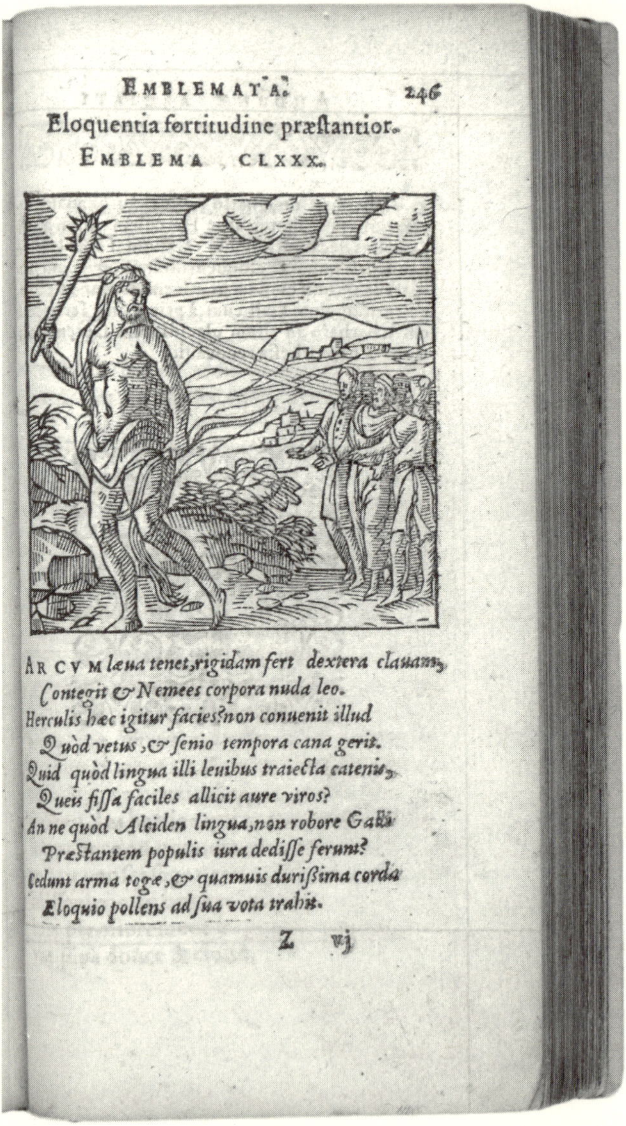

EMBLEMATA. 246

Eloquentia fortitudine præstantior.

EMBLEMA CLXXX.

ARCVM læua tenet, rigidam fert dextera clauam,
Contegit & Nemees corpora nuda leo.
Herculis hæc igitur facies? non conuenit illud
Quòd vetus, & senio tempora cana gerit.
Quid quòd lingua illi leuibus traiecta catenis,
Queis fissa faciles allicit aure viros?
An ne quòd Alciden lingua, non robore Galli
Præstantem populis iura dedisse ferunt?
Cedunt arma togæ, & quamuis durissima corda
Eloquio pollens ad sua vota trahit.

Z vj

Figure 3. "*Eloquentia fortitudine praestantior*," in Andrea Alciato, *Emblematum Liber* (Paris, 1584). Image courtesy of Glasgow University Library.

noble, *Scythians*" (223–24)? In an ironic reversal, the praise Mycetes conferred upon the Persian captain in scene 1—"thy words are swords, / And with thy looks thou conquerest all thy foes" (*One* 1.1.74–75)—comes to rest on his opponent, as Theridamas concedes to Tamburlaine without a fight: "Won with thy words, and conquered with thy looks, / I yield myself, my men and horse to thee" (*One* 1.2.227–28).

Thus far Marlowe's Tamburlaine makes good on the promise of bloodless conquest that underwrites Wilson's bid for vernacular eloquence. "[W]hat working words he hath!" the dazzled Theridamas exclaims (*One* 2.3.25). But the spectacle of Tamburlaine's rhetorical triumph over the Persian army is embedded in a scene that offers a more troubling account of the relationship between persuasion and conquest. For it is not until the middle of scene 2 that Tamburlaine encounters Theridamas; when the audience first sees him, his "working words"—and, more to the point, his weapons—are leveled not against the awesome forces of the Persian army but against the weak capacity of "a silly maid" (*One* 1.2.10): Zenocrate, the sultan's daughter ambushed by Tamburlaine's men and paraded before the Persions as proof of his imperial destiny. To be sure, the Tamburlaine who appears in scene 2 cuts a very different figure from "that sturdy Scythian thief" of the Persians' imaginings, who "with his lawless train / Daily commits incivil outrages" (*One* 1.1.36, 39–40). This Tamburlaine is courtly, even gentle, in his dealings with the Egyptian princess, addressing her as "lady" and "fair madam" (*One* 1.2.1, 252), assuring her that her "jewels and treasure . . . shall be reserved" (2) and she herself kept "in better state / Than . . . in the circle of your father's arms" (3, 5). But the dazzling oration that crowns the scene bears a queasy formal resemblance to the violence it seeks to conceal. Beginning with a series of short, measured questions, the speech opens out into a litany of declarations, each literally and figuratively more expansive than the one before:

> Disdains Zenocrate to live with me?
> Or you, my lords, to be my followers?
> Think you I weigh this treasure more than you?
> Not all the gold in India's wealthy arms
> Shall buy the meanest solder in my train.
> Zenocrate, lovelier than the love of Jove,
> Brighter than is the silver Rhodope,
> Fairer than the whitest snow on Scythian hills,
> Thy person is more worth to Tamburlaine,

Than the possession of the Persian crown,
Which gracious stars have promised at my birth.
A hundred Tartars shall attend on thee
Mounted on steeds swifter than Pegasus;
Thy garments shall be made of Median silk,
Enchased with precious jewels of mine own
More rich and valurous than Zenocrate's;
With milk-white harts upon an ivory sled
Thou shalt be drawn amidst the frozen pools
And scale the icy mountains' lofty tops,
Which with thy beauty will soon be resolved;
My martial prizes with five hundred men
Won on the fifty-headed Volga's waves
Shall all we offer to Zenocrate,
And then myself to fair Zenocrate. (82–105)

The dilatory power of Tamburlaine's rhetoric cannot be extricated from the scene of sexual violence that it both anticipates and seeks to assuage: the speech begins and ends with the invocation of Zenocrate's name, and her body is, ultimately, the territory it claims (and promises to enlarge).[49] Indeed listening from the perspective of Zenocrate, we can begin to understand the resentment expressed toward Marlowe's verse by so many of his early auditors. Like George Gascoigne, who penned his 1576 satire, *The Steel Glass*, "In rymeless verse, which thundreth mighty threats,"[50] Marlowe identifies the open-ended capaciousness of blank verse with aggression, although in Marlowe's case that aggression masquerades as generosity. The association is by no means strictly metaphorical: in a literal sense, the absence of end-rhyme creates a potentially limitless space for rhetorical amplification or *auxesis*, the steady accumulation of pentameter lines into the free-standing verse paragraph that James Shapiro identifies as the paradigmatic expressive unit of Marlovian poetry.[51] As Tamburlaine's address to Zenocrate makes plain, *auxesis* enacts a double display of dominance, as both syntax and audience are held hostage to the speaker's whim.

The reality of Zenocrate's situation, her position as one of Tamburlaine's "forced followers" (66), makes a mockery of the conventional association between rhetorical suasion and erotic seduction. "[W]omen must be flattered," Tamburlaine explains to his companions (107), but prisoners, of course, need not be, and once the threat of a Persian attack has been dispelled—thanks in part to the mute, unwilling testimony afforded by Zenocrate herself—Tamburlaine abandons his courtly pose: "If you will willingly remain with me / You shall have honours as your merits be— / Or else you shall be forced with slavery" (252–55). Neatly anticipating Milton's judgment against rhyme as a form of "bondage," the chiming end sounds of this triplet emphasize the truth of Zenocrate's predicament: whatever choice she makes, the result will be the same. But Marlowe is far more cynical than Milton when it comes to the asymmetric liberty afforded by unrhymed verse. Zenocrate's attendant Agydas replies promptly and politely on her behalf in terms that maintain the fiction of mutuality—"We yield unto thee, happy Tamburlaine" (256)—but the princess's own response is bitterer and more true: "I must be pleased perforce. Wretched Zenocrate!" (257). To be "pleased perforce" is a nasty paradox, a grim euphemism for the rape that has actually occurred, and an unsettling inversion of the idea that eloquence makes subjection pleasurable. By giving the Egyptian princess the last word—the scene concludes on this unhappy note—Marlowe makes Zenocrate the authority on all that has transpired, hinting at a much darker reading of the fantasy of rhetorical conquest. "Linking persuasion to coercion, Wilson minimizes the terror of that equation," as Barbour writes, but "Marlowe maximizes it . . . mak[ing] terms and swords not alternative but synergistic."[52] Blank verse is the crucial instrument of that synergy: it is what English poetry sounds like in the mouth of a tyrant who fancies himself a lover.

Of course Zenocrate does eventually fall in love with her captor, so that his once threatening words grow welcome to her ears, "his talk much sweeter than the Muses' song" (*One* 3.2.50). But even this development takes a nightmarish turn: when Zenocrate confesses her growing attraction to Agydas, he protests, not realizing that Tamburlaine is nearby, urging his mistress, "Let not a man so vile and barbarous . . . be honoured with your love, but for necessity" (26, 30). When Tamburlaine reveals himself, he pointedly says nothing, leaving Agydas "aghast" and "most astonied to see his choler shut in secret thoughts, / And wrapped in silence of his angry soul." As the unhappy Agydas prophesies, this uncharacteristic reticence bespeaks his doom, and when Tamburlaine's deputy enters bearing a dagger, he requires no further instruction: "It says, Agydas, thou shalt surely die" (95). "He needed not with words confirm my fear," the Egyptian lord mournfully observes, "For words are vain where working tools present / The naked action" (92–94). The observation is prescient. Although there is no diminution of his rhetoric, as Tamburlaine proceeds on his march toward global domination, eloquence plays less and less of a role in his successes. His crucial first victory, over the Persian army, may be attributable to the power of his "working words," but subsequent triumphs are openly reliant on the "naked action" of an increasingly baroque display of "working tools": "his sword, his shield, his horse, his armour, plumes, / And jetty feathers menace death and hell" (*One* 4.1.60–61), but so do his curtle axes and cannons, his cages and guns, even his bridles and harnesses. When Tamburlaine encounters the Turkish sultan Bajazeth, he delegates the task of rhetorical conquest to Zenocrate, urging her to abuse the Turkish queen Zabina, "vaunt of my worth, / And manage words with her as we will arms" (*One* 3.3.130–31). Zenocrate's insults infuriate Zabina, but it is Tamburlaine's military victory that stops her mouth: when she reproves him for his insolence to an empress, he bluntly informs her that "the pillars that have bolstered up those terms / Are fall'n in clusters at my conquering feet" (229–30).

It is precisely this shattering of linguistic distinction that Marlowe makes the paradoxical achievement of his distinctive poetic style. "There is no greater difference betwixt a ciuill and brutish vtteraunce then cleare distinction of voices," writes Puttenham in book 2 of his *Arte*: "the most laudable languages are always most plaine and distinct, and the barbarous the most confuse and indistinct" (61). Puttenham has in mind the civilized pauses—the commas and colons—built into Greek and Latin periods, and especially early on, Marlowe uses line breaks to achieve a similarly measured effect in Tamburlaine's sententious speeches. But the distinctions effected by meter are gradually effaced as Tamburlaine's charismatic style is aped by his followers: in this sense the more successful Marlowe's hero, the more brutish his play. For it is not only Zenocrate who adopts Tamburlaine's vaunting speech; as Tamburlaine's imperial might spreads across Asia and into Africa, so too does the influence of his "high astounding terms," and what was once a distinctive, indeed singular voice dissipates into a cacophony of competing tongues, each more outrageously boastful than the next.[53] Mark Thornton Burnett reads this as a sign of the waning of Tamburlaine's powers, as the rhetorical precedence he wields early on gives way in a world "inhabited by a number of rival speakers,"[54] but in fact Tamburlaine is the chief agent of that leveling of rhetorical distinction. For one thing, as Emily Bartels observes, many of his own best lines are stolen: "Even when Tamburlaine marks out his own distinctive rhetorical territory, claiming that '*will* and *shall* best fitteth Tamburlaine,' he does so after hearing Theridamas 'speak in that mood' (*One* 3.3.40–41) and applauding him for it. And . . . he first terms himself the scourge of god after noting that he has been 'term'd the Scourge and Wrath of God' (*One* 3.3.44) by others."[55]

Tamburlaine's rhetorical thievery—what Burnett calls his "magpie-like" appropriation of glittering words and well-turned phrases[56]—provides the template, even the impetus, for his thefts of land and titles. Thus when the Persian lord Menaphon congratulates the newly crowned Cosroe with the thought that they shall soon "ride in triumph through Persepolis" (*One* 2.5.49), Tamburlaine seizes on the phrase and makes it the theme of his own desires. So potent is the force of recitation that simply by repeating the phrase to himself, Tamburlaine is "strongly moved, / that if I should desire the Persian crown, / I could attain it with a wondrous ease" (*One* 2.5.75–77)—and so he does.

The inverse of this acquisitive talent is Tamburlaine's compulsion to see his own image and hear his own name wherever he goes. Thus when two of his sons wrangle over who, after their father's death, deserves to be called "the scourge and terror of the world," Tamburlaine insists that all three boys bear the epithet: "Be all a scourge and terror of the world / Or else you are not sons of Tamburlaine" (*Two* 1.3.62–64). It is because his third son, Calyphas, resists the impress of his father's character that Tamburlaine despises him. "Let me accompany my gracious mother," Calyphas requests, for two sons "are enough to conquer all the world, / and you have won enough for me to keep" (*Two* 1.3.67–68). In a world filled with the hyperbole of would-be Tamburlaines, Calyphas stands out as a proponent of witty understatement—"What a coil they keep!" he observes of the climactic encounter between Tamburlaine's army and the assembled forces of his rival kings; "I believe there will be some hurt done anon amongst them" (*Two* 4.1.74–75)—and it is this singularity that dooms him. "Thou shalt not have a foot" of empire, Tamburlaine rebukes him, and when he discovers that Calyphas has avoided the battle, he stabs him. Immediately after, Tamburlaine turns to his (literally) captive audience of fallen kings and boasts, "Now you shall feel the strength of Tamburlaine, / And by the state of his supremacy / Approve the difference twixt himself and you" (*Two* 4.1.135–37). But as Calyphas's corpse attests, difference is in fact precisely what Tamburlaine seeks to eradicate: his vision of empire entails the imposition of a radical sameness, a sameness achieved through total war and the passionate self-assertion that becomes its rhetorical equivalent.

It is a critical commonplace that "Marlowe takes particular delight in geographical nouns,"[57] and as we have seen, the recitation of those names possesses an incantatory power for Tamburlaine, as it must also have done for Marlowe's audience. But Tamburlaine's true gift, the real expression of his genius, is in unnaming and renaming. When he first meets the Turkish sultan, he asserts his authority over him by calling him "that Bajazeth" (*One* 3.3.65).

The sultan, understandably outraged, exclaims to his followers, "Kings of Fez, Moroccus, and Argier, / He calls me Bajazeth, whom you call lord! / Note the presumption of this Scythian slave" (*One* 3.3.66–68). But when the battle is won, so are the titles: Tamburlaine distributes the titles of Fez, Moroccus, and Argier to his own loyal deputies, and as for the sultan, "Bring out my footstool," Tamburlaine commands (*One* 4.2.1). Zenocrate's own Damascus is leveled as well, and the victor urges the conquered Egyptian king to regard his new role as Tamburlaine's father-in-law, "a title higher than thy Sultan's name" (*One* 5.1.435). Zenocrate begs that her homeland be spared, but Tamburlaine is adamant that nothing mar the uniform perfection of his empire, a world "reduce[d] . . . to a map" on which all "the provinces, cities, and towns" are "call[ed] . . . after thy name and mine" (*One* 4.4.82–84). So total is the scope of Tamburlaine's ambition to "see [his] name and honour . . . spread" (*One* 1.2.204) that even the alterity of the past becomes an affront to his self-regard: it is only because antiquity knew not Zenocrate, he claims, that Helen, Lesbia, and Corinna are named. "And had she lived before the siege of Troy," he insists, "Her name had been in every line" that Homer, Catullus, or Ovid wrote, herself "the argument / Of every epigram or elegy" (*Two* 2.4.90, 94–95).

The ceaseless echo of "Tamburlaine" and "Zenocrate" throughout the two plays is not simply evidence of the Scythian's boundless egotism; it is also a sheerly pragmatic feature of Marlowe's prosody, which depends on Tamburlaine's appetite for conquest to satisfy the demands of metrical form. Indeed there is an unmistakable kinship between the playwright's metrical strategies and his hero's ruthless course to empire. "[T]here can not be in a maker a fowler fault, then to falsifie his accent to serue his cadence, or by vntrue orthographie to wrench his words," Puttenham declares (67). Puttenham calls upon Temir Cutzclewe as the master of a poetic form—the shape-poem or the pattern-poem—that prevents this foul fault by making cadence and other aural effects secondary to visual appeal. As noted, the pattern-poem appealed to Puttenham partly because it depends on a formal rigor that has nothing to do with the way words sound: the wrenching on which Temir Cutzclewe's poems depend is entirely visual. But in other kinds of poetry, Puttenham cautions, the temptation to "falsify accents" and "wrench words" is strong for the vernacular poet, since "our naturall and primitiue language of the Saxon English, beares not any wordes (at least very few) of moe sillables then one (for whatsoeuer we see exceed, commeth to vs by the alterations of our language growen vpon many conquests and otherwise)" (56–57).

According to Puttenham, then, to the extent that English poets do possess the linguistic resources necessary to conform to the classical laws of prosody, it is only thanks to their own miserable history of invasion and subjugation. Here, yet again, the distinction between violence and generosity is uncomfortably blurred: the enrichment of monosyllabic England with the polysyllables of Latin and French cannot be extricated from its humiliation and defeat. *Tamburlaine's* far-flung plot returns repeatedly to this conundrum, but it also affords Marlowe the opportunity to reverse the unhappy association of poetic mastery and imperial conquest: to enrich his line with an enormous quantity of three- and four-syllable words drawn not only, or even primarily, from the Latin and French terms of England's colonial past but also from the new and strange fruits of Tamburlaine's own conquests. The names that most enchant Tamburlaine—"Zenocrate," "Persepolis"—are seductive not only because of what they describe but also because of how they sound, the regular iambs into which they fall; thus the march of Tamburlaine's conquering feet across the territories of Asia and Africa sustains the rhythm of Marlowe's own feet.

But not without violence: the wrenching and falsifying against which Puttenham inveighs is evident in many of Marlowe's lines, and it tends to mirror the protagonist's own outrageous impositions of will. Thus Bajazeth's humiliating turn as Tamburlaine's footstool is accompanied by what Cunningham calls "the play's most deviant metrical line," a spondaic command whose piling on of stressed monosyllables mimics the physical abuse it describes: "Stoop, villain, stoop, stoop, for so he bids" (*Two* 4.2.22). If, as Marjorie Garber says, the "dramatic tension" in *Tamburlaine* "derives from the dialectic between aspiration and limitation," ambition and enclosure, a similar tension is at work in the play's verse.[58] At the ends of his lines, Marlowe imposes strong syntactical breaks—as Russ McDonald writes, "For all Marlowe's reputation as an overreacher, only rarely did he overreach the poetic line"[59]—but what happens *within* those end-stopped lines is, as in Puttenham's pattern-poems, often rather irregular.[60] Cunningham notes that "reading Marlovian blank verse" is a delicate operation: "the ear seeks an appropriate tact of pace, breath-interval, and emphasis," for " 'Cosroe' sometimes, it seems, asks for two syllables, sometimes three; 'Fesse' two or one" (91). What Cunningham views as occasions for readerly tact might just as well be seen as the imprints of Tamburlaine's own extraordinarily tactless pace. For as Cunningham's examples help us notice, the disregard Tamburlaine shows for the boundaries of foreign kingdoms and the property of foreign kings has its counterpart in Marlowe's high-handed treatment of the names of those kings and their kingdoms. "Asia" and "Scythia," "Media" and "India," "Syria," "Parthia," and all the rest may have two syllables or three; "Egypt" has two, but "Egyptia" three or four; "Greece" possesses merely one, but "Graecia" a lordly four: the willful compressions and elongations of visual space with Puttenham's pattern-poems find an aural counterpart in Marlowe's manipulation of foreign polysyllables. When the deposed Turk protests that Tamburlaine's "Ambitious pride shall make thee fall as low / For treading of the back of Bajazeth," for instance, Tamburlaine responds, "Thy names and titles and thy dignities, / Are fled from Baj'zeth and remain with me," and he marks his entitlement by shearing a syllable from the Turk's once-proper name (*One* 4.2.76–77, 79–80).

So skeptical is Puttenham of such manipulations—or "metaplasms"— that he dubs the "joining or unjoining of syllables and letters, suppressing or confounding their several sounds" as "figures of the smallest importance" and "forbear[s] to give them any vulgar name" (246). In his view they verge on mere mispronunciation, the tell-tale sign of the barbarous outsider. In his *Notes on the Making of English Verse*, however, George Gascoigne dubs this Procrustean stretching and lopping of syllables "turkening"—a phrase whose etymological roots identify it with twisting or troping but whose contemporary associations, as observed in Chapter 2, inevitably summon the specter of Islam and of other violent conversions.[61] In *The Garden of Eloquence*, Henry Peacham allows fourteen distinct varieties of metaplasm to the English poet, permitting not simply "the cleauing a dipthong in sunder . . . as Aethiopia, for æthiopia," but even the alteration of emphasis in Greek or Latin words, "necessity of meter so compelling, as . . . Orphêus, for Orphěus": "our carpênter" may, according to Gabriel Harvey, be off-limits to the wrenching, lopping, and cleaving of the vernacular poet, but the father of classical eloquence receives no such consideration.[62]

Marlowe's imperious turkening of the geography of the East and his carelessness for the propriety of the proper noun, receive spectacular embodiment in Tamburlaine's most striking and barbarous display of power. Close to the end of part 2, on the road to Babylon, with his empire at what will prove to be its utmost bound, Tamburlaine celebrates his recent triumphs in Asia Minor by harnessing the former kings of Natolia, Jerusalem, Trebizond, and Soria and forcing them to draw his chariot. He represents the degrading treatment as apt repayment for the insults they have hurled at him, "bridl[ing] their contemptuous cursing tongues / That like unruly never-broken jades / Break through the hedges of their fateful mouths / And pass their fixed bounds exceedingly" (*Two* 4.3.44–47). This is hardly the outcome Wilson imagined for English eloquence, when, in the dedicatory epistle to his *Arte of Rhetorique*, he described that "greater delite" of "see[ing] a whole multitude, with the onely talke of man, rauished and drawne which way he liketh best to haue them."[63] Wilson's delightful spectacle is a fantasy of eloquence that Marlowe permits his audience—with qualifications—at the beginning of Tamburlaine's career, when he wins over the Persian general, but as Marlowe's hero enlarges his empire, the operations of eloquence and the mechanics of brute force are increasingly indistinguishable. In the notorious staging of the human chariot, tongues are not instruments of moral suasion but silent stubs of flesh. Here men are not "drawne" but made to draw, like beasts; here is not "onely talke" but its blunt objects—harnesses, whips, and "bits of burnished steel" (*Two* 4.1.183).

The mute lurching of those captive kings across the English stage is the antithesis of the sweet traction Wilson describes, the eloquence that drew beasts and bestial men to Orpheus, but it is an apt image for the violent methods on which Marlowe's verse often depends for its singularly potent effects. Tamburlaine comes to seem both the agent and the thrall of what George Gascoigne terms "poeticall license," that "shrewde fellow" who "maketh words longer, shorter, of mo syllables, of fewer, newer, older, truer, falser, and . . . turkeneth all things at pleasure."[64] "I love to live at liberty," he boasts in his first appearance onstage (*One* 1.2.26), but as he later confesses, "since I exercise a greater name, . . . I must apply myself to fit those terms" (*Two* 4.1.153–55). Applying oneself to fit the terms, applying the terms to fit oneself: such is the license that Marlowe claims for his play, whose exotic and elastic phrasing both defines and defies the limits of his native tongue.

"What Scythian Sorte Soeuer"

The most radical and unexpected articulation of this idea—the idea that eloquence is the exercise of an idiosyncratic and autocratic poetic will—appears in the work of a poet who did his utmost to confine *Tamburlaine*'s feet to the stage, a poet whose own verse struck many of his contemporaries as too restrained altogether.[65] A decade and a half after Marlowe announced his departure from rhyme, Samuel Daniel bowed to *Tamburlaine*'s influence, "confess[ing]" in his 1603 *Defence of Ryme* that his adversaries in the war over English measure had "wrought this much vpon me, that I thinke a Tragedie would indeede best comporte with a blank Verse, and dispence with Ryme."[66] But Daniel had his own uses for Tamburlaine, whom he invokes in the *Defence* as a counterweight to the humanist tendency to revile native poetic forms as signs of cultural and intellectual barbarism. In a lengthy digression Daniel argues that the notoriously immoderate battle tactics of the Scythian Tamburlaine ought to be recognized as the point of origin for what we now call the Renaissance: the revival of learning in fourteenth- and fifteenth-century Italy begins, he claims, at the margins of so-called civilization with a series of rather brutal acts of conquest (sig. H[1]$_{r-v}$). By tallying European humanism's debts to the inhumane achievements of a barbarian warlord, Daniel lays the ground for his critique of humanist rhetoric's own coercive tendencies, but he also advances his case for a more expansive and elastic version of literary history. His crude yet effective Tamburlaine stands as a rebuke to those who would make the boundaries of eloquence coextensive with those of ancient Athens and Rome, those who fail to recognize in homely rhyme a power that "swais th'affection of the Barbarian" as well as "the harts of Ciuill nations" (sig. G4$_r$).

Daniel may allow blank verse its dominion over English tragedy, but he insists on retaining the rest of the poetic landscape for rhyme, accusing partisans of quantitative meter of cultural and linguistic tyranny. The *Defence* begins by dismissing the familiar anxieties over numbers, accents, and feet as inconsequential. Where Puttenham and others—chiefly Thomas Campion, whose 1602 *Apologie of Poetrie* prompts Daniel's response—fretted over the difficulty of making English conform to cadences of classical measure, Daniel argues that English poets have no need for such artificial constraints, possessing already a much pleasanter and more natural method of giving shape to their lines. "[W]e are told," he writes, "that our measures go wrong, all Ryming is grosse, vulgare, barbarous," but this is mere chauvinism, for "[e]uery language hath her proper number or measure fitted to vse and delight," and in England rhyme "performes those offices" best, "delighting the eare, stirring the hart, and satisfying the iudgment in such sort as I doubt whether euer single numbers will doe in our Climate" (sigs. G3$_r$, G4$_v$–[G5$_r$]). But not only "our climate": rhyme, according to Daniel, has "so naturall a melodie" and "so vniuersall," that "it seemes to be generally borne with al the nations of the world." Thus the barbarism that is imputed to rhyme as its great defect in fact "argues the generall power of it: . . . it hath a power in nature on all" (sig. G4$_r$).

Daniel goes on to invent a genealogy for this universal melody, imagining the spread of rhyme across the globe as an unforced, triumphal march. It is an itinerary that uncannily replicates the course of Tamburlaine's own progress to world domination: "borne no doubt in Scythia," rhyming verse is "brought ouer Caucasus and Mount Taurus" to Turkey, carried to "a great part of Asia and Affrique," adopted by "the Muscouite, Polack, Hungarian, German, Italian, French, and Spaniard," and finally either brought thence or possessed already by "[t]he Irish, Briton, Scot, Dane, Saxon, English, and all the Inhabitours of this Iland" (sig. G4ᵥ). As for the "single numbers" of Greece and Rome, "notwithstanding their excellencie," they "seemed not sufficient to satisfie the eare of the world" (sig. [G5]ᵣ), and the veneration they are accorded is, according to Daniel, the fruit of tyranny. The Greeks and Romans, he argues, "may thanke their sword that made their tongues so famous and vniuersall as they are"—and their verses bear the impress of this history, being composed of the "scattered limbs" of severed clauses and "examples . . . of strange crueltie, in torturing and dismembering of words" (sig. [G5]ᵥ): according to Daniel, classical poets are the original turkeners of language. "We should not," he therefore urges, "so soone yield our consents captiue to the authoritie of Antiquitie"; although English poets may be accustomed to thinking of themselves as inhabitants of a remote corner of the world, "we are not so placed out of the way of iudgement, but that the same Sun of Discretion shineth vpon vs" (sig. [G6]ᵥ). To exchange rhyme for "single numbers" would be a bad bargain indeed, an exchange of native discretion for strange cruelty, and the loss of "an hereditary eloquence proper to all mankind" (sig. G4ᵣ).

But in order to claim this status for rhyme, Daniel must confront the foundational myth of Renaissance humanism, whereby eloquence is always already defined in relation to the classical literary tradition and Goths are the natural antagonists of Greeks. According to Daniel's mocking summary of this myth, "all things lay pitifully deformed in those lacke-learning times from the declining of the Roman Empire, till the light of the latine tongue was revived by Rewcline, Erasmus and Moore." This, Daniel says, is "a most apparent ignorance," for "three hundred yeeres before them about the coming downe of Tamburlaine into Europe," the "best notions of learning" in the same "degree of excellencie" were already at work, and "our nation . . . concurrent with the best of all this lettered world" (sig. H[1]ᵣ). Indeed, Daniel claims, it is thanks to Tamburlaine that the Renaissance happened at all. By taking "Bajazeth . . . prisoner," he argues, Tamburlaine inadvertently triggered an intellectual and literary revival: for upon learning of the Turk's defeat, the learned inhabitants of Constantinople, who had traveled to Italy in hopes of forging political alliances against Bajazeth, were now free to remain in Italy as scholars and teachers, "transport[ing] Philosophie beaten by the Turke out of Greece into Christendome." "Heereuppon," Daniel concludes, "came that mighty confluence of learning in these parts," which "meeting with the new inuented stampe of Printing, spread itself indeede in a more vniuersall sort then the world euer heretofore had it" (sig. H[1]ᵥ). Instead of being the achievement of dedicated scholars, intent on redeeming ancient beauty and truth, Daniel's Renaissance is the accidental by-product of war and new technologies. Eloquence, meanwhile, is not the instrument of imperial conquest but the sole surviving property of a transient community of refugees: a Gothic barbarian rescues Greek civilization, and poetic measure survives thanks to barbarous excess.

Daniel derives this account of Tamburlaine's role in the preservation of classical learning and literature from a French historian, Louis Le Roy, whose treatise *De la vicissitude ou variété des choses en l'univers* (1576; English translation, 1594) takes "the great and inuincible TAMBERLAN" as the emblem of "the power, learning, and other excellence of this age."⁶⁷ For Le Roy, the Scythian Timur appeals as a counterweight to humanism's obligatory sense of indebtedness to the classical past: as Mary Floyd-Wilson argues, his Tamberlan "embodies the paradoxically barbaric origins of early modern cultural advancement" and "refute[s] the geographic truisms of the conventional civilizing narrative—that barbarousness flows from the north and civilization emerges in the south."⁶⁸ But Le Roy also dwells on Tamberlan as the embodiment of a historiographic injustice: having created the circumstances for "the restitution of the tongues; and of all sciences," the Scythian warlord has been written out of the record by the beneficiaries of that restitution, men whose study of antiquity taught them to disdain his achievements as those of an unlettered barbarian. "Yet fortune hauing allwaies fauoured him, without euer hauing bin contrary vnto him," Le Roy laments, "seemeth among so many admirable euents, which exceed the ordinary course of Conquerours, to haue denyed him an Historyographer of excellent learning, and eloquence; agreeable to his vertues: to celebrate them worthily" (fol. 108ᵥ).

Le Roy's account of Tamberlan as the victim of his own radically transformative power—a figure who made history happen and was promptly shut out of it—authorizes Daniel's own revisionary project, in which Tamburlaine stands at the head of a long list of those whose contributions to learning and eloquence have been unfairly neglected: "witnesse," he commands his readers, "the venerable *Bede*, that flourished about a thousand yeeres since: *Aldelmus Durotelmus* that lived in the yere 739, . . . *Walterus Mape, Gulielmus Nigellus, Geruasius Tilburiensis, Bracton, Bacon, Ockam*, and an infinite Catalogue of excellent men" (sigs. H[1]ᵥ–H2ᵣ). To claim the authors of medieval Latin texts, even the scholastics—the most barbarous of barbarians, according to humanist orthodoxy—as "excellent men" in the cause of learning is to deny that the so-called revival of learning and letters was any such thing. The very idea that such institutions should need reviving is founded, Daniel insists, on a misguided assumption about the identification of eloquence with particular times and places: in truth, he writes, "[t]he distribution of giftes are vniuersall, and all seasons hath them in some sort" (sig. H2$_r$).

The theory of eloquence Daniel formulates in concert with this leveling of cultural history is at once homely and expansive, firm in its commitment to English forms but catholic in its appreciation of local variation. Daniel may be an apologist for rhyme, but he does not pretend that it possesses any merits beyond that of satisfying the ear and swaying the judgment; that satisfaction, vulgar as it may be, is sufficient guarantee of its value. "Suffer then the world to injoy that which it knows, and what it likes," he pleads. "Seeing that whatsoeuer forme of words doth mooue, delight and sway the affections of men, in what Scythian sorte soeuer it be disposed or vttered, that is true number, measure, eloquence, and the perfection of speech: which I said, hath as many shapes as there be tongues or nations in the world" (sig. [G5]$_v$). "In what Scythian sorte soeuer": the example of Le Roy's Tamberlan authorizes Daniel in bestowing an unprecedented degree of latitude upon the English author, and in granting an unprecedented weight to the enjoyment of the English tongue and ear. Of course, the "suffering" that Daniel commends to his readers somewhat collapses the distinction between ease and difficulty: like the appalled delight English audiences took in the spectacular barbarity and forceful rhythms of Marlowe's *Tamburlaine*, or the rigorous fascination George Puttenham finds in the unforgiving boundaries of the Tartarian shape-poem, Daniel's idea of "the perfection of speech" marries seemingly intuitive pleasure to the shock of alienation.

But we should not gloss over the differences between—indeed the outright incommensurability of—the forms that perfection assumes for each writer. Although they find inspiration in the same unlikely figure of eloquence, Puttenham, Marlowe, and Daniel arrive at radically disparate versions of vernacularity: oriental pattern-poems, blank verse, and rhyming couplets resist incorporation into any unified account of linguistic progress. Nor should we be too quick to assume that sixteenth-century readers would have found the choice between them an obvious one: Marlowe's spectacularly successful stage play offers one extremely influential account of where English poetry was headed at the end of the sixteenth century, but it is not the only story, then or now. By charting the unexpected range of associations between the Scythian warlord and the problem of measure, it is thus possible to defamiliarize ourselves with the trajectory of vernacular literature, recovering the confusion and excitement of a moment when the shape of England's literary history and its literary future were, as Daniel argues, no more distinct or fixed than "a superficiall figure of a region in a Mappe" (sig. H2$_r$)

The Scythian Timur may prove useful to the modern literary critic as well, insofar as his curious position within Renaissance culture—where he is at once ubiquitous and marginal, a catalyst of widespread change and the begetter of a degenerate line—forecasts the roles assumed by writers such as Lyly, Spenser, and Marlowe, whose self-consciously strange versions of vernacularity inaugurate a literary culture from which they are rather quickly exiled, marked as eccentric, idiosyncratic, and unfitting of imitation. What G. K. Hunter says of euphuism, that "though it contributed to the clarification of vernacular style . . . it had no real heirs,"[69] is equally true of Spenser's pseudo-archaism: even the tolerant (and otherwise admiring) Daniel politely declined to imitate his "aged accents and untimely words."[70] Marlowe's blank-verse line may seem the exception to this rule, for it has come to sound like the natural and inevitable voice of English eloquence, certainly so far as Renaissance drama is concerned. But blank verse survived the close of the sixteenth century only by being severed from the person of the strutting Scythian, who within a little more than a decade had come to seem, once again, rather lame. "[B]y the turn of the century," observes Alexander Legatt, "[n]o one was writing plays like *Tamburlaine* any more, and you could raise a laugh by quoting it."[71] There was worse to come. In 1681 a playwright by the name of Charles Saunders published a play titled *Tamerlane the Great,* with an epilogue by John Dryden and a preface in which Saunders defends himself from charges of plagiarism. Addressing those malefactors who have "give[n] out, that this was only an Old-Play Transcrib'd," Saunders writes:

> I hope I may easily unload my self of that Calumny, when I shall
> testifie that I never heard of any Play on the same Subject, untill
> my own was Acted, neither have I since seen it, though it hath
> been told me, there is a Cock-Pit Play, going under the name of the
> *Scythian Shepherd,* or *Tamberlain the Great,* which how good it is,
> any one may Iudge by its obscurity, being a thing, not a Bookseller
> in *London,* or scarce the Players themselves, who Acted it formerly,
> cou'd call to Remembrance, so far, that I believe that whoever was
> the Author, he might e'en keep it to himself secure from invasion,
> or Plagiary.[72]

Jonson's caution to playwrights against following in Marlowe's footsteps seems to have succeeded better than he could have hoped: like Milton, who disregards Surrey's *Aeneid* in claiming to originate the blank-verse English epic, Saunders appears sincere in his belief that he was the first English writer to take up the life of Tamburlaine. In an irony the Earl of Surrey might well have savored, the great stage poet of imperial ambition is himself relegated to the margins, the anonymous proprietor of a plot so obscure that no one would bother to usurp his place in it.

Eccentric Shakespeare

The period of theoretical and formal innovation that we now claim as a point of origin for modern literary history appeared to its immediate successors as a dead end. Neither the ministrations of Latin-speaking nursemaids nor the rigors of double translation succeeded in naturalizing classical eloquence in Renaissance England. No English compiler of tropes and figures achieved the authority of an Aristotle, a Cicero, or a Quintilian, nor did rhetoric long maintain its reign as the queen of the liberal arts: as early as 1605, Francis Bacon looked back with disdain at the sixteenth century's "affectionate study of eloquence"; by the mid-seventeenth century the tide of rhetorical handbooks had receded; and in 1691 John Locke dismissed "all the Art of Rhetoric, besides Order and Clearness, all the artificial and figurative application of Words Eloquence hath invented, are for nothing," as a "perfect cheat."[1] To a seventeenth-century eye—Ben Jonson's, for instance—Lyly's ornate prose, Spenser's odd diction, and Marlowe's thundering verse looked like failed experiments, useful only insofar as they marked the outer limits of vernacular decorum. A century later Samuel Johnson would describe the age of Elizabeth I as a period of violent and self-inflicted upheaval, in which "above all others experiments were made upon our language which distorted its combinations, and disturbed its uniformity."[2]

Johnson articulates that view in his 1756 "Proposals for Printing . . . the Dramatick Works of Shakespeare," and if we are now likely to regard the late sixteenth century in a rather different light—as a period in which English received the refinements that ushered it into a graceful and uniform maturity—that perspective has much to do with Shakespeare. Lyly, Spenser, and Marlowe may rapidly assume the status of linguistic outsiders and, to varying degrees, still hover at the margins of literary culture, but Shakespeare is the ultimate insider: "the exemplary author of the English canon," as Margreta de Grazia puts it.[3] And yet, as she points out, for a century and a half after his death—until Edmond Malone's pioneering 1790 edition of the complete works fashioned for him a legitimating carapace of scholarly respectability—the circumstances of Shakespeare's renown were decidedly otherwise: both his life and his art were judged wayward by early critics, as his famously extravagant fancy was matched by equally extravagant lapses in judgment.[4] Thus Johnson offers his judgment of the Elizabethan period not in order to rescue Shakespeare from it but to place him firmly within it: the reader of Shakespeare's text, he confesses, is "embarrassed at once with dead and with foreign languages, with obsoleteness and with innovation," the disorienting stylistic impress of a "desultory and vagrant" wit.[5]

Embarrassment—in both the eighteenth-century sense of perplexity or difficulty and our own sense of cringing awkwardness—seems indeed to have been a primary effect of reading Shakespeare throughout the seventeenth and much of the eighteenth centuries. For such readers Shakespeare did not transcend the eccentricities of his contemporaries; he epitomized them. Although Jonson's elegy for Shakespeare in the opening pages of the 1623 Folio hails the playwright as far greater than the "disproportion'd Muses" of Lyly, Spenser, and Marlowe,[6] his commonplace book lumps all four writers together in its disparaging account of the stylistic extremity of what he calls "the late age." In the same pages that record his judgments against Lyly's unrestrained *copia*, Spenser's queer pseudo-archaisms, and Marlowe's strutting bombast, Jonson laments the judgment of "the multitude," who "commend Writers, as they doe Fencers or Wrastlers; who if they come robustiously, and put for it, with a deale of violence, are received for the braver-fellows," and implies that Shakespeare was just such a robustious and violent sort: "His Wit was in his own Power, would Rule of it had been so too."[7]

Subsequent critics tended to agree in finding Shakespeare unruly: his genius, as Walter Harte wrote in 1730 with both admiration and dismay, "soar'd beyond the reach of Art"; his plots were deficient (or nonexistent); his style was passionately irregular; and his diction, as Francis Atterbury complained to Alexander Pope, less intelligible than "the hardest part of Chaucer."[8] In 1693 Thomas Rymer notoriously judged Shakespeare so eccentric as to be downright un-English, calling *Othello* a play whose absurdities and excesses "can only be calculated for the latitude of Gotham,"[9] the proverbial home of fools and simpletons. John Dryden rebuked Rymer for his want of generosity but allowed that Shakespeare's "whole stile is so pester'd with Figurative expressions, that it is as affected as it is obscure."[10] Lewis Theobold diagnosed Shakespeare's obscure style as the outworking of a wondering, wandering mind, whose "Acquaintance [with the world] was rather That of a Traveller, than a Native," addicted "to the Effect of Admiration begot by Novelty";[11] while Oliver Goldsmith found him prone to "far-fetch't conceit, and unnatural hyperbole."[12] "To judge . . . of *Shakespear* by *Aristotle's* rules," Pope cautioned, "is like trying a man by the Laws of one Country, who acted under those of another"—but if Shakespeare's country was not Aristotle's, nor was it obviously the English reader's own. Rather, Pope advised readers of his 1725 edition of the plays to approach the text as they would "an ancient majestick piece of *Gothick* Architecture," admiring its "nobler apartments; tho' we are often conducted to them by dark, odd, and uncouth passages."[13]

As de Grazia suggests, it was because he remained stubbornly outside the norms of vernacular decorum that Shakespeare became so central to the concerns of critics eager, in Pope's words, "to form the Judgment and Taste of our nation": "It was precisely because Shakespeare had traditionally been associated with irregular and artless Nature that he served this purpose so well."[14] As Michael Dobson has shown, it took the strenuous labor of scholars, politicians, and theatrical entrepreneurs in the late eighteenth century to groom this outlandish Shakespeare into the poet of English empire: ruled by their judgment, Shakespeare could proceed to rule Britannia.[15] Of course, certain parts of Shakespeare's corpus resisted this chastening. The most striking example is the eloquence of Othello, that "extravagant and wheeling stranger / Of here and everywhere": Coleridge sought refuge in the "pleasing possibility" that Shakespeare intended Othello as a light-skinned Moor, not a black African, but in 1920 it was still possible for T. S. Eliot to claim that he had "never seen a cogent refutation of Rymer's objections to *Othello*."[16] The character of Falstaff too was persistently associated with Shakespeare's immoderate and licentious pen and became the focus of a (still ongoing) argument about his creator's tolerance or promotion of subversion. For Dryden, writing in 1668, Falstaff was proof of Shakespeare's "largest and most comprehensive Soul," a marvel of "ridiculous extravagance,"[17] but for the straight-laced Jeremy Collier, writing in 1698, Falstaff's banishment by Henry V was crucial evidence of Shakespeare's capacity for moral and aesthetic judgment: the poet, like the newly crowned king, "was not so partial as to let his Humour compound for his lewdness."[18]

Modern critics continue to debate the implications of Hal's transformation from libertine prince to authoritarian king and to highlight the banishing of Falstaff as a turning point, if not in Shakespeare's personal psychology, at least in the ideological orientation of the English history play: a critical step toward Henry's apotheosis as "England" and Shakespeare's as England's "national poet."[19] Indeed for all the disagreement over the ethics and politics of the second tetralogy,[20] critics concur in identifying the ideal that emerges by way of Henry's famous eloquence: "the model of an English community";[21] "an emerging English nationalism";[22] "a fantasy of national (male) bondedness";[23] "an acceptable national self";[24] a "unitary state";[25] "a secure English polity";[26] "a nation conceived in strikingly modern terms."[27] If one wishes to make a case for the sixteenth-century origins of the English national community, it is Shakespeare's Henry V who, as one critic puts it, "springs to mind."[28] Within the second tetralogy, however, eloquence is not so easily domesticated. Although the banishment of Falstaff consigns one particular embodiment of linguistic extravagance to the margins of Shakespeare's plot, it signals the ascendancy of another. For it is not simply the case that, as a number of critics have pointed out, the second tetralogy permits a number of rival voices to threaten the dominance of the king's "good English."[29] That "good English" is itself the product of studied eccentricity: indeed of an apprenticeship to the strange literary vernaculars this book highlights.

Hal foregrounds the link between willfully outlandish speech and his own royal authority early in his career, when he claims his aptitude for tavern slang as a sign of his fitness to rule: "When I am King of England I shall command all the good lads in Eastcheap," he boasts to Poins. "I am so good a proficient in one quarter of an hour that I can drink with any tinker in his own language during my life" (*1 Henry IV* 2.5.12–17).[30] Of course this "proficiency" can also be read as a defect, the sign of a loose tongue and an unstable realm. The prince's worried father, for instance, hears in his son's indiscriminate talk a dangerously inverted form of Orphic eloquence: "For the fifth Harry from curbed licence plucks the muzzle of restraint," he laments on his deathbed, "O my poor kingdom! . . . O thou wilt be a wilderness again, / Peopled with wolves, thy old inhabitants!" (*2 Henry IV* 4.3.258–59, 261–65). The Earl of Warwick reconciles these opposed views by urging the king to regard Hal's waywardness as a mode of progress toward political mastery—which he too likens to the cultivation of a strange tongue:

The prince but studies his companions
Like a strange tongue wherein, to gain the language,
'Tis needful that the most immodest word
Be look'd upon and learn'd; which once attain'd,

> Your highness knows, comes to no further use
> But to be known and hated. So, like gross terms,
> The prince will in the perfectness of time
> Cast off his followers. . . . (*2 Henry IV* 4.3.67–75)

Warwick's analogy points up the fact that throughout the two parts of *Henry IV*, linguistic eccentricity is both an index of political insubordination and a repeated strategy of self-promotion. Most famously there is Falstaff, who adopts the sing-song rhythm, showy similitudes, and moralizing sententiousness of *Euphues* when impersonating the king in the tavern at Eastcheap.[31] In the scene that immediately follows, Spenser's self-consciously obscure style is parodied in the faux-mystical raving of Owen Glendower, the Welsh magician, who claims to have "framed to the harp / many an English ditty lovely well, / And gave the tongue a helpful ornament" (3.1.120–22) and who annoys Hotspur with his fanciful tales of Arthur and Merlin, occult prophecies and mythical beasts.[32] Finally, in *Henry IV, Part Two*, Marlowe's "high astounding terms" are lampooned in the bluster of ensign Pistol, who speaks exclusively in the ranting voice of a stage Scythian.[33] Like the vagabonds and rebels with whom they are aligned, Lyly's, Spenser's, and Marlowe's styles are forced to the margins of Shakespeare's plot—first indulged and then indicted—becoming, as Stephen Greenblatt writes of the play's Welsh and French speakers, "voices that . . . dwell outside the realms ruled by the potentates of the land."[34]

As each of these potentially disruptive figures is, as Warwick predicts, finally cast off,[35] Shakespeare clears the way for Hal to assert his own distinctive style: the blend of sonorous formality and folksy directness in which so many critics have heard the voice of an emergent English national community, a refined yet homely vernacular whose Orphic appeal transforms strangers into brothers. But those onstage perceive Henry, and his eloquence, rather differently: from the moment he ascends his father's throne, the magic of his presence and the charisma of his speech reside not in intimacy or familiarity but in the residue of his earlier estrangement. Early on, Henry IV warns Hal that his indiscriminate mixing with the likes of Falstaff and Pistol has made him "almost an alien to the hearts / Of all the court and princes of my blood" (*1 Henry IV* 3.2.34–35), and when Hal greets his father's courtiers for the first time as Henry V, we see that this is so: noting their anxious faces, he teases, "This is the English, not the Turkish court; / Not Amurath an Amurath succeeds, / But Harry Harry" (*2 Henry IV* 5.2.47–49).

As Benedict Robinson observes, the unexpected invocation of Elizabeth I's Ottoman counterpart, Sultan Murad, may be meant as an assertion of Henry's fundamental kinship both to his father and to his countrymen, but it also raises the specter of his permanent alienation from them. Indeed no sooner has Henry moved to allay the sense of distance, assuring the court, "I'll be your father and your brother, too," then he returns to it, saying with some satisfaction, "You all look strangely on me" (5.2.57, 63). Robinson notes that Henry's thoughts "turn to the Turks" with some regularity once he is king—in his proposal to Katherine that they "compound a boy, half French, half English, that shall go to Constantinople and take the Turk by the beard" (*Henry V* 5.2.204–7) and in his vision of failure as burial in an unmarked urn, "like a Turkish mute" with "a tongueless mouth" (1.2.232)—and reads in such asides the haunting traces of Henry's own bloody and illegitimate origins.[36] Henry's eloquence is, Robinson suggests, the antidote to this haunting, for it "tactically displaces attention from the vexed question of dynastic inheritance" by "turning Englishness into . . . common property."[37]

But that vision of intimacy through vernacularity was dispelled long before, banished from the second tetralogy along with Thomas Mowbray in the opening act of *Richard II*. The "heavy sentence" of his exile prompts Mowbray to protest the infliction of "so deep a maim" (1.3.148, 150):

> The language I have learn'd these forty years,
> My native English, now I must forego:
> And now my tongue's use is to me no more
> Than an unstringed viol or a harp,
> Or like a cunning instrument cased up,
> Or, being open, put into his hands
> That knows no touch to tune the harmony. (153–59)

As Mowbray makes clear, language is not a "common property"; rather it is what he loses by being "cast forth in the common air" (1.3.151). Nor is his "native English" a purely natural inheritance: it is the tongue he has "learn'd these forty years," a "cunning instrument" requiring a knowing touch. In this regard his lament charts a kind of progress for the mother tongue, but it is progress away from the ideals of commonness and accessibility, toward the incommensurable values of intricacy and art. Speaking *this* English is no durable means of cultural identification but a rare privilege, bestowed and rescinded at the whim of a fickle king.

Henry's own eloquence does not redress the "maim" done to English by Richard's "heavy sentence"—its severing from the fantasy of a shared and inalienable identity—so much as transform that injury into an enticement. In the opening scene of *Henry V*, the Archbishop of Canterbury marvels at the strange power of his tongue, which seems to solicit the very transgressive desires it also reproves:

> . . . when he speaks,
> The air, a chartered libertine, is still,
> And the mute wonder lurketh in men's ears
> To steal his sweet and honeyed sentences:
> So that the art and practic part of life
> Must be the mistress of his theoric. (1.1.48–53)

Like the imperious sultan who trims the tongues of his harem attendants (and their other parts as well), Henry's masterful speech makes mistresses and mutes of all who hear. It indicts and indulges, threatens and seduces, penning up the chartered libertine even as it turns the wondering listener to a lurker and a thief. Although "speechless death"—the fate of Thomas Mowbray—is what Henry particularly hopes to avoid for himself, his desire that "history shall with full mouth / Speak freely of our acts" (*Henry V* 1.2.230–31) depends on his ability to induce speechlessness in those around him: his sweet and honeyed sentences are precisely what they are not invited to share. While Robinson traces "the fragility of Henry's fraternal rhetoric"[38] to the uneasy political kinship of Englishman and Saracen, we might therefore trace it as well to the uneasy rhetorical kinship of enticement and alienation, to the honeyed sentences and turkened phrases that made English both eloquent and strange—eloquent *because* strange, just as Henry's "happy few" (4.3.60) are happy *because* few. Indeed where modern critics see fragility—fissures and flaws in Henry's attempt to fashion a perfect rhetorical union—their sixteenth-century counterparts might rather have seen strength: the persistent if paradoxical appeal of language that refuses identification with the common tongue.

This appeal is at the core of Henry's famous speech at Agincourt, which, although it has so often been read as a transcendent (if transitory) evocation of national unity, fashions its "band of brothers" both outside of and in opposition to England. To the extent that, as many critics have suggested, Henry relies on xenophobia to secure the boundaries of his imagined community, that xenophobia is here directed most forcefully at the supposed home front, at "gentlemen in England now abed" who "shall think themselves accursed they were not here" (4.3.64–65). The speech is prompted by Warwick's wish for the company of his countrymen—"O that we now had here / But one ten thousand of those men in England / That do no work today" (17–19)—to which Henry sternly replies, "No, faith, my coz, wish not a man from England. . . . O do not wish one more" (30, 33). From the beginning, then, the rhetoric of kinship and belonging—"my coz," Henry calls Warwick—is predicated on the exclusion of those at home. The remainder of the speech develops this opposition into a prolonged fantasy of privileged isolation from a broad and undifferentiated English community. Although we tend to interpret it as if it were addressed to the whole of Henry's host, "inscribing these men together in a shared and all but hagiographic history and a glorious future," as one critic writes,[39] it is addressed primarily to Warwick, who proves its success when he responds by wishing away not only the ten thousand Englishmen of his earlier imagining but also the five thousand actual Englishmen waiting close at hand: "God's will, my liege, would you and I alone, / without more help, could fight this royal battle" (74–75). His reaction reminds us that the only element of the speech extended to its general audience is an invitation to leave with passport in hand:

> Rather proclaim it presently throughout my host
> That he which hath no stomach to this fight
> Let him depart. His passport shall be made
> And crowns for convoy put into his purse.
> We would not die in that man's company
> That fears his fellowship to die with us. (34–39)

From a practical perspective, of course, the widespread defection of Henry's troops would mean disaster, but the appeal of his rhetoric is concentrated in the image of "you and I alone": a vision of belonging so exclusive as to verge on exile. "Perish the man whose mind is backward now," Warwick declares (72): this is no time to think of England.

Indeed even as Henry imagines his army returned "safe home" again, feasting their neighbors and teaching their sons, he insists that they will remain men apart, a select community oriented around a language that—while it resembles ordinary speech—belongs singularly and strangely to them:

He that shall see this day and live to old age
Will yearly on the vigil feast his neighbours
And say, "Tomorrow is Saint Crispian."
Then will he strip his sleeve and show his scars
And say, "These wounds I had on Crispin's day."
Old men forget: yet all shall be forgot,
But he'll remember with advantages
What feats he did that day: then shall our names,
Familiar in his mouth as household words—
Harry the king, Bedford and Exeter,
Warwick and Talbot, Salisbury and Gloucester—
Be in their flowing cups freshly remember'd. (44–55)

Familiar in *his* mouth as household words: the point is not that proper aristocratic names will be familiar to everyone, as the value of participation in Henry's royal condition is distributed down the social scale; on the contrary, other Englishmen will "hold their manhoods cheap whiles any speaks / That fought with us" (66–67). Once again the familiarity Henry invokes is ultimately a mode of estrangement: his rhetoric carves out of the common tongue—the tongue of actual families and households—a peculiar language belonging exclusively to those whose bodies bear the foreign tracery of his war. The soldier who strips his sleeve and shows his scars and says, "These wounds I had on Crispin's day" speaks the plainest English, but his speech inscribes a boundary between himself and his neighbors; no less than Lyly's ornate periphrases, Spenser's archaic diction, or Marlowe's mighty line, what such language is meant to produce is the alluring and alienating effect of *style*.

To the extent that Henry's famous speech conjures a national community, then, it does so only in order to assert the desirability of distance from it. "You know your places," Henry concludes (78), dismissing Warwick and the rest to battle. His eloquence teaches them their places, positioning them at the privileged and perilous extremity of linguistic community. That margin is not where we are now accustomed to locate Shakespeare, but it is where his eloquent English king finds it useful to reside: Henry may banish Euphues, Colin Clout, and Tamburlaine, but he also seems determined to join them. They hold their strangeness in common.

Notes

INTRODUCTION

1. In Richard Foster Jones, *The Triumph of the English Language* (Stanford, CA: Stanford University Press, 1953), the author argues that the publication and reception of *Euphues*, *The Shepheardes Calender*, and *Tamburlaine* mark the culmination of a decades-long process of linguistic self-assertion: "eloquence in English compositions becomes an accomplished fact, and the rhetorical potentialities of the mother tongue are revealed once and for all. The rude, gross, base, and barbarous mother tongue recedes into the past, and its place is taken by an eloquent language, confidence in which mounts higher and higher until it yields nothing even to Latin and Greek" (169–70).

2. Edward Blount, "To the Reader," *Sixe Court Comedies . . . by Iohn Lilly* (London: Edward Blount, 1632), sig. [A5v]; Philip Sidney, *An Apologie for Poetrie* (London: Henry Olney, 1595), sigs. [K4]ᵣ₋ᵥ.

3. Joseph Hall, "Virgidimarium," in *Christopher Marlowe: The Critical Heritage*, ed. Millar MacLure (New York: Routledge, 1995), 42.

4. Ben Jonson, *Discoveries: A Critical Edition*, ed. Maurice Castelain (Paris: Librairie Hachette, 1906), 41, 90.

5. For a thorough account of the extension of this myth into twentieth-century theories of civic discourse and the public sphere, see Walter Jost and Michael J. Hyde, "Introduction," in *Rhetoric and Hermeneutics in Our Time: A Reader*, ed. Walter Jost and Michael J. Hyde (New Haven, CT: Yale University Press, 1997), 1–31. Wayne Rebhorn, *The Emperor of Men's Minds: Literature and the Renaissance Discourse of Rhetoric* (Ithaca, NY: Cornell University Press, 1995), 23–29, provides a lengthy consideration of classical and Renaissance accounts of the origins of rhetoric, paying particular attention to the distinctive political ideologies that inflect versions of the foundational myth offered in republican and monarchic societies. Neil Rhodes, *The Power of Eloquence and English Renaissance Literature* (New York: St. Martin's, 1999), chap. 1, likewise reflects on Renaissance ideas of eloquence. See also Heinrich F. Plett, *Rhetoric and Renaissance Culture* (Berlin: de Gruyter, 2004), 396–410.

6. Isocrates, *Antidosis*, trans. G. Norlin (Cambridge, MA: Harvard University Press, 1982), 253–56, qtd. in Jost and Hyde, 2.

7. Marcus Tullius Cicero, *De Inventione*, trans. H. M. Hubbell (Cambridge, MA: Harvard University Press, 1949), 5–7.

8. Horace, *Ars Poetica*, in *The Works of Horace*, trans. C. Smart (New York: Harper and Brothers, 1896), 322.

9. Quintilian, *Institutio Oratoria*, 4 vols., trans. Donald Russell (Cambridge, MA: Harvard University Press, 2001), 1:373.

10. Thomas Wilson, *The Arte of Rhetorique* (London: Richard Grafton, 1560), sig. Aiii,, fol. 48,.

11. George Puttenham, *The Arte of English Poesie* (London: Richard Field, 1589), sigs. C,–Cii,.

12. Richard Rainolde, *A Book called the Foundacion of Rhetorike* (London: John Kingston, 1563), sig. Ai,.

13. Henry Peacham, "The Epistle," in Henry Peacham, *The Garden of Eloquence* (London: H. Jackson, 1577), sig. Aiii,–v.

14. Benedict Anderson, *Imagined Communities: Reflections on the Origin and Spread of Nationalism*, rev. ed. (New York: Verso, 2006), 7, 44.

15. David J. Baker, *Between Nations: Shakespeare, Spenser, Marvell, and the Question of Britain* (Stanford, CA: Stanford University Press, 1997), argues that the collective identity produced by sixteenth- and early seventeenth-century literature is "only ambiguously" English and that Britishness is an equally important site of literary and cultural identification (16). Andrew Hadfield, *Shakespeare, Spenser, and the Matter of Britain* (New York: Palgrave Macmillan, 2004), argues as well that it is "the notion of Britain" that "loomed so large in the horizons and imaginations of sixteenth- and seventeenth-century writers" (4). See also Adrian Hastings, *The Construction of Nationhood: Ethnicity, Religion, and Nationalism* (Cambridge: Cambridge University Press, 1997), which credits the English Bible with fostering a sense of linguistic commonality; and Joan Fitzpatrick, *Shakespeare, Spenser, and the Contours of Britain: Reshaping the Atlantic Archipelago* (Hertfordshire: University of Hertfordshire Press, 2004). Other authors have traced the stirrings of national imagining, both English and British, to earlier Tudor literature: see Cathy Shrank, *Writing the Nation in Reformation England, 1530–1580* (Oxford: Oxford University Press, 2004); Philip Schwyzer, *Literature, Nationalism, and Memory in Early Modern England and Wales* (Cambridge: Cambridge University Press, 2004)—although Schwyzer cautions that "[w]hat we discern in some early modern texts is not the nation *per se* so much as the nation *in potential*" (9); Herbert Grabes, "England or the Queen?: Public Conflict of Opinion and National Identity under Mary Tudor," in *Writing the Early Modern English Nation: The Transformation of National Identity in Sixteenth- and Seventeenth-Century England*, ed. Herbert Grabes (Amsterdam: Rodopi, 2001), 47–87; and Stewart Mottram, *Empire and Nation in Early English Renaissance Literature* (Cambridge: D. S. Brewer, 2008).

16. Richard Helgerson, *Forms of Nationhood: The Elizabethan Writing of England* (Chicago: University of Chicago Press, 1992), 1–2.

17. Claire McEachern, *The Poetics of English Nationhood, 1590–1612* (Cambridge: Cambridge University Press, 1996), 4.

18. Andrew Escobedo, *Nationalism and Historical Loss in Renaissance England* (Ithaca, NY: Cornell University Press, 2004), 3.

19. Ian Smith, "Barbarian Errors: Performing Race in Early Modern England," *Shakespeare Quarterly* 49:2 (Summer 1998): 172–73.

20. Derek Attridge, *Peculiar Language: Literature as Difference from the Renaissance to James Joyce* (Ithaca, NY: Cornell University Press, 1988), 3.

21. Aristotle, *Art of Rhetoric* 1.1356, 2.1395; translated and edited by George A. Kennedy as *On Rhetoric: A Theory of Civic Discourse* (Oxford: Oxford University Press, 1991), 41, 187.

22. Aristotle, *Rhetoric* 3.1404; trans. Kennedy, 221.

23. On the value-laden (and often specious) distinction between Attic and Asiatic styles, see Chapter 2, below, and Jeffrey Walker, *Rhetoric and Poetics in Antiquity* (Oxford: Oxford University Press, 2000). For a more thorough account of the afterlives of specific classical theories of style in Renaissance rhetorical handbooks and literary texts, see George A. Kennedy, *Classical Rhetoric and Its Christian and Secular Tradition from Ancient to Modern Times*, 2nd ed. (Chapel Hill: University of North Carolina Press, 1999); Kenneth Graham, *The Performance of Conviction: Plainness and Rhetoric in the Early English Renaissance* (Ithaca, NY: Cornell University Press, 1994); Debora Shuger, *Sacred Rhetoric: The Christian Grand Style in the English Renaissance* (Princeton, NJ: Princeton University Press, 1988); and Annabel Patterson, *Hermogenes and the Renaissance: Seven Ideas of Style* (Princeton, NJ: Princeton University Press, 1970).

24. Puttenham, 147.

25. Puttenham, 147.

26. Marcus Fabius Quintilian, *Institutio Oratoria*, 4 vols., trans. H. E. Butler (Cambridge, MA: Harvard University Press, 1966), 3:212–13.

27. As Kathy Eden, *Hermeneutics and the Rhetorical Tradition: Chapters in the Ancient Legacy and Its Humanist Reception* (New Haven, CT: Yale University Press, 1997), observes, in his *Rhetoric* Aristotle makes very little distinction between *to prepon* and *to oikeon*, between "appropriateness" and "homeliness"; Cicero follows him in defining decorum "as the ability to accommodate the occasion, taking account of times, places, and persons" and identifying this capacity as the key to success as an orator, a poet, and more broadly speaking, a moral being (25–26). See also Kathy Eden, "Petrarchan Hermeneutics and the Rediscovery of Intimacy," in *Petrarch and the Textual Origins of Interpretation*, ed. Teodolinda Barolini and H. Wayne Storey (New York: Columbia University Press, 2007), 233–34.

28. Arthur Golding, *The xv. bookes of P. Ouidius Naso, entytuled Metamorphosis* (London: William Seres, 1567), fols. 135ᵥ–136ᵣ. As Sean Keilen, *Vulgar Eloquence: On the Renaissance Invention of English Literature* (New Haven, CT: Yale University Press, 2006), notes, Renaissance emblem books sometimes conflate these two aspects of the classical myth, depicting the civilizing poet as himself half-wild—disheveled, barefoot, and perpetually on the verge of retreat to the untamed woods from which he emerged. Keilen argues that such hybrid images provided a particularly nourishing form of sustenance to vernacular authors, encouraging "the idea that Orpheus' eloquence was inseparable from his barbarism" and fostering the hope that their own unseemly origins might prove similarly generative (84–88).

29. Jeffrey Knapp, *An Empire Nowhere: England, America, and Literature from* Utopia *to* The Tempest (Berkeley: University of California Press, 1992), 21.

30. Jones, 212.

31. Jones, 169.

32. William Harrison, "The Description and Historie of England," in Raphael Holinshed, *The first and second volume of Chronicles* (London, 1577), 14.

33. Samuel Daniel, *The Defence of Ryme* (London: Edward Blount, 1603), sig. H7ᵣ; Robert Cawdrey, "To the Reader," in Robert Cawdrey, *A Table Alphabeticall* (London: Edmund Weaver, 1604), sig. [A3]ᵥ. Cawdrey lifts his epistle wholesale from the pages of Wilson's *Arte*, but the passage has a very different import when used as a justification for the first vernacular dictionary: Cawdrey clearly believes that "making a difference of English" is an absurdity; Wilson, as we shall see, and somewhat in spite of himself, does not.

34. David Wallace, *Premodern Places: Calais to Surinam, Chaucer to Aphra Behn* (Malden, MA: Blackwell, 2004), 53.

35. Richard Hakluyt, *Principle Navigations of the English Nation* (London, 1589), 33.

36. Thomas Nashe, "Have With You to Saffron Walden," in *The Unfortunate Traveller and Other Works*, ed. J. B. Steane (New York: Penguin Books, 1973), 490.

37. Thomas Nashe, "Nashe's Lenten Stuff," in *The Unfortunate Traveller and Other Works*, ed. J. B. Steane (New York: Penguin Books, 1973), 377.

38. Thomas Wilson, *The three orations of Demosthenes* (London: Henrie Denham, 1570), "To the right Honorable Sir William Cecill," sigs. A1ᵣ₋ᵥ.

39. Cloth is a particularly suggestive metaphor for the virtues and limitations of the mother tongue. Throughout the sixteenth and seventeenth centuries, wool and unfinished cloth constituted England's most valuable exports and the foundation of its economic stature abroad, but English clothiers "remained incapable of producing the sophisticated dyeing and finishing processes that were established in the Low Countries, Italy, Persia, India, and China," and attempts to redress the imbalance by mandating the sale of finished cloth ended in "catastrophic failure": Flemish merchants imposed an embargo, and as it turned out, "no one wanted to buy finished cloth of such poor quality anyway" (Peter Stallybrass, "Marginal England: The View from Aleppo," in *Center or Margin: Revisions of the English Renaissance in Honor of Leeds Barroll*, ed. Lena Cowen Orlin [Selinsgrove: Susquehanna University Press, 2006], 31).

40. George Chapman, "A Defence of Homer," in *Elizabethan Critical Essays*, ed. Gregory Smith (London: Oxford University Press, 1904), 304.

41. Richard Mulcaster, *The First Parte of the Elementarie* (London: T. Vautroullier, 1582), 257.

42. As Gabriele Stein has shown in her work on European polyglot dictionaries, English was a late and lesser object of study abroad, playing a "subordinate role," if any, in the most popular dictionaries and phrase books on the Continent; not until 1580, for instance, was English added to the eleven-language edition of Calepinus's *Dictionarium*, in which it "constituted a final group together with Polish and Hungarian and within that group . . . occupied the final position" ("The Emerging Role of English in the Dictionaries of Renaissance Europe," *Folia Linguistica Historica* 9:1 [1989], 30, 58). Barbara

Strang estimates that in 1570 English was "spoken by a population of about four and a half million and lacking all overseas branches" (*A History of English* [London: Methuen, 1970], 104).

43. Puttenham, 158.

44. Paula Blank, *Broken English: Dialects and the Politics of Language in Renaissance Writings* (London: Routledge, 1996), 16–23.

45. Harrison, 14.

46. Although the *Oxford English Dictionary* (hereafter *OED*) attests its use in the late fifteenth century (s.v. "ornature"), "ornature" still merits inclusion in Edward Phillips's 1658 dictionary of neologisms and hard words, the *New World of English Words*; more tellingly, it is a favored term of Ben Jonson's "poetaster" Crispinus—precisely the sort of would-be Orpheus whose corrupt phrasing Harrison decries. "Ornature" particularly offends Jonson's Horace, the voice of poetic reason: "Is't not possible to make an escape from him?" he pleads upon hearing Crispinus use the word (Ben Jonson, *Poetaster, or The Arraignment* [London: M. L., 1602], sig. D3ᵥ).

47. Wayne Rebhorn, "Outlandish Fears: Defining Decorum in Renaissance Rhetoric," *Intertexts* 4:1 (Spring 2000): 22.

48. Graham, 16. Graham's account jibes with the emphasis placed on the social and political contexts of rhetoric within a number of foundational studies of Renaissance humanism: see especially Joel B. Altman, *The Tudor Play of Mind: Rhetorical Inquiry and the Development of Elizabethan Drama* (Berkeley: University of California Press, 1978); Lisa Jardine, *Francis Bacon: Discovery and the Art of Discourse* (Cambridge: Cambridge University Press, 1974); Victoria Kahn, *Rhetoric, Prudence, and Skepticism* (Ithaca, NY: Cornell University Press, 1985); and Anthony Grafton and Lisa Jardine, *From Humanism to the Humanities: Education and the Liberal Arts in Fifteenth and Sixteenth Century Europe* (Cambridge, MA: Harvard University Press, 1986).

49. Citing the demise of the myth of Brutus and the discovery, by English antiquarians, of physical remnants of Britain's colonial past, Keilen argues that in the late sixteenth century, "England's broader relationship to Rome was suffering an unprecedented strain. . . . [H]istory obliged English poets to regard themselves as the victims of the Roman Conquest, rather than the rightful heirs of classical Latin culture"; what is more, as the assiduous study of that culture revealed, "derogatory passages about ancient Britain were scattered throughout the corpus of Latin literature. The most infamous of these occurred in texts whose authority and value were unimpeachable, like Virgil's *Eclogues* and Cicero's *Letters*" (15–16). In Chapters 1 and 4 I consider how two particular English writers, Roger Ascham and Edmund Spenser, respond to the sting of those insults.

50. Jenny Mann, *Outlaw Rhetoric: Figuring Vernacular Eloquence in Shakespeare's England* (Ithaca, NY: Cornell University Press, 2012), 13, 14.

51. See Carla Mazzio, *The Inarticulate Renaissance: Language Trouble in an Age of Eloquence* (Philadelphia: University of Pennsylvania Press, 2009). "Speech located at the nexus of classical and vernacular organization," whether grammatical or rhetorical, often "prove[d] vividly inarticulate," Mazzio observes (6). Mazzio's reading of *The Spanish Tragedy* offers a useful critique too of the assumption that cultivating the vernacular promoted

national unity: Kyd's play and, especially, its play-within-a-play expose "the ambivalence about forms of cultural fusion and confusion inherent in the establishment of a national tongue" (103).

52. Anderson, 19.

53. Wilson, *Rhetorique* 162, 171–72.

54. Richard Sherry, *A Treatise of Schemes and Tropes* (London, 1550), sigs. A1ᵥ–A2ᵣ.

55. Puttenham, 157, 143, 159–60.

56. Daniel, *Defence*, sig. [G5]r.

CHAPTER 1

1. See, for example, T. W. Baldwin, *Shakespere's Small Latine & Lesse Greeke* (Urbana: University of Illinois Press, 1944); Joel B. Altman, *The Tudor Play of Mind: Rhetorical Inquiry and the Development of Elizabethan Drama* (Berkeley: University of California Press, 1978); Jonathan Bate, *Shakespeare and Ovid* (Oxford: Clarendon Paperbacks, 1994); Rebecca Bushnell, *A Culture of Teaching: Early Modern Humanism in Theory and Practice* (Ithaca, NY: Cornell University Press, 1996); Leonard Barkan, "What Did Shakespeare Read?," in *The Cambridge Companion to Shakespeare*, ed. Margreta de Grazia and Stanley Wells (Cambridge: Cambridge University Press, 2001), 31–47; and Colin Burrow, "Shakespeare and Humanistic Culture," in *Shakespeare and the Classics*, ed. Charles Martindale and A. B. Taylor (Cambridge: Cambridge University Press, 2004), 9–27.

2. Ardis Butterfield, *The Familiar Enemy: Chaucer, Language, and Nation in the Hundred Years War* (Oxford: Oxford University Press, 2009), describes the written English of such writers, for whom either French or Latin would have been the usual language of composition, as a "neo-language" (342).

3. Jones, 13–15.

4. The rivalry is implicit throughout Jones's book but is made explicit in its final paragraph, which identifies the pursuit of vernacular eloquence by late Elizabethan writers as the generative spirit of a world in which "English reigns supreme" and "Latin, Greek, and the classical spirit have all but disappeared" (323). A similar premise undergirds Benedict Anderson's narrative in *Imagined Communities*, whereby the rise of national vernaculars coincides with and is contingent upon "the fall of Latin" (18).

5. Helgerson, *Forms of Nationhood*, 3.

6. C. S. Lewis, *English Literature in the Sixteenth Century Excluding Drama* (Oxford: Clarendon, 1944), 274–75, 279–81.

7. Anthony Grafton and Lisa Jardine offer the strongest and most influential version of this argument in *From Humanism to the Humanities*.

8. Burrow, "Shakespeare and Humanistic Culture," 15.

9. Richard Helgerson credits the flourishing of romance in the late sixteenth century to the rebellious efforts of "Elizabethan prodigals," whose literary ambitions for the vernacular simultaneously refuse and reframe the devoutly classicized, civic-minded precepts of their fathers' generation (*The Elizabethan Prodigals* [Berkeley: University of California

Press, 1976]; Helgerson recapitulates this argument in the introduction and first chapter of *Forms of Nationhood*). Arthur Kinney offers a similar account of late sixteenth-century poetic practice, discerning in it a pointed critique of its authors' humanist training in rhetoric (*Humanist Poetics: Thought, Rhetoric, and Fiction in Sixteenth-Century England* [Amherst: University of Massachusetts Press, 1986]). More recently Georgia Brown has identified in the 1590s novel "forms of authorship defined by their opposition to . . . the principles of humanist morality" (*Redefining Elizabethan Literature* [Cambridge: Cambridge University Press, 2004], 24), while Jeff Dolven reads the self-undermining tendencies of Elizabethan romance as "artifacts . . . of an unresolved opposition between story and school" (*Scenes of Instruction in Renaissance Romance* [Chicago: University of Chicago Press, 2007], 59), and Lynn Enterline finds that "Shakespeare creates convincing effects of character and emotion . . . precisely when undercutting the socially normative categories schoolmasters invoked as the goal of their new form of pedagogy" (*Shakespeare's Schoolroom: Rhetoric, Discipline, Emotion* [Philadelphia: University of Pennsylvania Press, 2012], 10).

10. Thomas M. Greene, "Roger Ascham: The Perfect End of Shooting," *English Literary History* 36:4 (December 1969): 623.

11. Roger Ascham, *The Scholemaster* (1570; reprinted, Menston, UK: Scolar Press, 1967), [2]–3. All subsequent citations to this work refer to this edition.

12. Richard Halpern, *The Poetics of Primitive Accumulation: English Renaissance Culture and the Genealogy of Capital* (Ithaca, NY: Cornell University Press, 1991), 24.

13. Ascham, *The Scholemaster*, 46,.

14. Thomas Elyot, *The Proheme,* in Elyot, *The Boke named the Governour* (1531; reprinted, Menston, UK: Scolar Press, 1970), sig. aii,. All subsequent citations to this work refer to this edition.

15. "Of education in its nursery stage Elyot has nothing of value to say," Lewis sniffs. "Like all his kind he issues rigid instructions which would be scattered to the winds by ten minutes' experience of any real child or any real nurse" (Lewis, 274–75).

16. "We have long accepted the word of humanist teachers and theorists about the effects of their pedagogy," Enterline writes. "It is time to listen to the testimony of grammar school students" (Enterline, 10). This chapter may seem to flout that sensible advice: Elyot's pronouncements about wet nurses, like Ascham's prescriptions for double translation, interest me precisely because they are so self-consciously unrealistic. It is my belief, however, that such impracticable fantasies are, in large part, how English writers trained in humanist schoolrooms learned to think of eloquence.

17. The example of the young Michel de Montaigne, born the year after Elyot published *The Governour*, is the exception that proves the rule. As Montaigne recalls in his essay "Of the Institution and Education of Children," his father, Pierre, went to extraordinary lengths to establish Latin as his son's first language, insisting that all household staff communicate with the child exclusively in Latin and supplying the boy with a tutor who spoke no French. Thanks to his father's "exquisite toile," Montaigne writes, by the age of six he spoke fluent Latin but knew "no more French . . . then Arabike" (*Essays written in French by Michael Lord of Montaigne*, trans. John Florio [London, 1613], 84–85).

18. On the afterlife of the English nurse as a locus of cultural anxieties about class,

language, and national identity, see Katie Trumpener, *Bardic Nationalism: The Romantic Novel and the British Empire* (Princeton, NJ: Princeton University Press, 1997), 196–241.

19. Robert Matz, *Defending Literature in Early Modern England* (Cambridge: Cambridge University Press, 2000), 36–48.

20. J. S. C. Eidinow, "Dido, Aeneas, and Iulus: Heirship and Obligation in *Aeneid* 4," *Classical Quarterly*, n.s., 53:1 (May 2003): 260–67.

21. As Eidinow points out, Virgil fixes attention of the empty space of Dido's "lap" or "womb" (*gremio*), and on her various and unsuccessful efforts to fill it. As book 4 draws to its embittered conclusion, Dido abandons these efforts, recasting nursing as the primal scene of abandonment and neglect: "No goddess was your mother," she rails at Aeneas. "Hyrcanian tigresses suckled you" (nec tibi diva parens . . . Hyrcanaeque admorunt ubera tigres). The narrator undercuts the potential pathos of the scene by noting, as an aside, that Dido's own nurse, who might have comforted her, is now just ashes in the land she left behind when she married (namque suam [nutricem] patria antique cinis ater habebat). The aside has a clear bearing on the Carthaginian queen's present predicament: "We, too, have the right to seek a foreign realm" (et nos fas extera quaerere regna), Aeneas says pointedly, reminding Dido of all that she herself has abandoned in pursuit of empire (*Aeneid*, trans. H. R. Fairclough [Cambridge, MA: Harvard University Press, 1916], 445–47).

22. David Baker, " 'To Divulgate or Set Forth': Humanism and Heresy in Sir Thomas Elyot's *The Book named the Governor*," *Studies in Philology* 90:1 (Winter 1993): 46.

23. And was said, as I mention in the following chapter: in the dedicatory epistle to his 1550 *Treatise of Schemes and Tropes*, Richard Sherry hails "ye right worshipfull knight syr Thomas Eliot," who "as it were generally searching out the copye of oure language in all kynde of wordes and phrases, . . . hath hereby declared the plentyfulnes of our mother tounge, loue toward hys country, hys tyme not spent in vanitye and trifles" (sig. [A3]_{r–v}).

24. Stephen Merriam Foley, "Coming to Terms: Thomas Elyot's Definitions and the Particularity of Human Letters," *English Literary History* 61:2 (Summer 1994): 221.

25. Thomas Elyot, *Of the knowledge whiche maketh a wise man* (London: Thomas Berthelet, 1533), sig. A3_{r–v}.

26. For a reading of the phrase's possible associations with a more dangerous sense of vulgarization, verging on threats of sedition and popular revolt, see Baker, "To Divulgate or Set Forth."

27. Foley, 221.

28. Elyot, *Of the knowledge*, sig. A2_v.

29. Ascham claims to have had a conversation with Elyot about the origins of longbow shooting, during which Elyot claimed to be writing a much longer work treating that subject and other "olde monuments of England"; Ascham's anecdote is the only surviving record of this (lost? never completed?) treatise, *De rebus memorabilibus Angliae*. See Roger Ascham, *Toxophilus: The Schole of Shoting*, in *English Works*, ed. William Aldis Wright (Cambridge: Cambridge University Press, 1904), 53. All subsequent citations to this work refer to this edition.

30. Ryan J. Stark, "Protestant Theology and Apocalyptic Rhetoric in Roger Ascham's

The Schoolmaster," *Journal of the History of Ideas* 69:4 (October 2008): 517–32. Greene points out that archery is Ascham's favorite metaphor for the arts of language, "recur[ring] so often in *The Scholemaster* as to almost seem obsessive." Of the goose, Greene notes, Ascham writes in *Toxophilus*, "How fit, even as her fethers be onlye for shootynge, so be her quylls fytte onlye for wrytyng" (qtd. in Greene, 619).

31. Dolven, 55–56.

32. Enterline, 12.

33. Helgerson, *Forms of Nationhood*, 22.

34. He charts both Lyly's and Spenser's careers in terms of their progress away from "Aschamite" values (Helgerson, *Forms of Nationhood*, 25–59).

35. So concludes William E. Miller, judging from the preponderance of "vulgars," or English crib sheets for Latin phrases, in surviving documents; see Miller, "Double Translation in English Humanist Education," *Studies in the Renaissance* 10 (1963): 163–74. We have as well the testimony of William Kempe, whose treatise *The Education of Children in Learning* (London: Thomas Orwin, 1588) offers an account of his experience as schoolmaster at the Plymouth School. Kempe says that Ascham's method is "good" but is to be used only "when opportunitie and leisure will serve" (sig. G1ᵥ).

36. Precisely this fear motivated Stephen Gardiner when, as chancellor of Cambridge University in the 1540s, he forbade Cheke and his colleague Thomas Smith from promulgating their new method of pronouncing ancient Greek; see Bror Danielsson's introduction to *Sir Thomas Smith, Literary and Linguistic Works*, part 1, *Stockholm Studies in English* 50 (Stockholm: Almquist and Wiksell, 1978), 13–20. In a 1542 letter Gardiner objects that, in their eagerness to bridge "the distance in time and space that separates us from them," the pair have "treat[ed] our English tongue as though it were a Lesbian measuring stick in accordance with which you take the measure of the Greek diphthongs." He goes on, "For just as Lesbian craftsmen adapt their measuring-stick to the marble, so you from time to time adapt English to Greek and, employing a new method of spelling, write our word *pay* with an *I* instead of a *y* . . . so that if we were to follow your example we should to that extent transform English orthography. . . . It was in order that this might not happen that I issued my edict" (qtd. in Danielsson, 213). Cheke made a politic retreat, but Smith persisted. In 1568 he published a fresh edition of *De Recta et Emendata Linguae Graecae Pronuntiatione*, bound together—just as Gardiner feared—with a new dialogue, *De Recta et Emendata Linguae Anglicae Scriptione*, proposing a reformed orthography for the English language: "vagabond" *C* and "beggarly, intruding" *Q* are to be "exile[d] far away"; while other English sounds, "so far vagrant"—the "th" in "father," for instance, which has been forced to share a grapheme with "th" in "thief"—are to be given "place[s] of eternal habitation" through the revival of the Anglo-Saxon letters þ and ð (Danielsson, 140). For more on spelling controversies, see Blank, *Broken English*, 24–29.

37. Richard Mulcaster, *Positions . . . for the training vp of children* (London: Thomas Vautroullier, 1581), 8, 11. All subsequent citations to this work refer to this edition.

38. Richard Mulcaster, *The First Part of the Elementarie Which Entreateth Chieflie of the Right Writing of Our English Tongue* (London: Thomas Vautroullier, 1582), 254. Mulcaster's was

one of the first English grammars; for an account of subsequent approaches to analyzing and standardizing vernacular usage, see Blank, *Broken English*; and Emma Vorlat, *The Development of English Grammatical Theory, 1586–1737* (Leuven: Leuven University Press, 1975).

39. Mulcaster, *First Part of the Elementarie*, 75.

CHAPTER 2

1. Elyot, *The Boke named the Governour* (1970), fol. 49ᵥ. All subsequent citations to this work refer to this edition.

2. Leonard Cox, *The Arte or Crafte of Rhetoryke* (London, 1532), sigs. [Fvi]ᵣ–[Fvii]ᵣ; Ascham, *The Scholemaster*, fol. 46ᵣ.

3. Sherry, (1550), sigs. A1ᵥ–A2ᵣ. All subsequent citations to this work refer to this edition.

4. Ascham, *The Scholemaster*, fol. 35ᵣ–ᵥ.

5. Jenny Mann identifies only one sixteenth-century vernacular rhetoric, Wilson's *Arte of Rhetorique,* that addresses the full classical complement of rhetorical techniques, from invention through pronunciation; the majority of the rest deal exclusively with style, although a few address only invention and arrangement, most often under the auspices of logic or dialectic (17–18 and appendix, 219–20). As style consumed rhetoric, it grew proportionally: as Sylvia Adamson, Gavin Alexander, and Katrin Ettenhuber note, the pseudo-Ciceronian *Ad Herennium* "gave its students sixty-five figures to learn," while "the second edition of Peacham's *Garden of Eloquence* (1593) raised the number to two hundred" ("Introduction," in *Renaissance Figures of Speech*, ed. Sylvia Adamson, Gavin Alexander, and Katrin Ettenhuber [Cambridge: Cambridge University Press, 2007], 3).

6. Lee Sonnino, *A Handbook to Sixteenth-Century Rhetoric* (London: Routledge and Kegan Paul, 1968), 7; Thomas Conley, *Rhetoric in the European Tradition* (Chicago: University of Chicago Press, 1990), 134.

7. Wolfgang G. Müller, "Directions for English: Thomas Wilson's *Art of Rhetoric,* George Puttenham's *Art of English Poesy,* and the Search for Vernacular Eloquence," in *The Oxford Handbook of Tudor Literature, 1485–1603,* ed. Mike Pincombe and Cathy Shrank (Oxford: Oxford University Press, 2009), 317, 320–21.

8. Adamson et al., 3.

9. Mann, 41.

10. The program he proposes is in fact rather lavish in its expense of time and money: ideally, he believes, the reading of classical poetry, oratory, and philosophy would occupy young men until the age of twenty-one—a full seven years after most Tudor youths began their professional training (see Elyot, *The Governour,* fol. 46ᵥ–55ᵥ).

11. Cox, sig. Fviᵥ.

12. Thomas Wilson, *The Arte of Rhetorique,* rev. and exp. 2nd ed. (London: Richard Grafton, 1560), fol. 1ᵣ. All subsequent citations to this work refer to this edition.

13. Ascham, *The Scholemaster*, 146.

14. Peter E. Medine, "Introduction," in Thomas Wilson, *The Art of Rhetoric (1560)*, ed.

Peter E. Medine (University Park: Pennsylvania State University Press, 1994), 5. "Wilson seems to have deliberately made his book look as English as may be," Müller notes, citing his *Arte* as "a significant contribution to the growth of national identity" (311, 321). "More than any other early guide, Wilson's *Arte of Rhetoric* reminds the reader that *England* is the site" of the eloquence it imagines, Mann argues: "Wilson repeatedly cites the topic of the nation as the most fitting subject of vernacular discourse" and offers "examples of rhetorical speech . . . ever more particularized to the geography of England" (44). His lexical and syntactical precepts reflect what Cathy Shrank describes as the "ideal of a self-regulating island nation": a "vision of a unified, obedient nation rest[ing] on the reformation of English speech" and the exclusion of "the polluting effect of foreign words" (*Writing the Nation in Reformation England 1530–1580* [Oxford: Oxford University Press, 2004], 188, 189–90). Shrank's account highlights the authoritarian political cast of Wilson's writings, situating the publication of the two editions of his *Rhetorique* in the context of his suffering under the Marian regime. For more on this context, see Peter E. Medine, *Thomas Wilson* (Boston: Twayne, 1986); and Martin Elsky, *Authorizing Words: Speech, Writing, and Print in the English Renaissance* (Ithaca, NY: Cornell University Press, 1989).

15. Albert J. Schmidt, "Thomas Wilson and the Tudor Commonwealth: An Essay in Civic Humanism," *Huntington Library Quarterly* 23:1 (1959): 50.

16. B. M. Cotton MSS, Titus, F. i., fol. 163 (qtd. in Schmidt, 59).

17. Thomas Wilson, *The Rule of Reason, Conteinyng the Arte of Logique, Set Forth in Englishe* ([London], 1551), sigs. A2ᵥ–A4ᵣ. All subsequent citations to this work refer to this edition.

18. Especially as concerns the importance of invention and its "places," Wilson makes no strong distinction between logic and rhetoric, regarding "both these Artes as much like" in their concern with probable argumentation, differing only in that the former "doeth playnly and nakedly set furthe with apt wordes the summe of thinges," while the latter "vseth gay paincted Sentences, and setteth furth those matters with fresh colours and goodly ornamentes" (*Logique*, sigs. B3ᵣ–ᵥ). Thus, although he calls his treatise an art of logic, he includes in it discussions of enthymemes, commonplaces, arguments from literature, and even sophistical tricks, all of which might more properly be considered elements of rhetoric.

19. Quintilian, *Institutio Oratoria*, 4 vols., trans. H. E. Butler (Cambridge, MA: Harvard University Press, 1966), 5.10.21, 2:213.

20. The *topoi* appear in Isocrates's *Encomium of Helen* and other sophistic texts in reference to tried-and-true strategies of argumentation and their material counterparts, the "places" in rhetorical handbooks where lists of such strategies could be found by an orator in need of guidance or inspiration. These topics, however, differ from Aristotle's in that they serve a primarily conservative function: they are textual repositories of "key ideas" or particular "forms of expression" available for imitation or replication, especially by novice orators. Aristotle, by contrast, seeks to endow rhetoric with the capacity for innovative rational thought; his topics redress the perceived imbalance between rhetorical and logical argument by serving as the engine of a uniquely rhetorical strategy of invention and persuasion. See William M. A. Grimaldi, *Studies in the Philosophy of Aristotle's Rhetoric*

(Wiesbaden: Franz Steiner Verlag GMBH, 1972), 121; and George Kennedy, *A New History of Classical Rhetoric* (Princeton, NJ: Princeton University Press, 1994), 28.

21. Jost and Hyde, "Introduction," 2, 12.

22. Dilip Parmeshwar Gaonkar, "Introduction: Contingency and Probability," in *A Companion to Rhetoric and Rhetorical Criticism*, ed. Walter Jost and Wendy Olmsted (Oxford: Blackwell, 2004), 7.

23. Plato, *Gorgias,* trans. Robin Waterfield (Oxford: Oxford University Press, 1998), 45. In the *Gorgias* Socrates challenges the chief of the sophists to identify the actual knowledge on which the attainment of rhetorical success depends. His critique amounts to the charge that, as Gaonkar puts it, eloquence is untrustworthy "precisely because it is rootless": because it is grounded in no particular realm of expertise, its claims are malleable to the expectations and desires of a given audience (5). Asked by Socrates to identify "the particular province" of his art, Gorgias finally claims that rhetorical expertise excludes no form of knowledge as alien to its purposes—a claim that Socrates argues amounts to saying that rhetoric has no knowledge of its own to impart. In the *Phaedrus*, by contrast, Plato's other major antirhetorical dialogue, Socrates alleges that rhetoric is inferior to dialectic because its arguments are too deeply rooted in circumstances (geographic, cultural, historical, political, and personal) irrelevant to the determination of universal truths; the *Gorgias* suggests that this local particularity is the symptom of a misguided aspiration to generality—rhetoric is both too narrow and too expansive in its claims.

24. Aristotle, *Rhetoric* 1.2.11, trans. Kennedy (1991), 41. For more on the relationship between consensus and topical argument, see John D. Schaeffer, "Commonplaces: *Sensus Communis,*" in *A Companion to Rhetoric and Rhetorical Criticism*, ed. Walter Jost and Wendy Olmsted (Oxford: Blackwell, 2004), 278–93; and Carolyn R. Miller, "The Aristotelian *Topos*: Hunting for Novelty," in *Re-Reading Aristotle's Rhetoric*, ed. Alan G. Gross and Arthur E. Walzer (Carbondale: Southern Illinois University Press, 2000), 130–46.

25. As Barbara Warnick points out, much recent rhetorical criticism has obscured Aristotle's emphasis on the contextual, local character of the rhetorical topics precisely because it has failed to take seriously the relationship between topics and the actual, physical places that define a community: "The topics are often referred to in spatial terms—as 'seats' of argument, 'regions' in which argument resides, containers, receptacles, and places where one can 'find' an argument, [but] few authors have speculated as to where these 'places' might be." Warnick observes that Aristotle's theory of topics goes beyond the strategies and formulas of the sophists' handbooks in this emphasis on locale: "[T]he rhetor must also know the values, presumptions, predispositions, and expectations of the audience, and he must locate both his starting points (special topics) *and* forms of inference (common topics) with these in mind. Thus, in addition to the cognitive processes of the individual [orator], one must look to another 'space' to locate the reservoir of common topics available to a speaker. One must look to the habits of thought, value hierarchies, forms of knowledge, and cultural conventions of the host society." See Barbara Warnick, "Two Systems of Invention: The Topics in the *Rhetoric* and *The New Rhetoric*," in *Re-Reading Aristotle's Rhetoric*, ed. Alan G. Gross and Arthur E. Walzer (Carbondale: Southern Illinois University Press, 2000), 107–8.

26. Aristotle, *Rhetoric* 2.22.1, trans. Kennedy (1991), 187.

27. Plato, *Gorgias* 465c, trans. Waterfield, 33.

28. Aristotle, *Rhetoric* 2.22.1, trans. Kennedy (1991), 187.

29. Mann elaborates on the significance of these, especially the conspicuously English *Shire* (44–45).

30. The observation is penciled on the final page of Harvey's copy of Quintilian's *Institutio Oratoria* (qtd. in Medine, *Thomas Wilson*, 55).

31. Barnes's remark dates to 1593 (qtd. in Schmidt, 55).

32. Qtd. in Kennedy (1994), 91.

33. Qtd. in Kennedy (1994), 18.

34. Aristotle, *Rhetoric* 3.1.6, trans. Kennedy (1991), 219.

35. Aristotle, *Rhetoric* 3.1.9, trans. Kennedy (1991), 219.

36. Aristotle, *Rhetoric* 3.2.1–2, trans. Kennedy (1991), 221.

37. Aristotle, *Rhetoric* 3.2.2–3, trans. Kennedy (1991), 221.

38. Aristotle, *Rhetoric* 3.2.3, trans. Kennedy (1991), 221–22.

39. Aristotle, *Rhetoric* 3.2.2, trans. Kennedy (1991), 221.

40. Aristotle, *Poetics*, trans. Malcolm Heath (London: Penguin Books, 1996), 34 (section 9.3).

41. Aristotle, *Poetics* 9.3, trans. Heath, 34.

42. Aristotle, *Poetics* 9.3; the first translation is Heath's (34), and the second is Kennedy's (1991, 222n25).

43. Quintilian, *Institutia Oratoriae* 8.3.58, trans. Butler (1966), 3:243.

44. Quintilian, *Institutia Oratoriae* 8.2.6, trans. Butler (1966), 3:199.

45. Quintilian, *Institutia Oratoriae* 9.3.2–5, trans. Butler (1966), 3:444–45.

46. Quintilian, *Institutia Oratoriae* 8.2.6, trans. Butler (1966), 3:199.

47. Kennedy (1994), 96.

48. Jeffrey Walker, *Rhetoric and Poetics in Antiquity* (Oxford: Oxford University Press, 2000), 55.

49. Kennedy (1994), 160–61.

50. Qtd. in Walker, 68–69.

51. Walker, 69.

52. Abraham Fraunce, *The Arcadian Rhetorike,* (London: Thomas Orwin, 1588), sig. D1$_v$.

53. Peacham, sig. B1$_r$.

54. Puttenham, 120–21. All subsequent citations to this work refer to this edition.

55. Jonson, *Discoveries*, 95.

56. Jonson, *Discoveries*, 75, 103–4.

57. Indeed, as Paula Blank, *Broken English*, argues, "words usually characterized as examples of Renaissance 'poetic diction'" may be "better understood as dialects of early modern English" (3). Blank cites Alexander Gill's Latin history of the English language, *Logonomia Anglica* (1619), which places the "Poetic" alongside "the general, the Northern, the Southern, the Eastern, [and] the Western" as one of the "major dialects." "Along with regional languages implicitly defined, geographically and socially, by their relation to the

'general' language (i.e., an elite variety of London English)," Blank writes, we might consider " 'Poetic' language as a province of the vernacular." For a discussion of the "generic intertextuality" enacted by Puttenham's conflation of poetry and eloquence, see Heinrich F. Plett, *Rhetoric and Renaissance Culture* (New York: Walter de Gruyter, 2004), 151–52, 162–73.

58. George Gascoigne. "Certayne Notes of Instruction Concerning the Making of Verse or Ryme in English," in *Ancient Critical Essays upon English Poets and Poesy*, vol. 2, ed. Joseph Haslewood (London: Robert Triphook, 1815), 53. All subsequent citations to this work refer to this edition.

59. *OED*, s.v. "turkesse."

CHAPTER 3

1. For a record of surviving editions from 1578 through 1902, see the table of editions in John Lyly, *Euphues: The Anatomy of Wit; Euphues and His England*, ed. Morris William Croll and Harry Clemens (New York: E. P. Dutton, 1916), x. All subsequent citations to this work refer to this edition. Leah Guenther cites a spate of imitations, including John Dickenson's *Arisbas, Euphues amidst His Slumbers* (1594); Robert Greene's *Euphues, His Censure to Philatus* (1597) and *Menaphon, Camilla's Alarum to Slumbering Euphues* (1589); and Thomas Lodge's *Rosalynde, Euphues Golden Legacy* and *Euphues Shadow, the Battaile of the Sences* (1592), which as she says, "effectively saturated the market" for euphuism "during the last two decades of the sixteenth century" (" 'To Parley Euphuism': Fashioning English as a Linguistic Fad," *Renaissance Studies* 16:1 [2002]: 25n5).

2. Francis Meres, *Palladis Tamia Wits Treasury being the second part of Wits Commonwealth* (London: P. Short, 1598), 627.

3. Qtd. in R. Warwick Bond, "Life of John Lyly," in *The Complete Works of John Lyly*, vol. 1, ed. R. Warwick Bond (Oxford: Clarendon, 1902), 80n2. This, Bond says, is "the absolutely earliest instance of direct disapproval of Euphuism": it appears in a pamphlet written in 1589, *Advertisement to Papp-Hatchett* (1593), Harvey's retort to *Pappe with a Hatchett*, Lyly's contribution to the virulent Martin Marprelate controversy.

4. Leah Scragg, "Introduction," in John Lyly, *"Euphues: The Anatomy of Wit" and "Euphues and His England*," ed. Leah Scragg (Manchester: Manchester University Press, 2003), 1.

5. Graham Tulloch, "Sir Walter Scott's Excursion into Euphuism," *Neuphilologische Mitteilungen* 78 (1977): 70.

6. William Webbe, *A Discourse of English Poetry* (London: Robert Walley, 1586), sig. C1v. All subsequent citations to this work refer to this edition.

7. Philip Sidney, *An Apologie for Poetry* (London: Robert Olney, 1595), sigs. [K4]r–v.

8. Philip Sidney, *Syr P. S. His Astrophel and Stella* (London: Thomas Newman, 1591), 2.

9. Lyly, 5.

10. C. S. Lewis, *English Literature in the Sixteenth Century Excluding Drama* (Oxford: Clarendon, 1954), 314–15. Lewis loathes *Euphues*—Lyly's "fatal success," as he terms it, and the work that prevents him from classing Lyly among the "golden" authors of his period.

Lewis's criticisms of the text are, to a certain extent, just—Euphues *is* least interesting once he reforms his ways and takes up the mantle of moral exemplarity—but Lyly's narrative, as I will show, is less indulgent of its protagonist's "confident fatuity" than Lewis allows (315).

11. Judith Rice Henderson, "Euphues and His Erasmus," *English Literary Renaissance* 12:2 (1982): 161.

12. Arthur Kinney, *Humanist Poetics: Thought, Rhetoric, and Fiction in Sixteenth-Century England* (Amherst: University of Massachusetts Press, 1986), 136.

13. Janel Mueller, *The Native Tongue and the Word: Developments in English Prose Style, 1380–1580* (Chicago: University of Chicago Press, 1984), 390.

14. Demetrius, *Demetrius On Style: The Greek Text of Demetrius' De Elocutione*, trans. W. Rhys Roberts (Cambridge: Cambridge University Press, 1902), 75.

15. Philip Sidney, *Apologie*, sig. L[1]r.

16. Aristotle, *Rhetoric*, trans. Kennedy (1991), 240.

17. Wilson, *The three orations of Demosthenes*, "To the right Honorable Sir William Cecill," sigs. A1ᵣ₋ᵥ. All subsequent citations to this work refer to this edition. It is no surprise to find Wilson sounding so much like Lyly: his *Arte of Rhetorique* is, as Mueller shows, the most useful guide to the nuts and bolts of euphuistic style (see Mueller, 387–423). I do not believe she or others have considered the relevance of Wilson's efforts as a translator, however, and although it is not my intent to revive here the once lively debate over the source(s) of Lyly's style, which have been traced from Gorgias and Isocrates through the Middle Ages and to the Oxford lecture hall of John Rainolds (see Eduard Norden, *Die Antike Kunstprosa*, vol. 2 [Leipzig, 1898], 773–809; Albert Feuillerat, *John Lyly: Contribution à l'histoire de la Renaissance en Angleterre* [Cambridge: Cambridge University Press, 1910]; George Williamson, *The Senecan Amble: A Study of Prose Form from Bacon to Collier* [Chicago: University of Chicago Press, 1951], 11–120; G. K. Hunter, *John Lyly: The Humanist as Courtier* [Cambridge, MA: Harvard University Press, 1962], 280–89; Morris W. Croll, "Introduction," in Lyly, *"Euphues: The Anatomy of Wit" and "Euphues and His England,"* ed. Croll and Clemens, xxiv–lxiv; William A. Ringler Jr., "The Immediate Source of Euphuism," *PMLA* 53 [1938]: 678–86), it is worth adding Wilson's Demosthenes to the list.

18. "The etymologies of *copia*," writes Terrence Cave, "originate in a spectacularly successful outgrowth . . . from the parent form *ops*, which already embraces the domains of material riches, natural plenty (personified as the goddess Ops), and figurative abundance, . . . [and] draws into its semantic net connotations of military strength (pl. *copiae*, 'forces') and above all of eloquent speech (*copia dicendi*), while retaining its connection with riches and a broad range of more general notions—abundance, plenty, variety, satiety, resources" (*The Cornucopian Text: Problems of Writing in the French Renaissance* [Oxford: Clarendon, 1979], 3). Most, if not all, of these senses are relevant to the debate over euphuism, which, as Sidney's criticism suggests, can be framed as an argument over the virtues of English's native resources and those ornaments it might attain by force or artifice.

19. Walter J. Ong, "Commonplace Rhapsody: *Ravisius Textor*, Zwinger and Shakespeare," in *Classical Influences on European Culture, 1500–1700*, ed. R. R. Bolgar (Cambridge: Cambridge University Press, 1976), 94.

20. Henderson, 151.

21. Dolven, 78, 83, 95.

22. Ong, 102.

23. Rebecca Bushnell, *A Culture of Teaching: Early Modern Humanism in Theory and Practice* (Ithaca, NY: Cornell University Press, 1996), 133.

24. Qtd. in William Sherman, *John Dee: The Politics of Reading and Writing in the English Renaissance* (Amherst: University of Massachusetts Press, 1995), 61–62.

25. Peter Beal, "Notions in Garrison: The Seventeenth-Century Commonplace Book," in *New Ways of Looking at Old Texts: Papers of the Renaissance English Text Society, 1985–1991*, ed. W. Speed Hill (Binghamton, NY: Medieval and Renaissance Texts and Studies, 1993), 132, 134.

26. Desiderius Erasmus, Epistle 1204:12–19, trans. R. A. B. Mynors, in *Collected Works of Erasmus* (hereafter *CWE*), vol. 8, ed. R. A. B. Mynors (Toronto: University of Toronto Press, 1988), 212–13. See also William Barker, "Introduction," in *The Adages of Erasmus,* ed. William Barker (Toronto: University of Toronto Press, 2001), xxiiii.

27. Kathy Eden, *Friends Hold All Things in Common: Tradition, Intellectual Property, and the* Adages *of Erasmus* (New Haven: Yale University Press, 2001), 1, 4.

28. Ann Moss, *Printed Commonplace-Books and the Structuring of Renaissance Thought* (Oxford: Clarendon, 1996), 207.

29. *The Adages of Erasmus*, ed. Barker, 5. For a modern reader, Barker notes, the *Adagia*, or indeed any Renaissance commonplace book, may yet retain this force, as the encounter with a still current expression "gives us an uncanny realization that what seems to us to be of homely, local, and oral origin is in fact sophisticated, widely traveled, and literary" (xxxvi).

30. Desiderius Erasmus, *De duplici copia verborum ac rerum commentarii duo (De Copia)* (1512; revised and expanded, 1514, 1526, 1534), trans. Betty I. Knott, in *CWE*, vol. 24, ed. Craig R. Thompson (Toronto: University of Toronto Press, 1978), 295.

31. *CWE,* 24:606.

32. *CWE,* 24:301.

33. Desiderius Erasmus, *De Conscribendis Epistolis* (1522), trans. Charles Fantazzi, in *CWE*, vol. 25, ed. Craig R. Thompson (Toronto: University of Toronto Press, 1978), 87.

34. *CWE,* 24:607–8.

35. Ong, 114. Travel and commonplacing are, for Zwinger, more than metaphorically related; they are mutually illuminating activities. Zwinger's interest in the geographic dimensions of commonplacing—what Ong calls his "concern for a topography of the mind"—leads him to the *Methodus apodemica*, a treatise on "how to travel and to describe what one encounters" (115).

36. Ong, 100.

37. Erasmus, *De Conscribendis Epistolis,* in *CWE,* 25:87.

38. Erasmus, *De Copia,* in *CWE,* 24:636, 638.

39. *CWE,* 24:348.

40. See *CWE,* 24:348–54.

41. *CWE,* 24:354.

42. Erasmus, *De Conscribendis Epistolis*, in *CWE*, 25:19, 12.

43. Noted in the margins of Harvey's copy of the *Similia*, the text on which John Lyly relies most heavily; qtd. in David Norbrook, "Rhetoric, Ideology, and the Elizabethan World Picture," in *Renaissance Rhetoric*, ed. Peter Mack (London: Macmillan, 1994), 144.

44. DeWitt T. Starnes, "Introduction," in Richard Taverner, *Proverbs or Adages* (Gainesville, FL: Scholars' Facsimiles and Reprints, 1956), vi.

45. Elyot, *Governour*, fol. 48.

46. Steven N. Zwicker, "Habits of Reading and Early Modern Literary Culture," in *The Cambridge History of Early Modern English Literature*, ed. David Loewenstein and Janel Mueller (Cambridge: Cambridge University Press, 2002), 186.

47. Richard Taverner, *Proverbs or Adages* (Gainesville, FL: Scholars' Facsimiles and Reprints, 1956), sig. A2ᵣ.

48. Qtd. in Clarence H. Miller, "The Logic and Rhetoric of Proverbs in Erasmus's *Praise of Folly*," in *Essays on the Works of Erasmus*, ed. Richard L. DeMolen (New Haven, CT: Yale University Press, 1978), 83.

49. Qtd. in Barker, xxxvii. This is a version of the same peculiar coinage that George Gascoigne uses to describe the operations of "poetic license" upon language (see Chapter 2). In both cases the term suggests an illegitimate and perhaps violent wrenching of words; in Harvey's usage, the hint of barbarous or "turk"-like degeneracy is even more strongly implied.

50. Qtd. in Beal, 139.

51. Moss, 211.

52. Kinney, 149.

53. Henderson, 151.

54. Morris Croll and Harry Clemens's edition builds on that of R. W. Bond in tracing the sources of almost all of *Euphues*'s commonplace material; in the vast majority of cases, Erasmus is the "likely source" (Lyly, *Euphues*, ed. Croll and Clemens, 24n2).

55. Joel Altman, *The Tudor Play of Mind* (Berkeley: University of California Press, 1978), 205.

56. Qtd. in Edward Arbor, "Introduction," in *Euphues: The Anatomy of Wit; Euphues and His England*, English Reprints, vol. 2 (New York: AMS Press, 1966), 16. Lodge records his views of contemporary vernacular authors in a 1596 epistle; Lyly's fellow laureates are Spenser, Daniel, Drayton, and Nashe. For a modern assessment of *Euphues*'s contribution to the store of English commonplaces, see Morris Palmer Tilley, *Elizabethan Proverb Lore in Lyly's* Euphues *and in Petties's* Petite Pallace (New York: Macmillan, 1926), which credits Lyly with unprecedented skill in the incorporation of foreign—often Erasmian—proverbs into the vernacular.

57. Andrew Hadfield, *Shakespeare, Spenser, and the Matter of Britain* (New York: Palgrave Macmillan, 2004), 113.

58. Ascham, *Scholemaster*, 7. All subsequent citations to this work in this chapter refer to this edition. The many and complicated ways in which *Euphues* reflects and refashions *The Scholemaster* make Ascham's treatise, in Arthur Kinney's phrase, "a Senecan model"

for Lyly's fiction: a pretext that is so thoroughly digested and transmuted that its precise influence on the work it inspires can be hard to gauge (see Kinney, 164). For more on the interrelation of Lyly's romance and Ascham's pedagogical precepts, see Dolven, 65–79.

59. R. W. Maslen, *Elizabethan Fictions: Espionage, Counter-Espionage, and the Duplicity of Fiction in Early Elizabethan Prose Narratives* (Oxford: Clarendon, 1997), 5. Maslen links Lyly's impudence to his embrace of the novella form: "Where [Ascham] sought to stem [the] threatening tide [of Italianate fictions]," Lyly is one of a cluster of late sixteenth-century English authors who "reveled in the rich abundance of exotic objects it carried to their shore, and chose to make the problems and perils of writing fiction the subject of their fictions" (2).

60. Indeed the figure of wax is *especially* waxen: when Erasmus advises readers of *De Copia* to "take a group of sentences and deliberately set out to express each of them in as many versions as possible, as Quintilian advises, using the analogy of a piece of wax which can be molded into one shape after another" (*CWE*, 24:302–3), his analogy draws upon a long history of poetic and philosophical figuration. Behind the overt allusion to Quintilian's *Institutio Oratoria* lurk implicit allusions to Ovid's *Metamorphoses*, where wax represents for Pythagoras the constancy of the soul and the mutability of form, while it supplies Pygmalian and Daedalus with the substance of artistic creation; to Aristotle's theory of sensory impressions in *De Anima*; and to Plato's philosophy of memory in the *Theaetetas*.

61. See especially Altman, 204–6, on Lyly's indebtedness to Erasmus in fashioning his rhetoric of ambivalence.

62. *CWE*, 24:647.

63. Sidney mounts a nearly identical critique of argument-by-similitude in his comments on euphuism in the *Apologie*—the amassing of similitudes in defense of an argument is, he writes, "as absurd a surfet to the eares as is possible: for the force of a similitude not being to prove anything to a contrary disputer but onely to explain to a willing hearer, when that is done the rest is a most tedious prattling" (sig. [K4]ᵥ)—but he seems to give Lyly no credit for self-awareness.

64. Dolven, 83.

65. *CWE* 24, 364.

66. Erasmus, *Adagia* 1.4.1, in *CWE*, vol. 31, trans. Margaret Mann Phillips, annotated by R. A. B. Mynors (Toronto: University of Toronto Press, 1982), 317–19.

67. Roger Chartier and Peter Stallybrass, "Reading and Authorship: The Circulation of Shakespeare 1590–1619," in *A Concise Companion to Shakespeare and the Text*, ed. Andrew Murphy (Oxford: Blackwell, 2007), 12.

68. Eden, 4–5 and throughout.

69. Erasmus, *Adagia* 1.4.1, in *CWE*, 31:318.

70. Scragg, 10.

71. *CWE*, 25:20.

72. John Hoskins, *Directions for Speech and Style*, ed. Hoyt H. Hudson (Princeton, NJ: Princeton University Press, 1935), 16.

73. Edward Blount, "To the Reader," in John Lyly, *Sixe Court Comedies . . . by Iohn Lilly*, ed. Edward Blount (London: Edward Blount, 1632), sig. [A5ᵥ].

74. Moss, 209.

75. "[T]o use popular, contemporary writers as suitable materials for commonplacing" is, as Chartier and Stallybrass argue, "radical": it confers upon English texts an authority equal to that of the classical tradition (9–10).

76. See especially, and unsurprisingly, the sections devoted to "wit."

CHAPTER 4

1. E. K., "Epistle" to *The Shepheardes Calender*, in Edmund Spenser, *The Shorter Poems*, ed. Richard A. McCabe (New York: Penguin, 1999), 23. All subsequent citations to this work refer to this edition.

2. Anne Lake Prescott, "The Laurel and the Myrtle: Spenser and Ronsard," in *World-making Spenser: Explorations in the Early Modern Age*, ed. Patrick Cheney and Lauren Silberman (Lexington: University Press of Kentucky, 2000), 63.

3. Patrick Cheney, *Spenser's Famous Flight* (Toronto: University of Toronto Press, 1993), 19.

4. Louis Adrian Montrose, " 'The Perfecte Paterne of a Poete': The Poetics of Courtship in *The Shepheardes Calender*," in *Critical Essays on Edmund Spenser*, ed. Mihoko Suzuki (New York: G. K. Hall, 1996), 8.

5. My interest here is in the generic problems encountered if we take pastoral, especially Virgilian pastoral, as the normative locus of poetic birth or rebirth. For a related consideration of *The Shepheardes Calender*'s appropriation of and negotiations with Virgilian poetics, specifically the trope of "ruin," see Rebeca Helfer, "The Death of the 'New Poete': Virgilian Ruin and Ciceronian Recollection in Spenser's *The Shepheardes Calender*," *Renaissance Quarterly* 56:3 (Autumn 2003): 723–56.

6. Abraham Fleming, *The Bucoliks of Pvblivs Virgilius Maro, with Alphabeticall annotations vpon proper names of Gods, Goddesses, men, women, hilles, flouddes, cities, townes, and villages orderly placed in the margent* (London: John Charlewood, 1575), sigs. A2$_r$–A3$_r$. All subsequent citations to this work refer to this edition.

7. Fleming's second translation of Virgil's eclogues, published in 1589 along with his version of the *Georgics*, dispenses with the glosses of proper nouns and place names, substituting fewer and more general marginal notes. Indeed, although the preface to this later edition reiterates Fleming's desire to provide "weake Grammarians" with Virgil "in a familiar phrase," the new translation is less obviously positioned to orient and assist the unlearned vernacular reader—it repudiates, for instance, the "foolish" rhymed couplets of the 1575 translation in favor of an English line approximating the "due proportion and measure" of classical verse (*The Bucoliks of Publius Virgilus Maro . . . Together with his Geogiks or Ruralls* [London: Thomas Orwin, 1589], sigs. A2$_r$, A4$_v$).

8. Richard Mallette, *Spenser, Milton, and Renaissance Pastoral* (Lewisburg, PA: Bucknell University Press, 1981), 21. In his work on English pastoral, Patrick Cullen offers a similar interpretation of the genre's geography, arguing that while the urban spaces from which pastoral figures flee—Virgil's Rome, Dante's Florence, or Sannazaro's Naples—may

differ, the place to which they retreat—Arcadia—is eternally the same (*Spenser, Marvell, and Renaissance Pastoral* [Cambridge, MA: Harvard University Press, 1970], 99).

9. As Julia Reinhardt Lupton observes, "the pastoral genre, in this brilliant commencement of the Latin tradition, is instituted as performing the necessary yet often violent cultural work of finding a home," and this home, "the paradigmatic object of nostalgia, is a category of experience only fashioned in the alienated desiring distance from it" ("Home-Making in Ireland: Virgil's Eclogue I and Book VI of *The Faerie Queene*," *Spenser Studies* 8 [1987]: 120–21). Lupton's remark reminds us that in the early modern period nostalgia retained its etymological significance as an essentially *geographic* affliction: to feel nostalgia is to be, literally, homesick. Her argument, which anticipates this essay's interest in the paradoxical interdependence of home and exile in the pastoral mode, identifies the Meliboee episode in book 6 of *The Faerie Queene* as a "revision" of eclogue 1 that allows Spenser to "accommodate the positions of both exile and home-maker" (119).

10. The Latin reads: "At nos hinc alii sitientis ibimus Afros, / pars Scythiam et rapidum cretae veniemus Oaxen / et penitus toto divisos orbe Britannos."

11. In Virgil's equally blunt phrase, "carmina nulla canam."

12. And, in fact, Meliboeus reappears in eclogue 7, no longer in any apparent danger of losing his land, his flocks, or his poetic identity.

13. Keilen, 78.

14. Although this chapter seeks to articulate why, given Britain's pointed exclusion from the world of Virgil's *Eclogues*, pastoral might have posed a particular challenge—and opportunity—to an English poet, one might profitably pursue a similar line of argument with regard to either Marot or Sannazaro, each of whom suffered exile from his homeland. For more on the impact of political exile on Sannazaro's poetic career, see William Kennedy, *Jacopo Sannazaro and the Uses of Pastoral* (Hanover, NH: University Press of New England, 1983), 21–27. For a discussion of Marot's experiences as a religious exile, as well as an account of his influence on Spenser and other sixteenth-century English poets, see Anne Lake Prescott, *French Poets and the English Renaissance* (New Haven, CT: Yale University Press, 1978), 3–15.

15. Contra Nancy Jo Hoffman's assertion that Spenser "frees pastoral . . . from attachment to real geographic place" and "is the first to sense that pastoral can become an integral, inclusive landscape" (*Spenser's Pastorals:* The Shepheardes Calender *and Colin Clout* [Baltimore: Johns Hopkins University Press, 1977], 11), I would argue that Spenser forces pastoral to reckon with its attachment with real geographic place, and in particular with the limitations and exclusions incumbent upon England (and English) itself. In this regard, my reading of the poem is akin to that offered by Paula Blank in *Broken English*, which highlights Spenser's use of English rural dialects to construct a fragmented and alienated pastoral landscape.

16. Spenser, "To His Booke," ll. 2, 13–15.

17. Among many theories propounded as to the identity of the mysterious E. K., Louis Waldman has proposed a deliberately veiled and estranged version of Spenser himself: Edmundus Kedemon, with the Greek *khdemwn*, meaning "procurator" or "spencer," substituting for the poet's English surname ("Spenser's Pseudonym 'E. K.' and Humanist

Self-Naming," *Spenser Studies* 9 [1988]: 21–31). Louise Schleiner has similarly proposed that the initials be deciphered "Edmund Kent," a double pun signaling "of Kent" and "kenned" ("Spenser's 'E. K.' as Edmund Kent (Kenned / of Kent): Kyth (Couth), Kissed, and Kunning-Conning," *English Literary Renaissance* 20:3 [1990]: 374–407). Such conjectures jibe nicely with my own understanding of E. K.'s obfuscatory relation to the *Calender* and of Spenser's alienated and alienating mode of authorship, but for the purposes of this essay, I am content to take E. K. at face value—as the poem's first reader and critic.

18. Lynn Staley Johnson, *The Shepheardes Calender: An Introduction* (University Park: Pennsylvania State University Press, 1990), 31.

19. Alexander Barclay, *The Egloges of Alexander Barclay* (Southwark: P. Traveris, c. 1530), sig. [A3]ᵣ.

20. George Turbervile, *The Eglogs of the Poet B. Mantuan Carmelitas* (London: Henrie Bynneman, 1567), sigs. A2ᵣ, A3ᵥ.

21. The word "gloss" distills this tension between familiarization and estrangement, since it comes from a Greek word meaning "strange" or "foreign" but is used in English to describe practices whereby a word or passage is clarified or made more plain.

22. Robert Lane's *Shepheards Devises: Edmund Spenser's* Shepheardes Calender *and the Institutions of Elizabethan Society* (Athens: University of Georgia Press, 1993) is an exception: Lane considers both how Spenser's rustic diction might signal opposition to the elitism of contemporary homiletic practice and how E. K.'s often unhelpful glosses reflect the self-protective strategies of reformist authors in response to an increasingly centralized state religion (see esp. 28–35, 56–73).

23. For a history of vernacular glosses of scripture, see Lynne Long, *Translating the Bible: From the 7th to the 17th Century* (Burlington, VT: Ashgate, 2001).

24. Qtd. in Long, 47.

25. *The Geneva Bible: A Facsimile of the 1560 Edition*, with an introduction by Lloyd E. Berry (Madison: University of Wisconsin Press, 1969), sigs. ***iᵣ and ***iiiiᵣ.

26. William Tyndale, *Tyndale's New Testament*, ed. David Daniell (New Haven, CT: Yale University Press, 1989), 3–4.

27. *Geneva Bible*, sig. ***iiiiᵥ.

28. *Geneva Bible*, sig. ***iiiiᵥ.

29. Not just geography, of course, but temporality as well: however innovative their approach to biblical translation might seem from the perspective of Catholic tradition, Protestant translators (and Protestants more generally) insisted that their labors were in fact more consistent with the practices of the early church, and that their version of Christian revelation simply returned the faith to its true origins. Such a claim obviously also resonates with E. K.'s insistence that Spenser's apparently newfangled diction restores to English poetry a long-lost dignity and richness of expression.

30. *Geneva Bible*, sig. ***iᵣ.

31. From the preface to Tyndale's *Obedience of a Christian Man*, qtd. in Long, 148.

32. Indeed in the *Geneva Bible*, Paul's Epistle to the Romans is preceded by a map illustrating just how belated and marginal Rome's place was in the world of biblical antiquity: purporting to represent the spread of the gospel outward from Jerusalem, the map

includes Rome barely at all, relegating it to the far northwest corner of the world—precisely where English readers would have been accustomed to finding their own remote island. Such a map literalizes the ambitions of England's sixteenth-century Bible translators, whose insistence on the more-than-adequate character of the English vernacular was simply one aspect of their effort to displace Rome from the center of Christianity, restoring a more antique and authentic Church whose home was, properly, everywhere—and perhaps especially in England.

33. A promiscuity enacted in E. K.'s own words, since both "gallimaufray" and "hodge-podge" are borrowings from French: see *OED*, s.v. "gallimaufry" and "hotchpot."

34. Qtd. in Veré L. Rubel, *Poetic Diction in the English Renaissance from Skelton through Spenser* (London: Oxford University Press, 1941), 6.

35. Elyot, *The Governour*, fol. 55$_r$.

36. "W. T. to the Reader," in William Tyndale, *Tyndale's Old Testament*, ed. David Daniell (New Haven, CT: Yale University Press, 1992), 5.

37. *Geneva Bible*, Psalm 137, notes a and e.

38. *Geneva Bible*, Psalm 137:6.

39. Harry Berger, *Revisionary Play: Studies in the Spenserian Dynamics* (Berkeley: University of California Press, 1988), 288. Roland Greene's reading of the poem also focuses on the shepherds' desire to restore Colin to a dialogic model of poetic creativity: the "hypothetical discourse . . . associated since 'Januarye' with Colin's lost expression and defined by its absence . . . lies just beyond the circumscription of the poem" and is "hypostasize[d] as a kind of *place*. . . . It is invoked, one might say, as a pastoral within the general pastoral landscape of the *Calender*, a particularly ideal 'here'. . . . [T]o entice Colin 'here' would be to reinstall the common voice of those shepherds and so to cancel the curse of isolation and divergence" ("*The Shepheardes Calender*, Dialogue, and Periphrasis," *Spenser Studies* 8 [1990]: 16–17, emphasis added).

40. These lines, which cast Colin as Aeneas, suggest that Spenserian pastoral already incorporates the geographic restlessness usually identified with epic.

41. For more on the narcissistic pleasures and perils of "Januarye," see Berger's essay on "The Mirror Stage of Colin Clout" in *Revisionary Play*, 325–46.

42. Syrithe Pugh, *Spenser and Ovid* (Burlington, VT: Ashgate, 2005), 12. Pugh does not discuss the "Nouember" eclogue, which is my focus here, but her chapter on *The Shepheardes Calender* as a "New *Fasti*" shares many of this chapter's preoccupations, especially with regard to Spenser's emphasis on exile and alienation as the defining experiences of the English pastoral poet.

43. Colin's song is a translation of Clément Marot's "Eclogue sur le Trespas de ma Dame Loyse de Savoye, Mere du Roy Francoys," the first French eclogue, written in 1531, and also framed within a dialogue between two shepherds named Colin and Thenot, but the name "Dido" is Spenser's innovation.

44. Donald Cheney, "Spenser's Currencies," in *Edmund Spenser: Essays on Culture and Allegory*, ed. Jennifer Klein Morrison and Matthew Greenfield (Burlington, VT: Ashgate, 2000), 42. See also Donald Cheney, "The Circular Argument of *The Shepheardes Calender*,"

in *Unfolded Tales: Studies in Renaissance Romance*, ed. G. M. Logan and Gordon Teskey (Ithaca, NY: Cornell University Press, 1989), 137–61.

45. This message is driven home by the eclogue's emblem, *"La mort ny mord"* (l. 210), which, as E. K. explains, serves as a reminder that "death biteth not" since "being ouercome by the death of one, that dyed for all, it is now made (as Chaucer sayth) the grene path way to life" (147). For more on the "Nouember" eclogue's reworking of classical narratives of female suffering, see John Watkins, *The Specter of Dido: Spenser and Virgilian Epic* (New Haven, CT: Yale University Press, 1995), 79–82, although Watkins does not cite the Ovidian parallel.

46. The *Calender*'s verse coda seems to advertise this triumph by beginning in words that echo—and overgo—the famous boast at the end of the *Metamorphoses*: where Ovid brags of a poem that will last as long as Rome, Spenser declares, "I haue made a Calender for euery yeare, / That steele in strength, and time in durance shall outweare," a poem made to endure not to the end of an empire but to the very limits of the Christian eschaton, "to the worlds dissolution" (156).

47. For more on the murky circumstances surrounding Ovid's exile to Tomis, see the foreword and introduction to Peter Green's translation of Ovid's *Poems of Exile* (Berkeley: University of California Press, 2005), vii–xii, xxiv–xxxv.

48. Ovid., *Tristia*, 1.1.128. This and all subsequent citations from the *Tristia* are from Green's translation.

49. Elyot, *The Governour*, fol. 18ᵣ.

50. Gabriel Harvey, *Pierce's Supererogation, or A New Praise of the Old Asse* (London: John Wolfe, 1593), sig. B4ᵥ.

51. Colin Burrow, *Edmund Spenser* (Plymouth: Northcote House, 1996), 9.

52. For the full range of responses to *The Shepheardes Calender*, see R. M. Cummings, *Spenser: The Critical Heritage* (London: Routledge and Kegan Paul, 1971), which contains a section devoted to comments on Spenser's language.

53. Webbe, 35, 53, 20, 19.

54. Sidney, *An Apologie for Poetrie*, sig. [I4]ᵥ.

55. Jonson, *Discoveries*, 90.

56. Thomas Warton, *Observations on the Fairy Queen of Spenser*, 2nd ed., enlarged and corrected, vol. 1 (London, 1762), 133.

57. Roscoe E. Parker, "Spenser's Language and the Pastoral Tradition," *Language* 1:3 (1925): 80–87.

58. Rubel, 145.

59. Qtd. in Rubel, 136n11.

60. Lynn Staley Johnson notes, furthermore, that E. K. encourages a kind of linguistic disorientation in his own readers, when, for instance, he categorizes the *Calender*'s eclogues as "moral," "plaintive," and "recreative": "His tone implies that he speaks of what everyone knows, that the terms he uses are standard critical usage. . . . But 'moral,' 'plaintive,' and 'recreative' are in no dictionary of rhetorical terms, no handbook of poetic forms. . . . [T]hey exist only within the closed world and language of *The Shepheardes Calender*" and

"are defined [only] in terms of what they define," so that the reader "seems to have stumbled into a particularly zany world [of] unknown but familiar-sounding words" (38).

61. See Megan L. Cook, "Making and Managing the Past: Lexical Commentary in Spenser's *Shepheardes Calendar* (1579) and Chaucer's *Works* (1598/1602)," *Spenser Studies* 26 (2011): 179–222. Cook identifies a number of suggestive parallels between Speght's editorial practice and that of E. K., including the identification of Chaucer with an exemplary and purified form of the vernacular and the application of classical rhetorical theory to the use of vernacular archaisms. She points out that E. K.'s gloss has been marshaled as a key piece of evidence in tracing the evolution of attitudes toward Chaucer's language, but that critics have failed to consider that the gloss might affect that trajectory as much or even more than it reflects it. And, in fact, most of the sixteenth-century comments on Chaucer's English that emphasize its difference from contemporary usage postdate *The Shepheardes Calender*.

62. Qtd. in Cook, 183.

63. Such type "would have looked decidedly old fashioned in 1579," notes Colin Burrow (*Edmund Spenser*, 12). For a broader discussion of typographical archaism in the sixteenth century, see Zachary Lesser, "Typographic Nostalgia: Play-Reading, Popularity, and the Meanings of Black Letter," in *The Book at the Play: Playwrights, Stationers, and Readers in Early Modern England*, ed. Marta Straznicky (Amherst: University of Massachusetts Press, 2006), 99–126.

64. Willy Maley, "Spenser's Languages: Writing in the Ruins of English," in *The Cambridge Companion to Spenser*, ed. Andrew Hadfield (Cambridge: Cambridge University Press, 2001), 169. See also Andrew Hadfield, *Shakespeare, Spenser, and the Matter of Britain* (New York: Palgrave Macmillan, 2004), esp. 32–33.

65. Edmund Spenser, *Colin Clout's Come Home Againe* (1595), ll. 16–17, in Spenser, *The Shorter Poems*, ed. Richard A. McCabe (New York: Penguin Books, 1999), 343–71. All subsequent citations to this poem refer to this edition.

66. Lupton, 141.

CHAPTER 5

1. Christopher Marlowe, *Tamburlaine the Great*, ed. J. S. Cunningham and Eithne Henson (Manchester: Manchester University Press, 1998), *One* prologue.1–6. All subsequent citations to this play refer to this edition.

2. The earliest evidence of *Tamburlaine*'s popularity comes in the prologue to part 2, which claims, "[t]he general welcomes Tamburlaine received / When he arrived last upon our stage" as justification for a sequel (*Two* prologue.1–2). See also Richmond Barbour, *Before Orientalism: London's Theatre of the East, 1576–1626* (Cambridge: Cambridge University Press, 2003), 39–41; and Russ McDonald, "Marlowe and Style," in *The Cambridge Companion to Christopher Marlowe*, ed. Patrick Cheney (Cambridge: Cambridge University Press, 2004), 56.

3. Hall, "Virgidimarium" (1597–98), in *Christopher Marlowe*, ed. MacLure, 42; Alvin

Kernan, "The Play and Playwrights," in J. Leeds Barroll, Alexander Leggatt, Richard Hosley, and Alvin Kernan, eds., *The Revels History of Drama in English*, 8 vols., gen. ed. Clifford Leech and T. W. Craik (London: Methuen, 1975), 3:255.

4. Gabriel Harvey, "A New Letter of Notable Contents" (1593), qtd. in *Christopher Marlowe: The Critical Heritage*, ed. Millar MacLure (New York: Routledge, 2005), 41.

5. Ascham, *The Scholemaster*, fol. 61ᵥ. All subsequent citations to this work refer to this edition.

6. Francis Meres, *Palladis Tamia: Wit's Treasury, being the second part of Wit's Commonwealth* (London: Cuthbert Barbie, 1598), 618.

7. Webbe, sig. Ciiiᵥ

8. O. B. Hardison, "Tudor Humanism and Surrey's Translation of the *Aeneid*," *Studies in Philology* 83:3 (Summer 1986): 243.

9. Derek Attridge, *Well-Weighed Syllables: Elizabethan Verse in Classical Metres* (Cambridge: Cambridge University Press, 1974), esp. 89–92.

10. Paula Blank, *Shakespeare and the Mismeasure of Renaissance Man* (Ithaca, NY: Cornell University Press, 2006), 54.

11. Hardison, 259.

12. Margaret Tudeau-Clayton, "What Is My Nation?: Language, Verse, and Politics in Tudor Translations of Virgil's *Aeneid*," in *The Oxford Handbook of Tudor Literature, 1485–1603*, ed. Mike Pincombe and Cathy Shrank (Oxford: Oxford University Press, 2009), 389–403, 390. See also Colin Burrow, "Virgil in English Translation," in *The Cambridge Companion to Virgil*, ed. C. Martindale (Cambridge: Cambridge University Press, 1997), 21–37.

13. Tudeau-Clayton discusses Surrey in relation to a number of rival translations: Gavin Douglas's 1513 rhyming translation appeared in 1553, a year before John Day printed Surrey's translation of book 4; in 1558, a year after Tottel published both books of Surrey's translation, John Kingston published Thomas Phaer's rhyming translation of books 1–7, Rowland Hall printed a nine-book translation by Phaer in 1562, and Thomas Twyne completed Phaer's translation in a 1573 edition of the poem, written in pseudo-quantitative meter; in 1582 the Catholic exile Richard Stanyhurst's translation of books 1–4, also "quantitative," was published in Leiden by John Pates (Tudeau-Clayton, 389–91).

14. Virgil, *Georgics*, trans. Janet Lembke (New Haven, CT: Yale University Press, 2005), 3.

15. Edmund Spenser, *Three proper, and wittie, familiar letters: Lately passed betvveene tvvo vniuersitie men; touching the earthquake in Aprill last, and our English refourmed versifying* (London: H. Bynnemen, 1580), 6.

16. Spenser, *Three . . . letters*, 6; Gabriel Harvey, *The Works of Gabriel Harvey, D.C.L.*, 3 vols., ed. Alexander Balloch Grosart (London: Camden Society, 1884), 1:100.

17. Helgerson, *Forms of Nationhood*, 27–30.

18. A similar question runs through the *Georgics*, verses composed during the bloody civil wars that marked the end of the Roman Republic and presented to the man whose victories made him the first Roman emperor: the *Georgics* are poems celebrating man's civilizing influence on unruly nature, but they are also poems that note the violence that

sustains and shadows the course of progress. Sixteenth-century English readers would have found "Britain's sons" ranked among "the victims felled," whose humiliation testifies to the triumph of imperial Rome, and the debate between Spenser and Harvey over how to interpret the stress imposed on English by quantitative versification resonates uneasily with that earlier narrative of colonial subjection.

19. Mary Floyd-Wilson, *English Ethnicity and Race in Early Modern Drama* (Cambridge: Cambridge University Press, 2003), 99, 103. Floyd-Wilson emphasizes Tamburlaine's supposed racial affinities with his English admirers, citing "England's intimate though fraught relationship with the Scythians," believed to be "among the earliest settlers of the British Isles," and the etymological conflation of "Scythian" with "Scots" as factors in Tamburlaine's cultural appeal. She notes that the Scythian warlord spoke to the insecurities and aspirations of "a culture that fears not only its native barbarism but also the subjugation and implicit softness inherent in adopting a classical model of civility" (89–90).

20. Hall, "Virgidemiarum" (1597–98), qtd. in *Christopher Marlowe*, ed. MacLure, 42.

21. David Riggs, "Marlowe's Life," in *The Cambridge Companion to Christopher Marlowe*, ed. Patrick Cheney (Cambridge: Cambridge University Press, 2004), 30.

22. Aristotle, *Rhetoric*, trans. Kennedy (1991), 237.

23. See Blank, *Shakespeare*, 42. As Blank notes, the confusion of these terms was common in sixteenth-century England—see *OED*, s.v. "rhyme," "rhythm," "arithmetic," and "arsmetry"—but Puttenham's conflations are more deliberate than most, for he is well aware of the spuriousness of the etymological link between rhyme and rhythm. Meter, he writes, "was in Greek called [rithmus]: whence we have deriued this word *ryme* but improperly & not wel because we haue no such feet or times or stirres in our meeters. . . . This *rithmus* of theirs, is not therfore our rime, but a certaine musicall numerositie in vtterance, and not a bare number as that of the Arithmetical computation is, which therfore is not called *rithmus* but *arithmus*" (Puttenham, 57).

24. Lawrence Manley, *Convention, 1500–1700* (Cambridge, MA: Harvard University Press, 1980), 2.

25. This identification of rhyme with the New World resonates with Sidney's appeal to Native American poets as "a sufficient probability" for the necessary and virtuous role of poetry in civilizing savage wits (*Apologie for Poetrie*, sig. B3ᵥ). It contrasts interestingly, however, with the rhetorical use to which Montaigne puts Native American poetry in his essay "Of the Caniballes," where as part of his argument that "there is nothing in that nation, that is either barbarous or savage," he cites two examples of supposed cannibal verse and concludes, "I am so conversant with Poesie, that I may judge, this invention hath no barbarisme at all in it, but is altogether Anacreontike. Their language is a kinde of pleasant speech, and hath a pleasing sound, and some affinitie with the Greeke terminations" (*Essays written in French by Michael Lord of Montaigne*, trans. John Florio [London, 1602], 101, 106). More broadly, we might observe that the tendency of Renaissance writers to look far East and West for confirmation of their poetic precepts bespeaks the contradictory status of eloquence as civilized discourse and exotic speech: that Indians and cannibals use verses like European or classical poets implies both that Indians and cannibals may be civilized and that poetry is itself, as Puttenham says, "a maner of foreign talk."

26. The actual page is unnumbered, as a gathering of eight pages appears to have been dropped from some printings of the *Arte* following page 84 and then re-added in subsequent printings. The pages remain unnumbered, and what would have been page 93 is labeled 85. When I refer to the unnumbered pages, I will provide what would have been the correct number in brackets.

27. In fact eight—not sixteen—pages later, since the pagination of the 1589 edition jumps from 92 to 101.

28. A. L. Korn, "Puttenham and the Orientall Pattern-Poem," *Comparative Literature* 6:4 (Autumn 1964): 290. Korn's article draws on the work of several earlier scholars who assess the poems as part of comparatist studies of Asian and European poetry. See, for instance, Chung-Su Chi'en, "China in the Literature of the Seventeenth Century," *Quarterly Bulletin of Chinese Bibliography* 1:4 (December 1940): 355–56; Margaret Church, "The First English Pattern Poems," *PMLA* 61 (1946): 648; William W. Appleton, *A Cycle of Cathay* (New York, 1951); and E. G. Browne, *A Literary History of Persia: From Firdawsi to Sa'di* (London, 1906), 60.

29. As Attridge argues, this debate was troubled by fundamental confusions of eye and ear: sixteenth-century poetic theorists might insist that they heard the "numbers" of classical verse, but in fact—because their mother tongue had no such numbers and because even the Latin they learned to speak retained little trace of the classical quantities—they reckoned syllabic quantities by rote, according to position, spelling, and other visual cues. The accentual patterns of English verse were, by contrast, invisible; neither syntax nor orthography determined the stress on a syllable. To early modern poetic theorists, Attridge suggests, those patterns were consequently—and curiously—inaudible: the jingling of rhyme was English poetry's only tonal quality (*Well-Weighed Syllables*, 108–11).

30. Emily C. Bartels, *Spectacles of Strangeness: Imperialism, Alienation, and Marlowe* (Philadelphia: University of Pennsylvania Press, 1993), xiii–xiv.

31. Barbour, 41.

32. Stephen Greenblatt, *Renaissance Self-Fashioning: From More to Shakespeare* (Chicago: University of Chicago Press, 1980), 194.

33. Harry Levin, *The Overreacher: A Study of Christopher Marlowe* (Cambridge, MA: Harvard University Press, 1952), 23, 31.

34. John Gillies, "Marlowe, the *Timur* Myth, and the Motives of Geography," in *Playing the Globe: Genre and Geography in English Renaissance Drama* (Madison, NJ: Fairleigh Dickinson University Press, 1998), 209.

35. McDonald, 56.

36. Thomas Nashe, "To the Gentlemen Students of Both Universities," in Robert Greene, *Menaphon* (London: Thomas Orwin, 1589), sig. **; Hall, "Virgidimarium" (1597–98), qtd. in *Christopher Marlowe*, ed. MacLure, 42.

37. Robert Greene, "Perimedes the Blacksmith" (1588), qtd. in *Christopher Marlowe: The Critical Heritage*, ed. Millar MacLure (New York: Routledge, 1995), 27.

38. Ben Jonson, "To the memory of my beloued, the Author, Mr. William Shakespeare: And what he hath left vs" in William Shakespeare, *Mr. William Shakespeares Comedies, Histories, and Tragedies* (London: Isaac Iaggard and Ed. Blount, 1623), sig. [A4]ᵣ, l. 30.

39. Jonson, *Discoveries*, 41.

40. McDonald, 56. See also Steven Mullaney, *The Place of the Stage: License, Play, and Power in Renaissance England* (Chicago: University of Chicago Press, 1988), 76–85. Before Marlowe, as Paula Blank observes, blank verse was a "means of translating or simulating the exotic grace of Latin quantitative verse," as in Surrey's Virgil, which advertises its use of "straunge metre" (*Shakespeare*, 60). In Thomas Sackville and Thomas Norton's *Gorboduc* (1561), Tucker Brooke notes, the same is true: blank verse is used to give English verse "an elevated, foreign character" ("Marlowe's Versification and Style," *Studies in Philology* 19:2 [1922]: 187–88).

41. Barbour, 41.

42. Whetstone's treatise is a gathering of historical anecdotes based on Claude Gruget's *Diverse Lecons* (1552) and Pedro Mexia's *Silva de varia lecon* (1540); Marlowe's other main source seems to have been Petrus Perondinus, *Magni Tamerlanis Scytharum Imperatoris* (Florence, 1553). See Ethel Seaton, "Fresh Sources for Marlowe," *Review of English Studies* 5:20 (1929): 385–401.

43. J. S. Cunningham, "Introduction," in Christopher Marlowe, *Tamburlaine*, ed. J. S. Cunningham (Manchester: Manchester University Press, 1981), 57.

44. Bartels, for instance, hears in Tamburlaine's blank verse the sound of internal division, a self "torn between two extremes": the barbarous and violent and the majestic and potent (60).

45. Wilson, *Arte of Rhetorique*, sigs. A2$_v$ [A7$_r$].

46. Keilen, 21–22.

47. See also the title page of Aulus Gellius's *Noctium Atticarum libri* (1519), which represents an exceptionally aggressive Gallic Hercules as the figure of eloquence: here Hercules actually points his loaded bow directly in the faces of his chained followers, making the threat of force rather explicit (reprinted in Müller, 314).

48. Müller, 313.

49. All this is contra the reading of Jonathan Burton, who argues that "the seduction of Zenocrate" is "carefully distinguished from coercion" (*Traffic and Turning: Islam and English Drama, 1579–1624* [Newark: University of Delaware Press, 2005], 86).

50. Qtd. in Levin, 11.

51. James Shapiro, "'Metre Meete to Furnish Lucans Style': Reconsidering Marlowe's *Lucan*," in *"A Poet and a Filthy Play-maker": New Essays on Christopher Marlowe*, ed. Kenneth Friedenreich, Roma Gill, and Constance B. Kuriyama (New York: AMS Press, 1988), 319.

52. Barbour, 53.

53. Jill Levenson catalogs the criticisms that have been leveled at this aspect of the play, beginning with Swinburne's dismissal of Marlowe's style as the "stormy monotony of Titanic truculence" (qtd. in Levenson, "'Working Words': The Verbal Dynamic of *Tamburlaine*," in *"A Poet and a Filthy Play-maker": New Essays on Christopher Marlowe*, ed. Friedenreich, Gill, and Kuriyama, 99–115, 99). T. B. Tomlinson observes, "The lines move with a firm deliberation which Marlowe applies equally to *any* situation, any imagery," while Donald Peet attributes the effect of sameness to Tamburlaine's favorite rhetorical strategy: "the

techniques of amplification . . . are quite impersonal; they may be effectively employed by any speaker without being significantly modified to reflect his individual nature. Relying almost exclusively upon these techniques, Marlowe thus was unable to distinguish his characters from one another by varying the tone, structure, or style, of their individual speeches. Every one of his characters must amplify all the time; and every one of them must amplify in very much the same manner. As a result, they all tend to talk alike" (qtd. in Levenson, 99–100). Levenson discovers uniformity at a more basic level, finding "the ultimate source of the plays' continuity" in "the most basic units of the dramas' composition: the words and the patterns of their distribution. . . . From Mycetes to Zenocrate, the personae employ the same lexicon, a collection of words both idiosyncratic and relatively large" (100). But she also notices more subtle rhetorical modulations, patterns of assonance and alliteration that give to particular speakers and dramatic occasions a distinct musicality.

54. Mark Thornton Burnett, "*Tamburlaine the Great, Parts One* and *Two*," in *The Cambridge Companion to Christopher Marlowe*, ed. Patrick Cheney (Cambridge: Cambridge University Press, 2004), 129.

55. Bartels, 67.

56. Burnett, 129. Patrick Cheney links Tamburlaine's copy-catting to Marlowe's own rivalry with Edmund Spenser: "[T]he *Tamburlaine* plays, which often hint at Tamburlaine's poetic powers, function as Marlowe's critically charged, metadiscursive project—his public attempt to overgo Spenser as England's new national poet. . . . The many documented borrowings from Spenser in the two plays insist that much of what we say about Tamburlaine we see as Marlowe's competitive rewriting of Spenser" (*Marlowe's Counterfeit Profession: Ovid, Spenser, Counternationhood* [Toronto: University of Toronto Press, 1997], 121). On patterns of repetition and citation and their relation to the problems of literary and genealogical succession, see Claire Harraway, *Re-citing Marlowe: Approaches to the Drama* (Aldershot: Ashgate, 2000).

57. McDonald, 61.

58. Marjorie Garber, " 'Infinite Riches in a Little Room': Closure and Enclosure in Marlowe," in *Two Renaissance Mythmakers: Christopher Marlowe and Ben Jonson*, ed. Alvin Kernan (Baltimore: Johns Hopkins University Press, 1977), 3, 8.

59. McDonald, 56.

60. M. R. Ridley ascribes this irregularity to the playwright's metrical sophistication: "Marlowe had an ear acute enough to perceive that though the base, the 'norm,' of English blank verse was to be the five-stress 'iambic' line, and though the hearer's awareness of that norm must not be lost, yet few lines should strictly conform to the norm, and that five is, so far from being the desirable, almost the forbidden, number" (*Marlowe's Poems and Plays*, ed. M. R. Ridley [London, 1955], 14).

61. Gascoigne, "Certayne Notes of Instruction," 53. *OED*, s.v. "turken" records the evolution in the word's connotations over the span of the late sixteenth and early seventeenth centuries: see Chapter 2 above.

62. Peacham, *Garden of Eloquence* (1577), sig. Ciii$_r$.

63. Wilson, *Arte of Rhetorique*, sig. Ai$_v$.

64. Gascoigne, *Certayne Notes*, 53–54.

65. Spenser's reaction is typical of the general view: he grants Daniel a prime position in the litany of English poets in *Colin Clouts Come Home Againe* (1595) but has Colin add, "Yet doth his trembling *Muse* but lowly flie, / As daring not too rashly mount on hight" (sig. C2ᵣ). Daniel writes "a very pure, and copious English, and words as warrantable as any Mans," grants Edmund Bolton, but "somewhat . . . flat" and "fitter perhaps for Prose than Measure" (*Hypercritica* [1622], in Joseph Haslewood, *English Poets and Poesy*, vol. 2 [London: Robert Triphook, 1815], 250). For more on the early reception of Daniel's work, see Raymond Himelick, "Introduction," in Samuel Daniel, *Samuel Daniel's* Musophilus, ed. Raymond Himelick (West Lafayette, IN: Purdue University Studies, 1965), 10.

66. Samuel Daniel, *Defence of Ryme*, sig. [H6]ᵥ. All subsequent citations to this work refer to this edition.

67. Louis, Leroy. *Of the Interchangeable Course, or variety of things in the whole world*, trans. R. A. (London: Charles Yetsweirt, 1594), fol. 107ᵣ₋₄.

68. This upending of geographical hierarchies is clearly a large part of what appeals to Daniel about Le Roy's historiography: "Le Roy's thesis," writes Floyd-Wilson, "allow[s] us to see how Tamburlaine's destruction of the order of things could potentially be interpreted by the English as a radically revisionist bid for the northerner's role in the progress of civilization (94).

69. Hunter, 280.

70. Samuel Daniel, *Delia: Contayning certayne Sonnets; with the Complaint of Rosamond* (London, 1592), sig. G3ᵥ.

71. Alexander Leggatt, "The Companies and Actors," in *The Revels History*, ed. Barroll et al., 3:101.

72. C. Saunders, "The Preface," in Saunders, *Tamerlane the Great, a Tragedy* (London: Richard Bentley, 1681), sig. aᵥ.

CODA

1. Francis Bacon, *The Advancement of Learning*, in *The Major Works*, ed. Brian Vickers (Oxford: Oxford University Press, 2002), 139; John Locke, *An Essay Concerning Human Understanding*, ed. Peter H. Nidditch (Oxford: Clarendon, 1975), 508. On the decline of rhetoric after the early seventeenth century, see Brian Vickers, *In Defense of Rhetoric* (Oxford: Clarendon, 1988); John Bender and David E. Wellbery, eds., *The Ends of Rhetoric* (Stanford, CA: Stanford University Press, 1990); and Mann, 201–18.

2. Samuel Johnson, "Proposals for Printing . . . the Dramatick Works of Shakespeare" (1756), in *Shakespeare: The Critical Heritage*, 6 vols., ed. Brian Vickers (London: Routledge and Kegan Paul, 1974), 4:270. For a thorough consideration of how Johnson and his contemporaries relied on characterizations of sixteenth-century English literature to consolidate their own sense of literary identity and authority, see Jack Lynch, *The Age of Elizabeth in the Age of Johnson* (Cambridge: Cambridge University Press, 2002).

3. Margreta de Grazia, *Shakespeare Verbatim: The Reproduction of Authenticity and the 1790 Apparatus* (Oxford: Clarendon, 1991), 1.

4. See, for instance, de Grazia's account of early anecdotal versions of Shakespeare's biography: "The repeated focus [in seventeenth- and eighteenth-century biographies] on Shakespeare in various indecorous and transgressive acts . . . may have reflected a certain unease about his particular bent of genius: its unruliness, or, in the terms repeated in commentary of this period, its 'extravagance' and 'licentiousness'" (76).

5. Samuel Johnson, "Preface" to *The Plays of William Shakespeare* (1765), in *Shakespeare: The Critical Heritage*, ed. Vickers, 5:92.

6. Ben Jonson, "To the memory of my beloved," in Shakespeare, *Comedies, Histories and Tragedies*, sig. [A4]ᵣ, l. 26.

7. Jonson, *Discoveries*, 22–23.

8. Vickers offers an excellent overview of neoclassicist objections to Shakespeare's art in his introduction to *Shakespeare: The Critical Heritage*, 2:1–12. Harte is quoted on 10, Atterbury on 7.

9. Thomas Rymer, *A Short View of Tragedy* (1693), in *Shakespeare: The Critical Heritage*, ed. Vickers, 2:28.

10. John Dryden, "The Preface," in Dryden, *Troilus and Cressida, or Truth Found Too Late* (London, 1717), 15.

11. Lewis Theobold, "The Preface" to *The Works of Shakespeare* (1733), in *Shakespeare: The Critical Heritage*, ed. Vickers, 2:489.

12. Oliver Goldsmith, "Of the Stage" (1759), in *Shakespeare: The Critical Heritage*, ed. Vickers, 4:373.

13. Alexander Pope, Preface to *The Works of Shakespeare* (1725), in *Shakespeare: The Critical Heritage*, ed. Vickers, 2:406, 415.

14. De Grazia, 196–97; Pope qtd. on 197. De Grazia also quotes Johnson's claim that "SHAKESPEARE stands in more need of critical assistance than any other of the English writers" (199).

15. See Michael Dobson, *The Making of the National Poet: Shakespeare, Adaptation, and Authorship, 1660–1769* (Oxford: Clarendon, 1992); and Michael Dobson, "Bowdler and Britannia: Shakespeare and the National Libido," *Shakespeare Survey* 46 (1994): 137–44.

16. *Othello* 1.1.137–38; S. T. Coleridge, *Notes and Lectures on Shakespeare* (Liverpool: Edward Howell, 1881), 248–49. Eliot's comment appears, unelaborated, as a note to his essay on "*Hamlet* and Its Problems," in T. S. Eliot, *The Sacred Wood: Essays on Poetry and Criticism* (London: Methuen, 1920), reprinted as *The Sacred Wood and Major Early Essays* (Mineola, NY: Dover, 1998), 55n1. On the tenacity of Rymer's critique and its implications for contemporary arguments about rhetoric and race, see Catherine Nicholson, "*Othello* and the Geography of Persuasion," *English Literary Renaissance* 40:1 (Winter 2010): 56–87.

17. John Dryden, "An Essay of Dramatick Poesie" (1668), in *Shakespeare: The Critical Heritage*, ed. Vickers, 1:138–39.

18. Jeremy Collier, "A Short View of the Immorality and Prophaneness of the English Stage" (1698), qtd. in Dobson, "Bowdler and Britannia," 138.

19. See especially Helgerson, *Forms of Nationhood*, 215–45.

20. On Shakespeare's courting of contrary views of Hal's authority, see Norman Rabkin, "Rabbits, Ducks, and *Henry V*," *Shakespeare Quarterly* 28:3 (1977): 279–96. On state

power and its mystification or subversion in the Henriad, see Stephen Greenblatt, *Shakespearean Negotiations: The Circulation of Social Energy in Renaissance England* (Berkeley: University of California Press, 1988), 21–65; Jonathan Dollimore and Alan Sinfield, "History and Ideology: The Instance of *Henry V*," in *Alternative Shakespeares*, ed. John Drakakis (New York: Routledge, 1985), 206–27; Jean Howard and Phyllis Rackin, *Engendering a Nation: A Feminist Account of Shakespeare's English Histories* (New York: Routledge, 1997), 137–215; and David Scott Kastan, *Shakespeare After Theory* (New York: Routledge, 1999), 99–133.

21. Benedict Robinson, "Harry and Amurath," *Shakespeare Quarterly* 60:4 (Winter 2009): 405.

22. Christopher Dowd, "Polysemic Brotherhoods in *Henry V*," *Studies in English Literature 1500–1900* 50:2 (Spring 2010): 377.

23. McEachern, *The Poetics of English Nationhood*, 107.

24. Helgerson, *Forms of Nationhood*, 243.

25. Kastan, *Shakespeare After Theory*, 118.

26. Allison Outland, "'Eat a Leek': Welsh Corrections, English Conditions, and British Cultural Communion," in *This England, That Shakespeare: New Perspectives on Englishness and the Bard*, ed. Willy Maley and Margaret Tudeau-Clayton (Burlington, VT: Ashgate, 2010), 88, 91.

27. Howard and Rackin, 187.

28. So writes Johann V. Sommerville in "Literature and National Identity [The Earlier Stuart Era]," in *The Cambridge History of Early Modern English Literature*, ed. David Loewenstein and Janel Mueller (Cambridge: Cambridge University Press, 2002), 461. Sommerville's observation is borne out by the fact that of the four essays on "Literature and National Identity" in the *Cambridge History*—one each for the Tudor period before Elizabeth I, the era of Elizabeth and James VI, the earlier Stuart era, and the Civil War period—all but the last cite the second tetralogy in their accounts of literary nationalism.

29. See, for instance, Michael Neill, "Broken English and Broken Irish: Nation, Language, and the Optic of Power in Shakespeare's Histories," *Shakespeare Quarterly* 45:1 (Spring 1994): 1–32; and Karen Newman, *Fashioning Femininity and English Renaissance Drama* (Chicago: University of Chicago Press, 1991), 95–108. Paula Blank highlights the unsettling function of both French and Welsh voices and accents in *Henry V* (*Broken English*, 136–39, 165–67), as does Patricia Parker in "Uncertain Unions: Welsh Leeks in *Henry V*," in *British Identities and English Renaissance Literature*, ed. David J. Baker and Willy Maley (Cambridge: Cambridge University Press, 2002), 81–100. Matthew Greenfield's essay in the same volume traces that linguistic unrest back to the generic and tonal diversity of *Henry IV, Part One*, whose unruly parts manifest a "distinct centrifugal tendency" that threatens to undo the "plot-magic" of the whole ("*I Henry IV*: Metatheatrical Britain," in *British Identities and English Renaissance Literature*, ed. Baker and Maley,74).

30. All Shakespeare citations are from William Shakespeare, *The Norton Shakespeare*, ed. Stephen Greenblatt, Walter Cohen, Jean E. Howard, and Katherine Eisaman Maus (New York: W. W. Norton, 1997)..

31. Bid by Hal to "stand for my father and examine me on the particulars of my life," Falstaff intones, "Harry, I do not only marvel where thou spendest thy time, but also how

thou art accompanied. For though the chamomile, the more it is trodden on, the faster it grows, so youth, the more it is wasted, the sooner it wears. . . . I do not speak to thee in drink, but in tears; not in pleasure, but in passion; not on words only, but in woes also" (2.5.342–43, 364–67, 378–80).

32. Hotspur scoffs, "I think there's no man speaketh better Welsh," and dismisses Glendower's "mincing poetry" as "such a deal of skimble-skamble stuff" (*1 Henry IV* 3.1.48, 130, 150). David Kastan hears in their heated exchange parodic echoes of the debate between Spenser and Harvey over metrical versification (William Shakespeare, *King Henry IV, Part One*, ed. David Scott Kastan [London: Arden Shakespeare, 2002], 248).

33. "Shall pack-horses / And hollow pamper'd jades of Asia, / Which cannot go but thirty mile a-day, / Compare with Caesars, and with Cannibals, / And Trojan Greeks?" he demands when Mistress Quickly begs him to moderate his tone; "Nay, rather damn them with / King Cerberus; and let the welkin roar" (*2 Henry IV* 2.4.140–46).

34. Greenblatt, *Shakespearean Negotiations*, 43.

35. "Dost thou speak like a king?" (*1 Henry IV* 2.5.394), Hal retorts to Falstaff and proceeds to bombard him with a fusillade of insults, culminating in a devastatingly terse promise of banishment, fulfilled at the end of *Henry IV, Part Two*, when he is ordered not to come within ten miles of the new-crowned king. Glendower simply vanishes from the plays following the defeat of his forces at the end of *Henry IV, Part One*. As for Pistol, the would-be Tamburlaine is exposed as a cowardly pretender on the battlefield of *Henry V*, his bombast much worse than his bite: "For Pistol, he hath a killing tongue and a quiet sword, by means whereof 'a breaks words and keeps whole weapons," jokes an onlooker (*Henry V* 3.3.32–34).

36. Robinson, 399.

37. Robinson, 415.

38. Robinson, 417.

39. Outland, 93. See also Dowd, who claims that Warwick's wish that he alone could fight with Harry expresses "the sentiments of all the soldiers at Agincourt after Henry's speech" and that the speech "unifies everyone who hears him into one proud force" ("Polysemic Brotherhood in *Henry V*," 344)—even though the two modes of feeling are hardly compatible.

Index

Acknowledgments

I am an avid and grateful reader of acknowledgments. Poring over others' books taught me what I wanted my book to be; poring over their acknowledgments taught me that I couldn't—and didn't have to—get there on my own. No doubt there are people for whom writing is an ideally solitary pursuit, but for me it's a necessarily communal endeavor (so much so that there's a long list of Philadelphia and New Haven coffee shops whose proprietors ought to get a mention here for their forbearance), and I've been incredibly fortunate in the company I keep.

That good fortune begins with two extraordinary teachers and mentors. Margreta de Grazia is my most generous, most rigorous, and most constant reader, whose good opinion is worth any number of revisions. I hope she likes this book because I wrote it for her. David Kastan is a bottomless well of enthusiasm, insight, and plain good sense; for the sake of its junior members, the profession should seriously consider cloning him.

Not far behind Margreta and David stand a host of advisers, colleagues, and friends who have been pressed into service (or offered themselves) as readers of this book in its many earlier forms: Sean Keilen and Ania Loomba, who got me started; David Quint, who helped me to the finish; Larry Manley and John Rogers, who give the role of senior colleague a good name; Barbara Fuchs, who invited me to California when I really needed the sunshine; J. K. Barret, who tells me what I want *and* what I need to hear (in that order); and Ian Cornelius, Wendy Lee, and Aaron Ritzenberg, partners in the struggle against the blank screen. Thanks are also due to Stephanie Elsky, John Guillory, Jenny Mann, Joe Roach, Caleb Smith, Peter Stallybrass, Brian Walsh, and John Williams for offering advice, encouragement, inspiration, and camaraderie and for sustaining my conviction that academia is a remarkably friendly place.

Briallen Hopper deserves a paragraph of her own: she's the best prose stylist, close reader, and godmother I know, and the most loyal friend I've got.

I owe an enormous debt to Jerry Singerman at the University of Pennsylvania Press, who has offered warm encouragement and savvy advice at every step of the publication process—I'm lucky to have had him as a reader and champion. The two anonymous readers for the press treated the manuscript with exceptional care, searching out its merits and its defects with unerring keenness and helping me to see, at last, what sort of book I wanted to write. I am most grateful to them both.

I've benefited as well from the opportunity to share portions of this project with smart and responsive audiences at the Yale Medieval-Renaissance Colloquium, the Center for Seventeenth- and Eighteenth-Century Studies at UCLA, the Medieval-Renaissance Colloquium at the University of Pennsylvania, and the Massachusetts Center for Interdisciplinary Renaissance Studies. Yale University provided essential and generous support in the form of a Morse Junior Faculty Fellowship for 2011–12. I'm grateful to *Spenser Studies* and Oxford University Press for permission to reuse previously published material: a portion of Chapter 2 appears as "Englishing Eloquence: Vernacular Rhetorics and Poetics," in *The Oxford Handbook of Renaissance Prose*, ed. Andrew Hadfield (Oxford University Press, forthcoming in 2013); an earlier version of Chapter 3 appeared as "Pastoral in Exile: Spenser and the Poetics of English Alienation," *Spenser Studies* 23 (2008).

Finally, there are those who don't read a word I write, and whose support is all the more precious for it. Diarmuid and Donna Nicholson are the best parents an early-career academic could ask for: serenely oblivious to the minutia of the profession, firmly convinced of my capacity to surmount all obstacles, undaunted by my setbacks, and delighted (but unsurprised) by my successes. Marc, Miriam, and Ruth Levenson are the source of my deepest and most durable joys. Marc makes writing possible, through endless gifts of time and reassurance; Miriam and Ruthie make it nearly impossible, but that can be a gift too. This book is also for them, with all my heart.